For Katherine,

In anticipation of
many more conversations
about hope and other
issues of mutual interest.

With very best wishes,

Hiro

9/24/04

The Method of Hope

The Method of Hope

ANTHROPOLOGY,

PHILOSOPHY,

AND FIJIAN KNOWLEDGE

Hirokazu Miyazaki

STANFORD UNIVERSITY PRESS
STANFORD, CALIFORNIA

Published with the assistance of
the Hull Memorial Publication Fund of Cornell University

Stanford University Press
Stanford, California
© 2004 by the Board of Trustees of the
Leland Stanford Junior University

Printed in the United States of America

Library of Congress Cataloging-in-Publication Data
Miyazaki, Hirokazu.
  The method of hope : anthropology, philosophy, and Fijian
knowledge / Hirokazu Miyazaki.
    p. cm.
  Includes bibliographical references and index.
  ISBN 0-8047-4886-1 (cloth : alk. paper)
    1. Ethnology—Fiji—Suva—Philosophy. 2. Ethnophilosophy—
Fiji—Suva. 3. Fijians—Land tenure—Fiji—Suva. 4. Fijians—Fiji—
Suva—Government relations. 5. Fijians—Legal status, laws, etc.—
Fiji—Suva. 6. Suva (Fiji)—Social life and customs. 7. Suva (Fiji)—
Politics and government. I. Title.

GN671.F5M59 2004
305.8'0099611—dc22   2004004764

This book is printed on acid-free, archival-quality paper

Original printing 2004
Last figure below indicates year of this printing:
13   12   11   10   09   08   07   06   05   04

Designed and typeset at Stanford University Press in 10/13 Sabon

For Annelise, my hope

☞ Acknowledgments

This book is an ethnographic demonstration of a very simple argument: hope is a method of knowledge formation, academic and otherwise. In more specific terms, it is a method for apprehending a present moment of knowing. As an instantiation of this method, the book juxtaposes hope in the philosophy of Ernst Bloch, Walter Benjamin, and Richard Rorty with the long-standing hope of a group of dispossessed Fijians, Suvavou people, to reclaim their ancestral land. Ultimately, it seeks to bring into view the work of hope in anthropological knowledge.

In the spirit of hope in this sense of the term, the book is also an instantiation of my own hope as a response to the hope friends and colleagues of mine have had in this project. The book draws upon archival and field research done in Fiji between August 1994 and March 1996, funded by the Division of Pacific and Asian History at the Research School of Pacific and Asian Studies at the Australian National University. I thank Donald Denoon for generous arrangements and my mother, Keiko Miyazaki, for additional financial support.

For granting a research permit expeditiously, I thank the Fiji government. The National Archives of Fiji provided me with a research base during the entire period of my fieldwork, and I thank Margaret Patel, then government archivist, and her staff for their assistance.

From August 1994 until June 1995, I lived at the Australian National University, Suva Flats, in Laucala Bay and engaged in extensive archival research at the National Archives of Fiji, as well as at other government departments. For generous access to gov-

ernment records, I thank Ratu Jone Radrodro, then permanent sec-
retary for Fijian Affairs, Ratu Viliame Tagivetaia of the Native
Lands and Fisheries Commission, Seru Naqase of the Native Land
Trust Board, Samu Levu of the Ministry of Lands and Mineral
Resources, and Samisoni Sawailau of the Ministry of Tourism. I
also thank the office of Roko Veivuke (Suva/Beqa) for assistance in
obtaining permission to access records at the Native Lands and
Fisheries Commission.

In late October 1994, I began my work in Suvavou, a Fijian village near Suva, and I spent almost every day thereafter in the village. From the beginning of July 1995, I lived near the village and
participated in Suvavou people's daily activities. I thank the chief of
the village, Tui Suva Ratu Epeli Kanakana, for generously allowing
me to conduct research in the village. I also thank Metui Muduna-
vosa, Seruveveli Dakai, and Pastor Samuela Ratulevu for their hos-
pitality. I also thank members of both Methodist and Seventh-Day
Adventist churches in Suvavou. In particular, I thank the *vakatawa*
(catechist) of the Suvavou Methodist church, Avisai Bokosa, and
William Dyer, Sakeasi Tuni Koroi, Uraia Kerekerelevu Rabuatoka,
and other senior members of the SDA church. Special thanks are
due to the Suvavou Soqosoqo Vakamarama (women's association)
for letting me participate in their meetings and activities. I thank
Alumita Koroi, Atelina Turagabeci, and Niko Tamani for research
assistance during the last five months of my fieldwork. Last, but
not least, I thank the Koroi family in Suvavou for taking such good
care of me during my research. In particular, I thank Makeresi,
who worked at the National Archives of Fiji, and Laisani, who is
now in Hawaii, for introducing me to the Tui Suva in October
1994. Subsequently, Sikeli and Ana accepted me into their family.

For critical comments in the early stages of this project, I thank
my teachers at the Australian National University, especially Donald Denoon, Bronwen Douglas, Jim Fox, Margaret Jolly, Brij Lal,
Nicholas Thomas, and R. Gerald Ward, as well as my dissertation
examiners, Don Brenneis, Stephen Hugh-Jones, and Marshall
Sahlins.

For their careful reading of an entire draft of this book and for their insightful comments, I thank Tom Boellstorff, Jane Campion, Tony Crook, Jane Fajans, Iris Jean-Klein, George Marcus, Adam Reed, Nicholas Thomas, Matt Tomlinson, Christina Toren, and especially Don Brenneis and Bill Maurer. Erica Bornstein, Vincent Crapanzano, Patrick Deneen, Davydd Greenwood, Jane Guyer, Bill Hanks, Naoki Kasuga, Webb Keane, Donald Moore, Bill Murphy, Kathy Rupp, and Allison Truit also read portions of the manuscript and provided me with consequential advice. Special thanks are due to Naoki Kasuga and Matt Tomlinson for generously sharing their knowledge of the Fijian language with me. Participants in my graduate and senior seminars at Cornell University during the 2002/2003 academic year also read an entire draft of the book. I thank them all for their challenging comments. The core argument of the book was presented at the 2001 meeting of the American Ethnological Society held in Montreal, the 2002 meeting of the American Anthropological Association held in New Orleans, and a conference on pragmatism held in March 2003 at Cornell University's Clarke Program in East Asian Law and Culture. I thank Webb Keane, Joel Robbins, and Steve Sangren for their helpful comments at these occasions. I am also deeply indebted to Muriel Bell for taking a leap of faith in this somewhat unusual project and for all her support and patience ever since. I also thank my copy editor, Peter Dreyer, for his careful reading. Special thanks are due to Jason Ettlinger for his assistance of many kinds at the last stage of this project.

The book could not have been written without witnessing firsthand the making of Annelise Riles's exemplary work. I am grateful for her care as well as for her uncompromising criticism at every step of this project. More than anything else, it is her faith in me and my work that has sustained my hope. In anticipation of and in the spirit of the argument of this book, she gave me both hope and method.

The argument of this book has developed in a series of essays I have written in both English and Japanese over the past few years, portions of which appear in the book. All chapters were written anew as book chapters, however, and the core argument of the book is presented here for the first time. More important, my argument is predicated on the particular shape of the entire book developed over the seven chapters. Portions of the following essays appear in this book, and I thank their respective editors and publishers for permitting me to use them here:

"Faith and Its Fulfillment: Agency, Exchange and the Fijian Aesthetics of Completion," *American Ethnologist* [American Anthropological Association] 27 (1) (2000): 31–51.

"The Limits of Politics," *People and Culture in Oceania* [Japanese Society for Oceanic Studies] 16 (2000): 109–22.

"Hoho toshite no kibo" ["Hope as a method"], *Shakai jinruigaku nenpo* [Tokyo Metropolitan University Society for Social Anthropology annual report on social anthropology] 27 (2001): 35–55.

"Bunka no seiji niokeru bubun to zentai" ["Parts and wholes in the politics of culture"], *Minzokugaku kenkyu* [Japanese Society for Ethnology journal of ethnology] 66 (2) (2001): 240–57.

"Delegating Closure," in *Law and Empire in the Pacific: Fiji and Hawai'i*, edited by Sally Engle Merry and Donald Brenneis (Santa Fe, N.M.: School of American Research Press, 2004), pp. 239–59.

The publication of this book was generously supported by the Hull Memorial Publication Fund of Cornell University. A grant from Cornell University's Department of Anthropology made possible the speedy preparation of the index.

Throughout the book, Bible passages are quoted from the King James Version and the standard Fijian translation. Some of the names of Suvavou kin groups (*i tokatoka*, *mataqali*, and *yavusa*) and individuals I use in this book are fictitious. As is the common practice in Fiji, I use the term "Fijian" to refer to "ethnic Fijian."

Contents

Maps and Photographs

Maps

Photographs

A Note on Fijian Orthography

b is pronounced *mb* as in number
c is pronounced *th* as in thus
d is pronounced *nd* as in mend
g is pronounced *ng* as in sing
q is pronounced *ng* as in anger

The Method of Hope

1   Hope as a Method

This book examines the place of hope in knowledge formation, academic and otherwise, in response to ongoing efforts in social theory to reclaim the category of hope (see, e.g., Hage 2003; Harvey 2000; Zournazi 2002; cf. Williams 1979, 1989). These efforts are part of divergent searches for alternative modes of critical thought that have followed the apparent decline of progressive politics and the rise of right-wing politics (cf. Lasch 1991). As David Harvey puts it: "The inability to find an 'optimism of the intellect' with which to work through alternatives has now become one of the most serious barriers to progressive politics. . . . I believe that in this moment in our history we have something of great import to accomplish by exercising an optimism of the intellect in order to open up ways of thinking that have for too long remained foreclosed" (Harvey 2000: 17).

Because these efforts constitute social theorists' response to conservative politicians' appropriation of the language of hope, for most social theorists, hope as a subject immediately triggers a series of ethical concerns regarding its content and its consequences (see Crapanzano 2003: 6; Zournazi 2002: 218). For example, in a series of interviews with renowned thinkers on the subject of hope, the philosopher Mary Zournazi has recently observed,

> The success of right-wing governments and sentiments lies in reworking hope in a negative frame. Hope masquerades as a vision, where the passion and insecurity felt by people become part of a call for national unity and identity, part of a community sentiment and future ideal of what we imagine ourselves to be. It is a kind of future nostalgia, a "fantastic hope" for national unity charged by a static vision of life and the

exclusion of difference. When, for the benefit of our security and belonging, we evoke a hope that ignores the suffering of others, we can only create a hope based on fear. (Zournazi 2002: 15)

Zournazi instead seeks to carve out a space for "a hope that does not narrow our visions of the world but instead allows different histories, memories and experiences to enter into present conversations on revolution, freedom and our cultural sense of belonging" (ibid.: 18).

In a more sociologically inspired effort, the anthropologist Ghassan Hage contends that we need to conceptualize societies as "mechanisms for the distribution of hope," arguing that "the kind of affective attachment (worrying or caring) that a society creates among its citizens is intimately connected to its capacity to distribute hope," and that neoliberal regimes have contributed to the "shrinking" of this capacity (Hage 2003: 3).

Although I am sympathetic to these efforts to reclaim hope in progressive thought, the focus of my investigation in this book does not concern either the ethical question of what the proper object of hope should be or the sociological question of what social condition increases or decreases actors' capacity to hope. Rather, I approach hope as a methodological problem for knowledge and, ultimately, as a *method* of knowledge deployed across a wide spectrum of knowledge practices, as well as of political persuasions. It is my conviction that any effort to reclaim the category of hope for a greater cause must begin with an examination of the predication of knowledge, academic or otherwise, on hope, and vice versa.

My investigation into hope draws on a comparative examination of very specific hopes in particular knowledge practices. The book is first of all my own response to the long-standing hope kept alive by the Fijians I came to know during ethnographic fieldwork in Suvavou, Fiji. Since the late nineteenth century, Suvavou people, the descendants of the original landowners of the Suva Peninsula, where the city of Suva stands today, have sought proper compensation from the government for the loss of their ancestral land. Because of its economic and political importance, the government has repeatedly maintained that the case cannot be reopened. De-

spite this repeated rejection, Suvavou people have continued to petition the government.

For Suvavou people, seeking this compensation has been more
than a matter of either monetary gains or identity. The long series
of petitions that they have sent to the government, I argue, represent an enduring hope to confirm their self-knowledge, the truth
about who they really are. In the Fijian context, what is true (*dina*)
is effective (*mana*), and vice versa. For Suvavou people, to receive
a large amount of compensation from the government for their
ancestral land would be an effect of and proof of the truthfulness
of their knowledge about themselves. In this book, I seek to answer
a seemingly self-evident question: How have Suvavou people kept
their hope alive for generation after generation when their knowledge has continued to fail them? In order to answer this simple
question, the book investigates the work of hope across different
genres of Suvavou people's self-knowledge, ranging from archival
research to gift-giving, Christian church rituals, and business practices. An investigation of the semantic peculiarity of the Fijian term
i nuinui (hope) and its relationship to Christian and more secular
discourses of hope would be an important ethnographic exercise
(cf. Crapanzano 2003: 11–14; Franklin 1997; Good et al. 1990;
Verdery 1995), but as I discuss below, the goal of the present study
is to shift from hope as a subject to hope as a method.

Ultimately, this book is an enactment of Suvavou people's hope
on another terrain, that of anthropological knowledge. In this sense,
the book is also an effort to bring into view the place of hope in academic knowledge. Some readers may find this juxtaposition controversial. As discussed in chapter 2, by the time of my field research
(1994–96), Suvavou people's struggle had been entangled with Fiji's
rising ethnic nationalism; moreover, the compensation Suvavou people had demanded from the government might also be seen as having potentially serious consequences for the country's economy (cf.
M. Kaplan 2004: 185, n. 7). How is it possible, the reader may ask,
to equate Suvavou people's hope with academic hope? My response
is to draw attention to a parallel between the ways in which Suvavou people, on the one hand, and philosophers such as Ernst Bloch,

Walter Benjamin, and Richard Rorty, on the other, generate hope, or prospective momentum. In other words, my focus is not so much on the divergent *objects* of these hopes as on the idea of hope as a method that *unites* different forms of knowing. I did not go to Fiji to study hope, and neither did I have the philosophies of Bloch, Benjamin, and Rorty in mind when I went there. The way my research focus shifted points to a broader theoretical issue that defines the character of my approach to the subject of hope. I arrived in Fiji in early August 1994 intending to conduct ethnohistorical research into contemporary Fijian perceptions of *turaga* ("chiefs") and *vanua* ("land" and "people"). The ritual complementarity of *turaga* and *vanua* has long been a central concern in Fijian ethnography (Hocart 1929; M. Kaplan 1988; M. Kaplan 1990b: 8; M. Kaplan 1995; Sahlins 1985; Toren 1990, 1999), and my ambition was to follow Marshall Sahlins's lead (Sahlins 1981, 1985, 1991) to examine this ritual relationship in the context of Fijian conceptions of the past (cf. M. Kaplan 1995). More specifically, my project concerned the character of the relationship of *turaga* to *vanua* as a context and consequence of land alienation during the mid nineteenth century.

I began archival research at the National Archives of Fiji in August 1994. My target was the extensive body of government records concerning land alienation during the nineteenth century, and in particular the so-called Land Claims Commission's reports (hereafter LCC reports) on the history of each tract of land originally claimed by European settlers. My archival research led, however, to the unexpected discovery of something more intriguing than archival records. Each day, I noticed a number of Fijian researchers at the archives who requested and read the same LCC reports as I did. Some were heads of *mataqali* (clans), and others were interested persons from throughout Fiji, including a number of Fijian lawyers and "consultants" in Suva who specialized in providing legal advice on land disputes. My project turned to archival research and its associated evidential practices, and, ultimately, to the hope that the researchers, including myself, all shared in our respective pursuits of documents. Numerous lawyers and consultants and Suvavou people had themselves conducted extensive archival research into the Suva land case, and Suvavou emerged as the focus of my ethnographic project.

The parallels among the divergent Fijian, philosophical, and anthropological forms of knowledge, and the unity I seek to bring to light, rest on a particular notion of hope. In the terms of this book, hope is not an emotional state of positive feeling about the future or a religious sense of expectation; it is not even a *subject* of analysis. Rather, following Bloch, Benjamin, and Rorty, I approach hope as a *method*. In these philosophers' work, hope serves as a method of radical temporal reorientation of knowledge. My insistence on using the category of hope derives precisely from this potential of hope as a method. As subjects of analysis, desire and hope are not easily distinguishable from each other, and the category of hope can easily be collapsed into the more thoroughly theorized category of desire.[1] Anthropologists have recently adopted desire as a cornerstone of analytical perspectives ranging from psychoanalysis to structural Marxism (see, e.g., Allison 2000; Sangren 2000). Unlike the subject of desire, which inherently invites one to analyze it with its infinitely deferrable quality, I argue, the conceptualization of hope as a method invites one to hope.

My investigation of hope as a common operative and method in Fijian, philosophical, and anthropological knowledge practices owes a particular debt to Marilyn Strathern's conscious efforts to juxtapose Melanesian knowledge and anthropological knowledge as comparable and parallel "analytical" forms (see Strathern 1988, 1990, 1991a, 1991b, 1997). Strathern has drawn attention to a series of aesthetic devices such as decomposition and substitution through which, according to her, Hageners in Papua New Guinea make visible their "inner capacities" (Strathern 1991a: 198). Strathern has made use of the parallel and contrast between "indigenous" and social analyses in her efforts, not only to question assumptions behind anthropological analytical constructs such as gender and part-whole relations (Strathern 1997; see also chapter 3), but also to *extend* Hageners' analytical devices to the shape of her own analysis (see Crook, in press).

Annelise Riles's work *The Network Inside Out* extends Strathern's concerns with analytical forms to analytical forms that resem-
ble forms of social analysis such as the network form (Riles 2000).
Whereas the distance and contrast between indigenous and social
analyses has enabled Strathern to extend the former to the latter,
the formal affinity and lack of distance between the knowledge
practices of NGO workers and those of social analysts has led Riles
to other analytical possibilities, not predicated on the existence of
distance. Here Riles tackles the broader analytical issues at stake in
divergent efforts to reinvent ethnography after the crisis of anthropological representation (see, e.g., Clifford 1988; Clifford and
Marcus 1986; Comaroff and Comaroff 1992; R. G. Fox 1991b;
Marcus and Fischer 1986; and see also Rabinow 1999: 167–82),
and, in particular, in ethnographic studies of expert knowledge
where the idea of difference, whether cultural, methodological, or
even epistemological, cannot be sustained as a useful analytical
framework (see Boyer 2001; Brenneis 1999; Holmes and Marcus,
in press; Jean-Klein, in press; Marcus 1998, 1999; Maurer 2002,
2003; Miyazaki and Riles, in press; Reed 2003; Strathern 2000).
    In this book, I seek to contribute to this broader debate by
proposing a somewhat different ethnographic possibility. Specifically, my investigation of the character of hope across different
forms of knowing, Fijian, philosophical, and anthropological,
points to *replication* as an anthropological technique (cf. Strathern
1988). By replication, I mean to allude to both the structuralist
notion of formal resemblance across different domains of social life
(see Fajans 1997: 5–6, 267) and the notion of replication as proof
in scientific methodology. Although Harry Collins and other science studies scholars have complicated our understanding of the
latter (see Collins 1985; Dear 1995: 95; M. Lynch 1993: 212; Shapin 1994: 21; and see also Gooding et al. 1989), I hope to demonstrate during the course of my argument that replication is a useful
analytical metaphor for the present investigation into the character
of hope. Throughout the book, I have consciously sought to *replicate* Suvavou people's hope as a modality of engagement with one
another, with their God, and with their government in my own

ethnographic engagement. In this sense, the book seeks to present a modality of ethnographic engagement that is predicated not so much on objectification, in the sense of analysis or critique, as on reception and response. It was once again through Strathern's work that I learned how acts of receiving and responding can be creative work (see, in particular, Strathern's response to Annette Weiner's critique in Strathern 1981). It is equally important to note that my discussion of Suvavou people's hope should not be mistaken as an effort to draw attention to a seemingly more general mode of engagement with the world that dispossessed people seem to exhibit elsewhere in the world. What is at issue for me is at once both more personal and more universal. More specifically, in this book, I seek to develop an account of hopeful moments whose shape replicates the way those moments are produced and experienced. Indeed, ultimately, I hope to generate a hopeful moment.

Hope as a Methodological Problem

Hope first of all emerged for me as a methodological problem. In the course of Fijian gift-giving, characterized by the interaction of two parties "facing" (*veiqaravi*) each other, there is a moment at which the gift-giving "side" subjects itself to the gift-receivers' evaluation, and quietly hopes that the other side will respond positively. After finishing a speech consisting of a series of apologies for the inadequacy of gifts, the spokesman for the gift-givers remains motionless holding a *tabua* (whale's tooth) in front of him until a spokesman for the gift-receivers takes it from him. In this moment of hope, the gift-givers place in abeyance their own agency, or capacity to create effects in the world (cf. Strathern 1987: 23–24; Strathern 1988: 268–74), at least temporarily (see Miyazaki 2000a). But what interests me most for present purposes is that once the gift-receivers accept the gifts, they deny the importance of the act of gift-giving among humans and collectively present the gifts to God. I have, for example, heard a spokesman for gift-receivers say, in accepting gifts: "Your valuables have been offered to Heaven so that we all may be given Heavenly blessing.

May [your chief] be blessed. May your descendants be blessed. . . . May God love us and may our duties be possible. Our love is the only valuable." At the moment at which the gift-givers' hope is fulfilled, it is replaced by another hope, hope of God's blessing on all those involved. My interpretation is that this second moment of hope is an echo of the first fulfilled hope: The first moment of fulfillment in ritual is an intimation of God's ultimate response. The production of hope of God's blessing, then, is a product of a carefully orchestrated discursive play of human agency.

It soon became clear to me, however, that my own analytical treatment of hope as the product of a ritual process was temporally incongruous with the prospective orientation of hope itself (see Miyazaki n.d.). The analysis was predicated on the assumption that the manipulation of ritual language produces something (a sense of collectivity, religious faith, hope, etc.). The retrospective treatment of hope as a subject of description forecloses the possibility of describing the prospective momentum inherent in hope. As soon as hope is approached as the end point of a process, the newness or freshness of the prospective moment that defines that moment as hopeful is lost.

I am seeking here to ask a somewhat different set of questions than those long explored in anthropological studies of the gift since Bronislaw Malinowski and Marcel Mauss (Malinowski 1922; Mauss 1966 [1925]). First of all, the focus of my attention is not so much on the question of reciprocity and the Maussian notion of *hau,* or the "spirit of the thing given," that prompts a return gift, which have preoccupied generations of anthropologists (see, e.g., Godelier 1999; Sahlins 1972: 149-83; A. Weiner 1992). Second, my attention to the temporal dimension of gift-giving may recall Pierre Bourdieu's attention to temporal strategies in gift-giving in the context of his critique of Claude Lévi-Strauss's structuralist treatment of exchange (Bourdieu 1977: 4–6), but, unlike Bourdieu, the methodological problem at stake for me is not the tension between subjective and objective standpoints but the interconnection between the hope entailed in gift-giving and the hope entailed in its analysis.

The argument of this book is that hope presents a set of methodological problems that in turn demand the temporal reorientation of knowledge. Looking at hope as a methodological problem, and ultimately a method, rather than a product or a strategic moment in a language game or a semiotic process, leads us to reconsider hope as a common operative in all knowledge formation. My claim is that thinking through hope as a method allows us to begin to confront the most fundamental problem—what knowledge is for.

My encounter with Fijian hope resonates with the German Marxist philosopher Ernst Bloch's discussion of a "not-yet" (*Noch-Nicht*) consciousness at the very moment at which hope is fulfilled in his philosophy of hope (Bloch 1986). I first encountered Bloch's concept of the not-yet through the work of the Japanese anthropologist and cultural theorist Naoki Kasuga, who has conducted extensive ethnographic and historical research in Fiji. In an article published in Japanese, Kasuga seeks to explain how Fijians maintain their faith in land as the ultimate source of everything good even when land continually fails to fulfill this faith. According to Kasuga, "Fijians' persistent attachment to land is a daily reminder of what has 'not-yet' come, to borrow Ernst Bloch's phrase (*Noch-Nicht*), and of its immanent arrival. In the midst of disappointment, [the attachment to land] once again allows them to discover that reality is still in a state of not-yet. This cycle in turn sustains Fijians' persistent attachment to land" (1999: 386; my translation). I shall return to this repetitive quality of Fijian hope later in the book.

Bloch's best-known work, *The Principle of Hope* (1986), has received enthusiastic praise (e.g., Hobsbawm 1973: Steiner 1967: 90–91), as well as criticism (e.g., Habermas 1983; Ricoeur 1986: xiv), from influential thinkers.[2] Bloch's argument has arguably had its most prominent influence in the German theologian Jürgen Moltmann's *Theology of Hope* (1993a [1967]).[3] Nevertheless, although there have been numerous efforts to recuperate the contemporary relevance of Bloch's philosophy (see, especially, Daniel and Moylan 1997; Hudson 1982; Jameson 1971; Jay 1984; Levinas 1998: 33-42; Roberts 1990),[4] unlike much-celebrated contemporaries and close friends of his such as Theodor Adorno, Walter Benjamin, and Georg Lukács,[5] Bloch (1885–1977) remains a marginal figure in anthropology and in social theory more generally (see Malkki 2001 for a notable exception).[6]

From my point of view, what emerged at the intersection of Bloch's philosophy of hope and my ethnographic encounter with Fijian hope was a methodological problem. In *The Principle of Hope*, Bloch focuses on the question of how to overcome the incongruity between the retrospective orientation of philosophy as a contemplative form of knowledge and the prospective orientation of hope. According to Bloch, it is this temporal incongruity that has prevented philosophy from apprehending the nature of hope. In Bloch's view, therefore, hope is a methodological problem, that is, a problem of the retrospective character of contemplative knowledge.[7]

Bloch's methodological framing of the subject of hope prompted me to rethink the temporal orientation of my analysis of Fijian gift-giving, referred to earlier (Miyazaki 2000b; Miyazaki n.d.). To the extent that my analysis followed the flow of the gift-giving event, tracking every step of the ritual, in sequence, the temporal orientation of my analysis mirrored that of the gift-giving event itself. However, this prospective orientation was enabled by a retrospective perspective of my own. My analysis was predicated on the assumption that the moment of hope of God's blessing was an effect of and part of the strategic manipulation of ritual language, that is, it foregrounded what was analytically conceived as an *end point*, or *result*. More precisely, my focus on the production of hope followed the studies of Michael Herzfeld, Webb Keane, and others of how actors' manipulation of the formal properties of ritual language results in the emergence of certain particular forms of consciousness (Herzfeld 1990, 1997; Keane 1997c). From this point of view, I understood the exchange of words and objects in Fijian gift-giving as carefully designed to generate hope of God's blessing among ritual participants (see chapter 5). The focus of my analysis, in other words, was on the ritual process as seen from the vantage point of its effects. As I would later come to understand, any analysis that foresees its own end point loses its open-endedness. The temporal orientation of this analysis and that of the ritual practices it described were incongruous. However, where the focus on production demands a retrospective perspective from the point of view of what is produced, ritual participants maintained a forward-looking orientation at every step of the ritual. More precisely, from ritual participants' point of view, the maintenance of a prospective perspective was at the heart of ritual performance. This was true even though the same participants engaged in the same ritual form repeatedly, and hence could be said to know the ritual's outcomes or effects (cf. Bourdieu 1977: 5).

Upon discovering this temporal incongruity, my initial urge was to pursue a framework of analysis that would replicate the temporality of every moment in the gift-giving event. In approximating the structure of the ritual moment, analysis would in a sense be in that moment. A framework of analysis that is completely synchronous with a present moment is an illusion, however. The challenge I faced is pertinent to a more general problem of how to approach the infinitely elusive quality of any present moment. As William Hanks has noted, "To say 'now' is already to have lost the moment. To say 'here' is to objectify part of a lived space whose extent is both greater and lesser than the referent" (Hanks 1996b: 295). This paradox of the present, according to Hanks, "produces a synchrony, only to be superseded, overtaken by its own momentum, unable to stop the motion of meaning" (ibid.: 295–96).

My investigation of hope in this book begins with the impossibility of achieving analytical synchronicity. Here, I once again turn to Bloch, whose solution to the problem of the incongruity between the direction of philosophy and that of hope is to reorient philosophy toward the future. In his view, hope can only be apprehended by hope. On the face of things, this move would seem to come up against the same limit. However, I argue below that the difference lies in the fact that Bloch's proposal does not treat hope as a *subject* of knowledge. Rather, it is a proposal to regard hope as a *method*. From this point of view, the impossibility of achieving synchronicity foregrounded in Bloch's concept of the "not-yet" becomes the means of apprehending hope itself. The remainder of this chapter is devoted to explicating this idea and examining its theoretical implications for anthropology and social theory more generally. For anthropology, this idea takes on the relevance of problems of agency and temporality. For social theory, it suggests an unexpected point of confluence between German social thought and American pragmatism as exemplified by the work of Bloch, Benjamin, and Rorty. The ultimate goal of this exercise, however, is not to theorize hope but to construct an analytical framework for approaching concrete moments of hope that I encountered across different domains of knowledge in Suvavou, ranging from archival research to religious discourse to gift-giving rituals to business. I first turn to philosophical arguments about the temporal orientation of knowledge entailed in efforts to capture hope as a subject of contemplation. The question of hope in turn naturally invites the question of God, that is, of the problem of the *limits* of human agency. The next section therefore turns to questions of agency to show how, for Bloch and others, questions of temporality displace questions of agency. The chapter concludes that this displacement is instrumental to hope as a method, that is, to these philosophers' efforts to deploy hope as a means of apprehending hope. I follow with an overview of the argument of the book as a whole, as it unfolds in each of the individual chapters.

Reorienting the Direction of Knowledge

If there is little empirical ground for hope, on what grounds and for what should one hope? For many philosophers, this deceptively simple observation is at the heart of the problem of hope.[8] Just as the focus of Christian eschatology shifted from a concrete hope for the second coming of Christ to an abstract hope for an afterlife (see Bultmann 1957: 51; Kermode 2000: 25; Moltmann 1993a [1967]), the insufficient empirical foundation of hope has led many philosophers to make a purely moral argument for hope (see Ricoeur 1986: xv). In *Critique of Pure Reason,* for example, Immanuel Kant asks the famous question, "What may I hope?" (1929 [1781]: 635), or "If I do what I ought to do, what may I then hope?" (636).

Kant's answer to this question derives from his assumption that "there really are pure moral laws which determine completely *a priori* (without regard to empirical motives, that is, to happiness) what is and is not to be done, that is, which determine the employment of the freedom of a rational being in general" (636). For Kant, "hope in the moral progress of human society" comes down to "moral faith," or faith beyond knowledge, the philosopher Robert Adams observes (1998: xxv, xxvi), that is, faith in the possibility of "a moral world" (Kant 1929 [1781]: 637), which is itself also the condition of that possibility (see also Peters 1993: 143). This understanding of hope is not so different from the notion of "hope against hope" often attributed to Saint Paul's comment on Abraham, who "against hope believed in hope" (Rom. 4:18; see Muyskens 1979: 136) or indeed of Kierkegaard's existentialist philosophy (cf. Adams 1987).

Ernst Bloch's philosophy of hope represents a significant departure from this conventional framework of philosophical contemplation on the subject of hope. In his magnum opus, *The Principle of Hope*, Bloch seeks to "bring philosophy to hope" (Bloch 1986: 6) and analyzes a variety of hopeful visions ranging from daydreams to fantasies about technology to detective stories and the Bible (see also Bloch 1988). However, I read *The Principle of Hope* not so much as a study of various manifestations of hope as an effort to reconstitute philosophy on what he calls the "principle hope" (*das Prinzip Hoffnung*). In my terms, Bloch's philosophy is a proposal for hope as a method of knowledge.

In *The Principle of Hope*, Bloch confronts the limits of philosophy in its capacity to comprehend "the world [as an entity] full of propensity towards something, tendency towards something, latency of something" (Bloch 1986: 18). According to Bloch, the limits of philosophy derive from its retrospective character: "Contemplative knowledge [such as philosophy] can only refer by definition to What Has Become"; in other words, it "presuppose[s] a closed world that has already become. . . . Future of the genuine, processively open kind is therefore sealed off from and alien to any mere contemplation" (ibid.: 8).

What Bloch points out here is the incongruity between the temporal orientation of knowledge and that of its object, the world. According to Bloch, this incongruity has also prevented philosophy from appreciating the character of hope. He proposes to substitute hope for contemplation as a method of engagement with the world. Bloch's philosophy of hope in this sense is a methodological move to reorient the direction of philosophy: he thus proposes to turn philosophy toward the future and to what has "not-yet" become. Bloch introduces the notion of the not-yet consciousness as the antithesis of the Freudian notion of the subconscious. If the power of psychoanalysis is predicated on the rebounding power of the repressed or suppressed, the power of hope as a method rests on a prospective momentum entailed in anticipation of what has not-yet become: "a relatively still Unconscious disposed towards its other side, forwards rather than backwards. Towards the side of something new that is dawning up that has never been conscious before, not, for example, something forgotten, something rememberable that has been, something that has sunk into the subconscious in repressed or archaic fashion" (Bloch 1986: 11).

Moreover, according to Bloch, the philosophy that is open to the future entails a commitment to changing the world: "Only thinking directed towards changing the world and informing the desire to change it does not confront the future (the unclosed space for new development in front of us) as embarrassment and the past as spell" (Bloch 1986: 8).

The German Marxist philosopher's intense concern with hope resonates, albeit in an unexpected manner, with the American pragmatist Richard Rorty's own turn to hope.[9] In a series of essays entitled "Hope in Place of Knowledge," Rorty reads John Dewey's pragmatism as a proposal to replace knowledge with hope. As in the case of Bloch, this turn to hope demands shifting the temporal orientations of philosophy. According to Rorty, Dewey's criticism of metaphysical philosophy for simply being "an attempt to lend the past the prestige of the eternal" (Rorty 1999: 29) sought to substitute "the notion of a better human future for the [metaphysical] notions of 'reality,' 'reason' and 'nature.' . . . [Pragmatism] is 'the

apotheosis of the future'" (ibid.: 27). The resonance between Bloch
and Rorty derives from their efforts to anchor their critique of philosophy in the problem of the temporal direction of knowledge.
More concretely, their shared pursuit of a transformative philosophy leads them to a shared concern with the future, that is, with the
direction of knowledge. American pragmatists' commitment to the
task of changing the world (that is, making it more democratic)
could also be described as a future-oriented faith in themselves.
Rorty emphasizes that Dewey sought to make philosophy "an
instrument of change rather than of conservation," even denying
that "philosophy is a form of knowledge" (ibid.: 29). "American
pragmatism is a diverse and heterogeneous tradition. But its common denominator consists of a future-oriented instrumentalism
that tries to deploy thought as a weapon to enable more effective
action," Cornel West observes (1989: 5).

Underlying Bloch's and Rorty's turn to the future is their critique
of the philosophical understanding of essence, or truth about
humanity that is given but is hidden from humans, captured in the
Greek notion of history as a teleological course of disclosure of this
essence. Bloch notes, for example, that "essence is not something
existing in finished form . . . [but] is that which is not yet" (Bloch
1986: 1373; emphasis removed). As Wayne Hudson puts it, Bloch
"replaces any conception of a settled world with the thought exper-
iment of a world kept open by the presence of futuristic properties
within it" (Hudson 1982: 92). Rorty similarly says: "What [prag-
matists] hope is not that the future will conform to a plan, will fulfill an immanent teleology, but rather the future will astonish and
exhilarate. . . . [What pragmatists share] is their principled and
deliberate fuzziness" (Rorty 1999: 28). Underlying Bloch and
Rorty's turn to the future is their critique of the Greek idea of
anamnesis and its associated teleological course of the world taken
for granted in metaphysics. For both, therefore, there is no God's
plan, no essential disposition of the world that will automatically
unfold. Both stress the indeterminate character of the direction of
the world; both abandon the notion of a predetermined end.

At the intersections of Bloch and Rorty's philosophy, therefore, hope emerges as a method of engagement with the world that has particular implications for the temporality of knowledge formation. In their view, hope invokes the limits of the retrospection of philosophical contemplation and serves as a method for a philosophy that is open to the future. In other words, the introduction of hope to philosophy reorients philosophy to the future. This reorientation of knowledge has some significant consequences for a range of issues that are central to the current concerns of social and cultural theory. I wish to focus here, in particular, on the problems of agency and temporality.

Sources of Hope: The Problem of Agency

The predication of hope on an understanding of the world as indeterminate is for both Bloch and Rorty preconditioned by a rejection of the possibility of God. This raises a question about the source of hope. For Rorty, that source is human agency. Rorty's self-consciously aggrandizing concept of human agency explicitly rejects humility as instrumental to the production of hope.

The notion of humility "presupposes that there is, already in existence, something better and greater than the human," according to Rorty, who proposes instead the notion of finitude, which "presupposes only that there are lots of things which are different from the human." He adds: "A pragmatic sense of limits requires us only to think that there are some projects for which our tools are presently inadequate, and to hope that the future may be better than the past in this respect" (Rorty 1999: 51–52).

Underlying Rorty's preference for the notion of finitude over humility is his anti-essentialist rejection of the pursuit of the essence of humanity as the goal of philosophy: "humanity is an open-ended notion, that the word 'human' names a fuzzy but promising project rather than an essence" (Rorty 1999: 52). This rejection of the notion of essence in turn leads him to emphasize human agency (or human capacity to create a better future) in place of God's agency:

> pragmatists transfer to the human future the sense of awe and mystery which the Greeks attached to the non-human; it is transformed into a

sense that the humanity of the future will be, although linked with us by a continuous narrative, superior to present-day humanity in as yet barely imaginable ways. It coalesces with the awe we feel before works of imagination, and becomes a sense of awe before humanity's ability to become what it once merely imagined, before its capacity for self-creation. (Rorty 1999: 52)

For this reason, following Christopher Lasch's distinction between hope and optimism (1991), Patrick Deneen has argued that Rorty's (and Dewey's) "hope" cannot be called hope. Rorty's hope is simply "optimism without hope," that is, "the disposition that human problems are tractable without needing to resort to any appeals to transcendence or the divine in their solution," according to Deneen, who contrasts Rorty's optimism without hope with Václav Havel's "hope without optimism," which, he says, is based on "a fundamental mistrust in the belief that humans have the ability to solve political and moral problems, but that the appeal to a transcendent source—through hope—can serve as a guiding standard, as well as an encouragement to action" (Deneen 1999: 578). In other words, for Deneen, Rorty's optimism cannot be considered hope, because hope is predicated on a concept of God, that is, of transcendent agency, which in turn implies limits to human agency.

Rorty's move to eliminate the notion of transcendence from his hope is deliberate and strategic. In fact, Rorty anticipates Deneen's line of criticism:

A typical first reaction to antiessentialism is that it is too anthropocentric, too much inclined to treat humanity as the measure of all things. To many people, antiessentialism seems to lack humility, a sense of mystery, a sense of human finitude. It seems to lack a common-sensical appreciation of the obdurate otherness of things of this world. The antiessentialist reply to this common-sensical reaction is that common sense is itself no more than the habit of using a certain set of descriptions. In the case at hand, what is called common sense is simply the habit of using language inherited from the Greeks, and especially from Plato and Aristotle. (Rorty 1999: 51)

Bloch's hope surfaces as an interesting counterpoint to both of these positions. The question for Bloch as a committed atheist is how to hope after the death of God (cf. Habermas 1983). Bloch's starting point is that God is not a possible solution. "[N]o one, not even the most religious person, today still believes in God as even the most lukewarm, indeed the doubters, believed in him two hundred years ago," he observes in *The Principle of Hope* (1986: 1291). He therefore seeks to decouple the problem of hope from the question of agency (human versus God) per se. More precisely, for Bloch, hope actually replaces the problem of agency: imagined nonhuman agents such as God are simply a manifestation of hope. From this point of view, it is not God that is the source of hope but hope that is the source of God:

> The place that has been occupied in individual religions by what is conceived as God, that has ostensibly been filled by that which is hypostatized as God, has not itself ceased after it has ceased to be ostensibly filled. For it is at all events preserved as a place of projection at the head of utopian-radical intention; and the metaphysical correlate of this projection remains the hidden, the still undefined—underdefinitive, the real Possible in the sense of mystery. The place allocated to the former God is thus not in itself a void; it would only be this if atheism were nihilism, and furthermore not merely a nihilism of theoretical hopelessness but of the universal-material annihilation of every possible goal- and perfection-content. (Bloch 1986: 1199)[10]

For Bloch, in other words, the important choice is not so much between God and humans as between nihilism and hope. Upon the death of God, the question of agency, whether human or nonhuman, fades into the background to the extent that it is understood as a simple manifestation of human hope. For Bloch, the source of hope is neither faith in God nor faith in humans. Hope is the source of such faith.

Moments of Hope: The Problem of the Present

Bloch thus practically substitutes the question of temporality for the question of agency. Underlying Bloch's turn to hope is his concern with the problem of the present.[11] In a series of essays entitled "On the Present in Literature," for example, Bloch confronts the difficulty of accessing the present. For Bloch, the difficulty arises from the lack of distance between oneself and the present moment in which one finds oneself:

> Without distance . . . you cannot even experience something, [much]
> less represent it or present it in a right way. . . . In general it is like this:
> all nearness makes matters difficult, and if it is too close, then one is
> blinded, at least made mute. This is true in a strict sense only for a pre-
> cise, on-the-spot experience, for the immediate moment that is as a dark
> "right-now" lacking all distance to itself. But this darkness of the
> moment, in its unique directness, is not true for an already more medi-
> ated right-now, which is of a different kind and which is a specific expe-
> rience called "present." . . . Nevertheless, something of the darkness of
> the immediate nearness is conveyed . . . to the more mediated, more
> widespread present by necessity, i.e., an increased difficulty to represent
> it. (Bloch 1998: 120)

For Bloch, therefore, the problem of the present is emblematic of
the problem of one's alienation from self-knowledge. In his first
major work, *The Spirit of Utopia*, originally published in 1918,
Bloch points out that our knowledge about who we are "represents
only an untrue form, to be considered only provisionally. We . . .
are located in our own blind spot, in the darkness of the lived
moment" (Bloch 2000: 200). For Bloch, hope emerges from this
condition of alienation from self-knowledge. Hope, according to
Bloch, "is in the darkness itself, partakes of its imperceptibility"
and "lifts itself precisely out of the Now and its darkness, into
itself" (ibid.: 201, 202).

The problem of how to approach the present has been one of the
most difficult puzzles in philosophy and exemplifies the problem of
the lack of analytical distance more generally. One solution has
been to move away from the idea of linear and clocklike temporal
flow that treats the present as an instant and to introduce uneven-
ness into the past-present-future relationship, of which the present
is the focal point (cf. Munn 1992: 115). The phenomenologist
Edmund Husserl, for example, understands actors' perception of
the present as an intersection of what he terms retention, or the
accumulation of past actions and their consequences, on the one
hand, and protention, or plans for future actions (Husserl 1964
[1887]; see also Schutz 1970: 137–38). From this perspective, Alfred Gell observes, as against the philosophical problem of the

"nothingness" of the present (Sartre 1956: 175–79), Husserl suggests that the present has its own "thickness" (Gell 1992: 223). The pragmatist Charles Sanders Peirce calls the present "inscrutable," a "Nascent State between the Determinate and the Indeterminate," adding, "the consciousness of the present is . . . that of a struggle over what shall be; and thus we emerge from the study with a confirmed belief that it is the Nascent State of the Actual" (Peirce 1960: 5: 459, 462, quoted in E. V. Daniel 1996: 125–26). William James's theory of the consciousness of self also draws on his redefinition of the notion of the present: "the practically cognized present is no knife-edge, but a saddle-back, with a certain breadth of its own on which we sit perched, and from which we look in two directions into time" (James 1981 [1890]: 574). In a similar fashion, George Herbert Mead famously develops the notion of the present as "the locus of reality" in his theory of the emergent self:

> A present then, as contrasted with the abstraction of mere passage, is not a piece cut out anywhere from the temporal dimension of uniformly passing reality. Its chief reference is to the emergent event, that is, to the occurrence of something which is more than the processes that have led up to it and which by its change, continuance, or disappearance, adds to later passages a content they would not otherwise have possessed. (Mead 1959: 23)

Nancy Munn (1990) shows that the present as a site of reality construction contains intersecting temporalities that actors seek to control.

In contrast to these efforts to develop a general theory of actors' apprehension of the present, Bloch and Benjamin theorize the problem of how to apprehend a particular kind of present that they call the "now" [*Jetzt*]. "The now [*Jetzt*] moves and propels itself through each day, whenever. It beats in all that happens with its shortest time span, and it knocks on the door," Bloch writes (1998: 127). Yet, as he notes, the now is not always accessible:

> [N]ot every present opens up for it. The actual impulses, the socially driving pulses, do not beat in each present fresh and vital. Not every time opens up for the now and the next now that stands exactly at that moment in front of the door and that has never "entered" before. It has

not unloaded its true contents with which and toward which it is on its way. . . . That which we call the propelling now evidently does not mean anything other than the tendencies within all that exists projected onto and atomized within the course of time. (Bloch 1998: 127)

Access to the now, in other words, demands another "now," that is, a moment of hope.

The problem of the now is precisely the problem Walter Benjamin tackles in his famous "Theses on the Philosophy of History" (1992 [1968]: 245–55). Let us consider for a moment Benjamin's discussion of "hope in the past" to which Peter Szondi has drawn attention (1986; see also Didi-Huberman 2000: 99). Benjamin was once a close friend of Bloch's, and the two thinkers' interests intersected (cf. Kaufmann 1997; Geoghegan 1996). In "Theses on the Philosophy of History," Benjamin criticizes the idea of history as a chain of cause and effect (see Weber 2001: 201) by pointing to the messianic role of the historian:

> To articulate the past historically does not mean to recognize it "the way it really was" (Ranke). It means to seize hold of a memory as it flashes up at a moment of danger. Historical materialism wishes to retain that image of the past which unexpectedly appears to man singled out by history at a moment of danger. The danger affects both the content of the tradition and its receivers. The same threat hangs over both: that of becoming a tool of the ruling classes. In every ear the attempt must be made anew to wrest tradition away from a conformism that is about to overpower it. The Messiah comes not only as the redeemer, he comes as the subduer of Antichrist. Only that historian will have the gift of fanning the spark of *hope in the past* who is firmly convinced that even the dead will not be safe from the enemy if he wins. And this enemy has not ceased to be victorious. (Benjamin 1992 [1968]: 247; my emphasis; original emphasis removed)

Benjamin's messianic historian searches for unfulfilled hope in the past and facilitates its fulfillment. We might call this attitude toward the now retrospective from the perspective of the past's future moment of its own salvation.[12]

In Benjamin's "hope in the past," Szondi sees the "joining of hope and despair" (1986: 156). In other words, the historian's self-assigned messianic mission becomes the basis for hope of the historian's own salvation. The historian's messianic retrospection is the source of hope in the future messianic historian even at a moment of despair. Benjamin therefore carves out a space for hope by changing the character of the direction of historical knowledge. We might say that Benjamin's hope is predicated on a dialectic of the past and the present, defined as the past's eschatological future moment (cf. Szondi 1986: 157).

According to Benjamin, this dialectic of the past and its own eschatological moment is conditioned by the past itself: "the past carries with it a temporal index, according to which it is assigned to salvation" (Benjamin 1980, vol. 1: 495, quoted in Szondi 1986: 157). In other words, the past points to the future moment of its own salvation. This view of the past is predicated on a view of the present as having an internal drive toward its own end point. What fans "the spark of hope in the past" is the historian's retrospective attention from the past's future end. The past has its own directionality, in other words, that invites the historian to participate in its internal drive toward its own fulfillment.

What Benjamin's critique of history and Bloch's critique of philosophy have in common are precisely this attention to the direction of knowledge and its associated reorientation of knowledge. Just as described in the previous section, Bloch introduces a prospective perspective to philosophy's retrospective contemplation, Benjamin reverses the direction of historical knowledge, and counters the linear temporality of conventional historical writing that relates past and present as cause and effect with a retrospective intervention that relates past and present as the past's eschatological future.

More important, both Bloch and Benjamin draw attention to the character of a hopeful moment. For both, hope is always disappointed. Yet, in Benjamin's view, hope in the present points to its own future moment of salvation. Likewise, Bloch draws attention to unfulfilled hope as "the repressed, the interrupted, the undischarged on which we can in one and the same act fall back upon while it reaches forward to us in order to develop in a better way" and points to how in this unfulfilled hope, "the corresponding points of the now sparkle and transmit each other" (1998: 129, 130). Both seek to apprehend a moment of hope, in other words, by striking it with a perspective whose direction is opposite to that of the moment. In other words, to borrow Benjamin's expression, the spark of hope flies up in the midst of the radical temporal reorientation in their own analyses.

For both Bloch and Benjamin, therefore, moments of hope can only be apprehended as other moments of hope. Any attempts to objectify these moments and turn them into outcomes of some process, as both philosophy and history tend to do, are destined to fail to capture the temporality of these moments. Bloch and Benjamin succeed in recapturing the temporality of these moments, rather, by reproducing another hopeful moment, the moment of hope in their own writing. According to Bloch, the hopeful moment, or the now-time, is "a turning point [that] gathers all the undischarged corresponding elements within this time that is to be shaped . . . [and that] is the resource that enables now-time to be seen and yet not contemplated, thus without the loss of goal, without the loss of its frontier characteristic" (Bloch 1998: 131).

From this perspective, I now wish to revisit my own initial impulse for synchronicity between the temporality of my analytical framework and that of the hope of Fijian ritual participants for God's blessing. I mentioned at the outset that my initial response to Fijians' ritual production of hope was an impulse to construct an analytical framework that would be synchronous with the temporality of every moment of hope in the ritual. Note that this hopeful impulse for synchronicity emerged for me at the moment of my apprehension of the temporal incongruity between my analytical attention and its object, that is, others' hope. In other words, for me, hope was simultaneously a *cause* and an *effect* of that incongruity.

In light of the above discussion, the problem of incongruity between the retrospective framework of production and that of hope becomes a methodological opportunity. It was precisely at that moment of incongruity that hope emerged as a driving force for my own inquiry. At the moment when I apprehended the tem-

poral incongruity between my own analysis of the ritual production of hope and Fijians' hope, in other words, I replicated Fijians'
hope on a methodological terrain. My point is that the real challenge posed by moments of hope is not so much the impossibility
of achieving the temporal congruity between knowledge and its
object as the immediacy of hope thus engendered, that is, hope's
demand for its own fulfilment. In the method of hope, this hope for
synchronicity is a "representation" of the hope to which it is
deployed. Moments of hope can only be apprehended as sparks on
another terrain, in other words. The sparks provide a simulated
view of the moments of hope as they fade away.

   In the five ethnographic chapters that follow, I wish to recapture
what Benjamin calls the sparks of hope that have flown up from
my encounter with the hope of Suvavou people. As I already have
suggested, these sparks are mostly products of incongruities
between the temporal direction of my own anthropological intervention and that of Suvavou people's hope as a method of self-
knowledge. The challenge I face is how to preserve these sparks
while resisting the immediate demand of hope for synchronicity
that emerges in these incongruities. In these chapters, I examine the
work of hope across different domains of Fijian knowledge ranging from archival research (chapter 2) to distribution of rent money
(chapter 3) to petition writing (chapter 4) to religious and gift-giving rituals (chapters 5 and 6) and to business activities (chapters 3
and 6).

An Overview of the Book

Underlying my turn to Bloch's philosophy is my hope to carve out
a space for a new kind of anthropological engagement with philosophy. Recently, against earlier efforts to deploy non-Western
thought to challenge Western metaphysics (e.g., Lévi-Strauss 1962),
anthropologists have begun to engage in a more substantial manner with the work of philosophers such as Wittgenstein (Das 1998),
Heidegger (J. F. Weiner 1992, 1993, 2001), Peirce (E. V. Daniel
1984, 1996; Lee 1997), and Charles Taylor (Geertz 2000). Al-

though I am sympathetic to these anthropological attempts to tackle philosophical problems, this book is not such an attempt.[13] That is, I am not interested in either extending Bloch's theoretical constructs to anthropology or reinterpreting the location of his work in social and cultural theory.[14] To do so would violate the spirit of Bloch's work. In other words, Bloch's particular concept of hope as a method has consequences for the character of the relationship between knowledge and its object that in turn demand a particular kind of response. That is, if as suggested above, the conception of hope as a *problem* has led many philosophers to look to moral faith for a solution, I argue that the reconceptualization of hope as a method simply demands its application and replication on a new terrain.

My investigation into the character of Fijian hope is therefore not so much a study of the hope of others as an effort to recapture that hope (Fijians' as well as Bloch's) as a method for anthropology. This general aim of the book manifests itself in the trajectory of my investigation as unfolded in the next six chapters. In this chapter, I have juxtaposed my encounter with hopeful moments in Fijian gift-giving with Ernst Bloch's conceptualization of hope as a methodological problem. Ultimately, I have suggested that a solution to this problem inheres in turning hope into a method of my inquiry, that is, in retrospectively making explicit my own analytical hope as a replication of the hope as an analytical object that had prompted me to strive for temporal congruity between knowledge and its object at the outset. In the following five chapters, with this hope in mind, I retrospectively investigate hopeful moments across different genres of Suvavou people's knowledge practices. My hope is that the constellation of "sparks of hope" in this zigzag juxtaposition between my own analytical hope and Suvavou people's hope will in turn point to yet another moment of replication, that is, hope latent in the present of anthropological knowledge of which this work is part. In this sense, the book is an ethnographically informed speculation about what comes after hope. This seems to be a particularly appropriate response to Bloch's philosophy of hope given that it is "a doctrine of hope and ontological anticipation, is itself an anticipation," as Fredric Jameson puts it (1971: 158–59).

In more concrete terms, in the chapters that follow, I demonstrate that for the Fijians I knew, as for Bloch, hope was a method of knowledge. More concretely, it was a method of self-knowledge, that is, knowledge about who they were. As a method of knowledge, I shall show, hope consistently introduced a prospective momentum that propelled their pursuit of self-knowledge. I wish to show how hope allowed the Fijians I knew to experience the limits of self-knowing without abandoning the possibility of self-knowing altogether.

Chapters 2 and 3 comprise an ethnographic introduction to Suvavou and also seek to situate Suvavou people's hope at the intersection of their pursuit of compensation for the loss of their ancestral land and their effort to confirm their knowledge about themselves. In chapter 2, "A History of Thwarted Hope," I discuss the shifting location of Suvavou people's hope in Fiji's political economy. My focus is on a history of Suvavou people's engagement with the government since the late nineteenth century and, in particular, on the government's evaluation of Suvavou people's knowledge about themselves. At the time of my research, the government treated Suvavou people with a certain degree of sympathy and also perceived Suvavou people's affairs to be "sensitive" because of their history. However, both colonial and postcolonial government officials approached Suvavou people with a patronizing and even condescending attitude. In these officials' view, Suvavou people were "illiterate" and "ignorant"; moreover they were not authentic traditional Fijians because of the negative effects of their longtime exposure to city life. Following the two military coups in 1987 that toppled the democratically elected coalition government of the multi-ethnic Labour Party and the Indo-Fijian dominated National Federation Party, however, Suvavou sympathizers emerged within and outside of the government owing to their status as an archetypical disenfranchised and dispossessed indigenous people. Yet even these sympathizers expressed some doubt about the authenticity of Suvavou people's self-knowledge. The ultimate goal of this chapter is to point to gaps between these sympathizers' hope for Suvavou people, as dispossessed indigenous people, and Suvavou people's own hope. This incongruity in turn sets the stage for my examination of the incongruities between the direction of anthropological intervention and that of Suvavou people's hope in the chapters that follow.

If chapter 2 situates Suvavou people in the wider politics of indigenous knowledge, in chapter 3, "A Politics of Self-Knowledge," I turn to the internal politics of Suvavou. My focus is on the character of reorientation of knowledge in the context of disputes among Suvavou *mataqali* over the method of distribution of rent money received from the government for the use of their lands. The disputes revolved around a contest between two notions of a whole: the whole defined by the act of combination of parts, and the whole defined by the act of division. In recent years, the emergence of a village company and associated concepts of company shares had introduced a new notion of a whole defined by exchangeable parts (shareholders). My argument is that these competing conceptions of wholes had different temporal implications for the politics of self-knowledge.

In chapters 4, 5, and 6, I address the question of how Suvavou people have kept alive their hope. My focus is on the interplay of agency and temporality in the production of hope. Drawing on my discussion of the politics of self-knowledge in chapters 2 and 3, I investigate how Suvavou people have striven to introduce a prospective momentum to a present moment constantly invaded by retrospection. In these three chapters, I also address three themes that are central to Bloch's philosophy of hope, that is, (1) indeterminacy as a condition of the possibility for hope; (2) the backgrounding of the problem of agency in the production of hope; and (3) the repetitive quality of hope.

In chapter 4, "Setting Knowledge in Motion," I draw attention to the predication of Suvavou people's hope on a delicate balance between an emphasis on future-oriented openness and an anticipation of a moment of closure. My focus is on the content and form of petitions that Suvavou people have sent to the government over the past hundred years. Fijian land officially known as "Native Land" is registered to *mataqali*. The *mataqali*'s ownership is founded on the records kept by the Native Lands Commission, a division of the government that created and has maintained these records. Access to these records is tightly controlled and is rarely granted to members of the public. In this sense, Fijians are alienated from their own self-knowledge. This alienation has conditioned the character of Suvavou people's petitions to reopen inquiry into their landownership. The problem the authors of these petitions have faced, I argue, is how to set in motion their self-knowledge. This has entailed an effort to render the frozen present of Fijian self-knowledge indeterminate, while at the same time indicating a method for alternative closure. My argument, contra the currently dominant treatment of reality, is that in this context, indeterminacy has been an achievement, not a given condition, and that the problem of indeterminacy has been inseparable from the problem of how to bring into view a point of closure.

In chapters 5 and 6, I turn to Suvavou people's religious and gift-giving rituals. On its surface, the highly religious quality of Fijian social life would seem to constitute such a contrast with the secular philosophical efforts to apprehend hope as to render them inapposite. Because most Fijians, including Suvavou people, are Christians, for them, unlike for Bloch and Rorty, God's presence is unquestionable.[15] At another level, however, certain parallels emerge. As in the case of the philosophical debates about hope mentioned above, Fijian hope entailed a discursive game in which conceptions of human and nonhuman agency were negotiated and redefined. Chapter 5, "Intimating Fulfillment," focuses on these moments of what I call the abeyance of agency. A comparison of Christian and gift-giving rituals draws attention to moments in these rituals at which the agency of some or all ritual participants was left in abeyance. I argue that these moments are instrumental in the production of hopeful moments.

In chapter 6, "Repeating Without Overlapping," I demonstrate the predication of hope as a method on replication, that is, on the effort to reproduce prospective momentum to knowledge from one domain to the next. In the first half of the chapter, I examine a series of events surrounding a Suvavou village company's construction project in order to draw attention to different kinds of retrospective perspectives that constantly invaded moments of hope. My focus is on the way Fijians reintroduced a prospective perspective to these moments. Fijians accomplish this task by redefining and reconfiguring the relationship between humans and God in order to repeatedly recapture the prospective momentum latent in retrospection. In the second half of the chapter, I turn to the public debate engendered by an apology Prime Minister Sitiveni Rabuka delivered to the nation for his past conduct. My focus here is on the limits of hope as a method. In this debate, in response to Rabuka's critics, Christian defenders of Rabuka pointed to those critics' failure to appreciate the moment of hope in the prime minister's act of apology. I argue, however, that in engaging in this kind of rhetoric, Rabuka's defenders failed precisely to recapture the hopeful content of Rabuka's apology. My point in this chapter is to demonstrate that hope can only be represented by further acts of hope. I conclude chapter 6 by considering the implications of the repetitive quality of hope for my own endeavor to recapture hopeful moments.

Chapter 7, "Inheriting Hope," concludes the book with a reflection on hopeful moments in anthropology since the 1980s. I focus on two examples of temporal incongruity between anthropological theory and its object: the problem of colonial legacies (Asad 1973; Clifford 1988; Thomas 1991; cf. Said 1978) and the problem of what Michael Fischer has termed "emergent forms of life" (Fischer 1999; see also Appadurai 1996; Strathern 1992). In both cases, anthropological knowledge has been imagined to lag behind what is emergent in its subject. The apprehension of these temporal incongruities has in turn prompted anthropologists to attempt to correct them.[16] This sense of belatedness, in other words, generated in anthropologists a hope of synchronicity. In light of my discussion above, however, this synchronicity must be understood as an illusion. If anthropologists have focused on the question of how to make their knowledge synchronous with the present moment of its subject, my discussion of hope begins with the limit of such synchronicity. The argument of this book is that hope as a method does not rest on an impulse to pursue analytical synchronicity but on an effort to *inherit* and *replicate* that impulse as a spark of hope on another terrain. The ultimate goal of this book, in other words, is to ignite sparks that illuminate the here and now of anthropology.

My turn to hope is a turn away from the now fashionable effort to pursue "new" subjects for ethnographic inquiry. Hope *is* a new subject for anthropology in a sense, but I do not approach hope as a subject. For me, as for the Fijians I knew (and Bloch), hope is a method. As a method, hope is not new, because it is latent in all academic ventures.

2 ⌒ A History of Thwarted Hope

> Money the government has reserved for you is large. It is
> just like water wrapped up in a taro leaf. If something pricks
> it, the money will pour out to you.

Suvavou people attributed the above statement to Ratu Sir Lala
Sukuna (commonly known as Ratu Sukuna), a high chief of Bau,
Fiji's most prominent island, and the architect of the modern Fijian
administrative system (see Scarr 1980). Suvavou people did not
know the exact circumstance under which Ratu Sukuna made this
statement, but they regarded it as evidence that the government has
kept money aside to compensate the descendants of Suva people,
the original landowners of the Suva Peninsula, where the city of
Suva stands today.

In 1882, in order to make room for the newly established colonial capital city, the government relocated Suva people to a tract of
land across the Suva Harbor. The newly established village was
named "Suvavou" ("New Suva"). In a colony where the government ostensibly made great efforts to preserve indigenous populations' land and customs (France 1969), the government in this way
explicitly deprived Suva people (and later Suvavou people) of their
land and their link with the past.[1] Since then, Suvavou people have
made a living on the margins of city life by selling souvenir articles
to tourists or by working at the wharf, in the factories, or as "house
girls" in expatriates' residences in Suva.[2]

Over the past hundred years, however, Suvavou people have
repeatedly demanded proper compensation from the government
for the loss of their ancestral land. The government has repeatedly
rejected these requests. Despite the government's rejections,
Suvavou people have continued to petition it. For the Suvavou people I knew, Ratu Sukuna's statement summarized their mission:
over the past hundred years, they have deployed a variety of strate-

gies in their petitions to the government and have searched for the
exact place to "prick the taro leaf" once and for all.

The image of a sudden flow of water out of a taro leaf in Ratu
Sukuna's statement may resonate with the "episodic" conception
of time that anthropologists have taken to underlie "cargo cult
thought" in Melanesia that culminates in a sudden arrival of a utopian world of abundance (see Errington 1974; McDowell 1985;
Trompf 1990: 188–211; cf. Lindstrom 1993: 59). It would be a
mistake, however, to reduce Suvavou people's pursuit of the promised money to simply either a quest for monetary gains or a quest
for identity. For Suvavou people, getting the promised money depended on finding the correct manner by which to convey their
grievances to the government. The promised money would be an
effect of and a response to the correct manner of presentation.

The Suva Land Case

In 1868, the most powerful Fijian chief of the day, the Vunivalu of
Bau,[3] Ratu Seru Cakobau, sold the Suva Peninsula to the Polynesia
Company of Melbourne, Australia, set up to attract potential settlers to Fiji. Prior to the cession of the Fiji islands to the British
Crown, Cakobau's government owed Washington U.S. $42,248 for
damages caused by some Fijians to some U.S. citizens,[4] and the
Polynesia Company offered to pay this in exchange for the Suva
Peninsula and other large tracts of land, which together amounted
to approximately 90,000 acres.[5] Cakobau offered the Suva Peninsula land for sale to the Polynesia Company on the strength of his
close kinship to Suva's chiefly line[6] (France 1969: 83). After the
sale, the Polynesia Company subdivided approximately 27,000
acres of the Suva Peninsula land for sale to individual European
settlers. Apparently, Suva people nevertheless remained on their
land and resisted some European settlers' attempt to occupy the
tracts of land they had purchased.[7]

Following the cession of the islands by Cakobau and other high
chiefs, the British government paid the Polynesia Company £9,000
and annulled all property transactions between the Cakobau gov-

ernment and the Polynesia Company (Whitelaw 1966: 39).[8] The government upheld the claims of European settlers who could show that they had occupied and made use of lands purchased from the Polynesia Company regardless of the conditions of the original sale (ibid.). However, the government managed to reclaim at least half of the titles it allowed, because many of the European claimants owed money to a certain James McEwan & Co., from which the government acquired their land without payment.[9]

On the face of it, the government's actions with regard to Suva land seem to have conformed to its wider policy of protecting Fijian interests in land. In 1875, the government established a commission to investigate European settlers' claims in Fiji (France 1969: 114–15, 200). Following the recommendations of this commission, the government rejected the majority of the European claims; as a result, Fijians retained approximately 83 percent of the total area of the Fiji Islands (see Ward 1969). The remaining 17 percent of the land was owned by European settlers as freehold property or by the government as Crown property (Ward 1969, 1995). Where European claims to Suva land were rejected by the government, however, the land was not returned to Suva people, unlike everywhere else in Fiji. The government kept all Suva land, except for those tracts already occupied by European settlers, as well as approximately three hundred acres of land that the Polynesia Company had set aside as a "Native Reserve."

In fact, a number of facts suggest that the government never intended to return the land to Suva people.[10] Some time between 1880 and 1882, the government began to construct public facilities in Suva such as a jail, an immigration depot, a hospital, a cemetery, and an asylum.[11] The government also subdivided the land acquired from James McEwan & Co. and sold some of it to government officials.[12] When the capital of Fiji was relocated from Levuka, on the island of Ovalau, to Suva in 1882, the inhabitants of the "Native Reserve" known as Old Suva Village or Naiqasiqasi were removed to Narikoso, a tract of land located diagonally across the Suva Harbor from Suva, where Suvavou is located today.[13] In 1882, the government arranged to pay Suvavou people

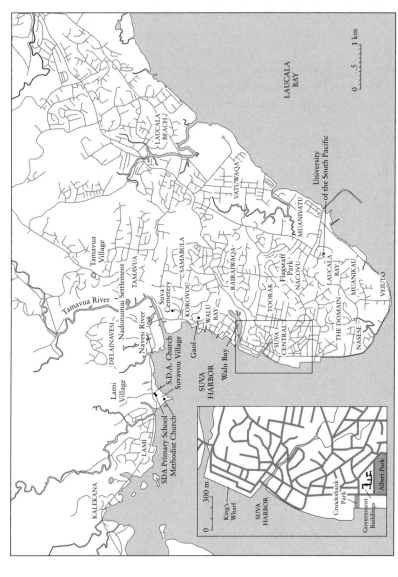

Map 1. The Suva Peninsula (based on map of Suva City, Lami Town, and Environs, FMS 1, 2d ed., Department of Lands and Surveys, 1986)

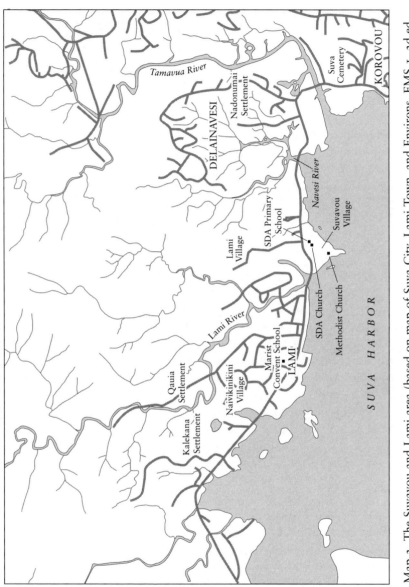

Map 2. The Suvavou and Lami area (based on map of Suva City, Lami Town, and Environs, FMS 1, 2d ed., Department of Lands and Surveys, 1986).

£200 annually, in what was vaguely framed as a form of compensation, although it was left unclear which lands the money pertained to, exactly what it was that was being compensated for, and whether the money was indeed compensation or in fact rent. The legal significance of this payment later became the subject of decades of debate between the government and Suvavou people.

It is important to note that Suvavou people did not challenge this arrangement until November 1898, sixteen years after they were removed from the Suva Peninsula. The timing is interesting, because it coincides with the conversion of the Roko Tui Suva, Ratu Avorosa Tuivuya, and some of Suvavou people to Seventh-Day Adventism earlier that year.[14] Since the first group of Fijians had converted to Christianity in 1835, the majority of Fijian Christians had been Methodists.[15] Suvavou was no exception: according to Methodist missionary records, Ratu Avorosa's father, Ratu Ravulo, converted to Christianity in 1840 (Cargill 1977: 179; Jaggar 1988: 45). Suvavou was the first Fijian village to embrace Seventh-Day Adventism, and the village remains the SDA Church's mission base in Fiji.[16] Ratu Avorosa's conversion to Seventh-Day Adventism must in itself have constituted a challenge to the authority of the government, because of SDA's American leadership and its explicit rejection of certain aspects of Fijian tradition, in contravention of the government's policy of preserving Fijian customs.

When Ratu Avorosa and eight others wrote to the government in 1898 expressing their dissatisfaction with the £200 they received annually and requesting some form of compensation for Suva land,[17] the government responded sharply. William L. Allardyce, assistant colonial secretary, summoned those who had signed the letter. In his minute, Allardyce described a meeting with them in which he had first confronted them by reading it aloud: "I read them their letter enclosed and asked them if they really intended me to take the matter up seriously. They said they did to which I replied 'Very well but you will first of all answer me the following questions.'" Allardyce then asked them:

Why have you waited for the last 20 years and not brought forward your claim until now? You have had many opportunities of doing so.

You admit to receiving and having received for many years past the sum of £200 annually on account of the lands within the yellow mark [including the entire area of the Suva Peninsula] on the accompanying sketch exclusive of lands granted to Europeans.[18]

In response, representatives of Suvavou asserted that the £200 was only compensation for the taking of the Native Reserve land originally allocated to them by the Polynesia Company, on which Government House was built, and was not compensation for the whole of the Suva Peninsula. Allardyce's response was unsympathetic. In his minute, he wrote:

It was too utterly preposterous, that as a matter of fact the whole block on the sketch had little or no value until Government came to Suva,— that they were now jealous because they saw the houses of the Europeans scattered all over what was once their lands, and I had besides been led to believe from what I had heard that they were being prompted by an [sic] European to put in a claim for the land,—that as a matter of fact the £200 paid to them annually and promised to them in perpetuity was, at the present very low rate of back interest, equal to about £10,000,—that this then was the sum which was paid for their lands by Government at a time when they had but very little value, thus showing the liberality of Government; and as it appeared to me that they had come to discuss a subject which they did not know anything whatsoever about I recommended their returning at once to Suvavou which they appeared somewhat anxious to do.[19]

The unsympathetic nature of the government's response to Suvavou people's petition is noteworthy in itself, considering that the government had ostensibly been concerned about the protection of Fijians' land rights since the very early stage of colonization. In 1903, however, Suvavou people again confronted the government in a letter demanding:

1. We wish to know who receives the purchase money or rent money derived from our land.
2. We are the true and only owners of the land, and we know the boundaries of it perfectly well. The reason for our enquiry is that there are a number of Indians building houses on the land, and we, who are the true owners, do not know to whom they pay rent. Please be of a good mind and assist us to obtain relief. We are unhappy because our land is being made use of without our knowledge. It is the wish of the

whole Mataqali [clan] that we be paid rent for our land according to custom.[20]

In response, a government investigation found that a portion of the land belonged to the government and the rest belonged to Europeans, and that the annual payment to the villagers of £200 was for all Suva land held by the government, including the particular portion of land in question.[21]

The following year, Suvavou people again wrote to the government and this time asked the government questions:

1. Who was the owner of the land who gave it away?
2. To whom was the land given?
3. For what reason or in payment of what was the land given?
4. In payment of whose debt was the land given?
5. Who arranged for the land being given?

With reference to the alleged sale of the land

6. Who was the owner of the land who sold it?
7. To whom was it sold?
8. What was the price of the land?
9. Who divided the money?

Every year £200 rent is paid for the piece of land on which the Governor lives, but we get nothing for our land. Why is this?

Section 5 of the Deed of Cession says "that Her Majesty shall have power, whenever it shall be deemed necessary for public purposes, to take any lands upon payment to the proprietor of a reasonable sum by way of compensation for the deprivation thereof." Section 7 Subsection 3 says "That all claims to titles of land, by whomsoever preferred . . . shall in due course be fully investigated and equitably adjusted." We are anxious to have our claim adjusted.

When we see the Indians' houses we are very unhappy as we do not know anything about their occupation of our land. Native Regulation 3 of 1880 Section 1, says "Any person planting on land which is not the property of his Mataqali without the permission of its owners . . ." The Indians have cut down our fruit trees, ivis, dawas, vutus and kavikas and breadfruit. It would be different if we were responsible for our unhappiness, but we are not.[22]

These questions, along with the sophisticated legal argument presented in the letter, led one government official to question its authenticity, writing: "I doubt if there is more than one writer in this case, or perhaps I should be more correct in saying 'inditer,' and that one person is *not* a Fijian."[23] In response, the governor simply decided that given that Suvavou people had accepted £200 every year for Suva land for the past twenty-two years, they had no good reason to make such a claim. Therefore, "[t]he question which was settled so long ago cannot now be reopened."[24] A brief letter to this effect was sent to Suvavou.[25]

In 1907, despite the government's repeated rejection of Suvavou people's claim, a series of letters from Suvavou once again flooded the government office. This time, Suvavou people adopted a new strategy. Assuming that it was impossible to determine the status of the yearly payment, Suvavou people requested that the government *purchase* Suvavou people's interest in whatever the government believed it had been paying £200 per annum for.

> We the people of Suvavou make application to the Government to buy the land outright [*volia vakadua*] on which Government House stands. We are all of one mind in the matter.
> The rent money is really not of much use to us now, it has to be split up into so many divisions. We want money to buy houses etc. with.[26]

This move neatly avoided the question of whether the government was paying for the whole of Suva Peninsula or for the Government House land only and simply asked that the government purchase the Government House land.

The governor at the time, Everald Im Thurn, was himself a critic of the early colonial government's policy of preserving Fijians' lands, and he had changed existing land policy to make room for new European settlers.[27] It was Im Thurn's opinion that the government should not accept Suvavou people's offer to sell the land outright: "I have little hesitation in saying that we should decline this offer—unless we have to accept it for a reason which will appear presently. . . . The really important question on the papers is not whether we should or should not buy the land but on what tenure, if any, we hold it and must continue to hold it."[28]

Im Thurn regarded this case as "important" and "very delicate," and he referred the matter to the Executive Council, which in turn decided to ask for legal advice from the acting chief justice and acting attorney general.[29] Gilchrist Alexander, acting attorney general, in turn referred to another documentary source, an 1887 opinion of a former acting attorney general, Sir Francis Winter, concerning the government's legal position that it had "absolute proprietorship" of the Suva land and that it should treat £200 as an "annuity,"[30] and not as "quit rent."[31] Alexander echoed the argument, writing: "Since the date of Sir Francis Winter's minute the position has been strengthened by the fact that the Crown has been in possession of the land as absolute owner for at least twenty five years and has exercised rights of absolute ownership with the knowledge and acquiescence of the natives."[32]

Therefore, in Alexander's opinion, "the title of the Crown to the lands could not now be successfully attacked."[33] Im Thurn was relieved. It was the government's belief that the issue had been resolved through reinterpreting the purpose of the payment of £200 yearly.

The legal ambiguity surrounding the annuity money continued to plague the government every time Suvavou people drew attention to it, however. In his book on the development of government policy concerning land in Fiji, D. T. Lloyd, who from 1954 to 1966 held appointments as director of lands, mines, and surveys and chairman of the Native Land Trust Board in Fiji, described what he perceived to be the delicate nature of the Suva land case. According to Lloyd, the government had in fact *purchased* a portion of Suva land from Suva people. In Lloyd's understanding, however, although "a generous purchase price was amicably agreed" between the government and Suva people, according to the strict interpretation of government policy to protect Fijian land rights, the government could not alienate any Fijian land, and therefore it was decided that "any capital sums arising from the sale of mataqali land to government should be treated likewise and invested on behalf of the mataqali, the interest accruing being distributed annually amongst the surviving members" (Lloyd 1982: 184). Lloyd claims that this was the origin of the annuity money Suvavou people have received since 1882. However, according to Lloyd, when Suvavou people sought an increase of the annuity money in 1960, a delicate legal issue was raised:

> The petition raised not only those very complex and virtually fathom-
> less financial issues of estate management associated with annuities, the
> intricacies of which were beyond the comprehension of the Fijians con-
> cerned, but it also brought to the notice of government and the Fijian
> administration that the disbursement of the money had hitherto not
> been effected in accordance with the stipulations laid down by the
> British government in 1905 and later enshrined in law by the regula-
> tions made in 1941 under the provisions of the Native Lands Trust
> Ordinance for the disbursement of interest and rents accruing from
> mataqali-owned land. Nevertheless, after protracted and patient dis-
> cussions with the recipients, and with the assistance of the Fijian admin-
> istration and the petitioners' own private legal advisers, the official
> explanation as to why the quantum could not be changed was accept-
> ed and the sum of £200 continued to be paid. (Lloyd 1982: 185)

The details of the discussions held with the government during
the 1960s were not available to either Suvavou people or myself at
the time of my fieldwork. What is important for current purposes
is that, as Lloyd put it, the government has dismissed Suvavou people's request by regarding them as not understanding "the intrica-
cies" of legal and financial implications of the Suva land case. The
government's initial unsympathetic treatment of Suvavou people's
request was therefore symptomatic of a more general condescending and patronizing attitude toward Suvavou people. In the opinion of many government officials, Suvavou people simply did not
understand the nature of the problem they were raising. In more
practical terms, extensive commercial and state interests are at
stake in the Suva land case, and over the past century, the colonial
and postcolonial governments have mobilized considerable legal
and administrative resources to reject Suvavou people's request.

The government's condescending attitude toward Suvavou people continued even after the 1987 coups d'état replaced the existing coalition government with a nationalist government ostensibly
dedicated to "indigenous rights," in which Suvavou people found
vocal sympathizers.[34] For many Fijian government officials, the
case of Suvavou people epitomized the plight of commoner landowners, and they looked upon Suvavou people with compassion

and pity. But they also had inherited the colonial view that because of their long exposure to city life, Suvavou people were not authentic traditional Fijians,[35] and they referred to Suvavou people as "ignorant" in terms of their own heritage. Several government officials even warned me to be careful of Suvavou people, because they would tell me all kinds of "lies," albeit out of "ignorance." This image of Suvavou people as, on the one hand, exemplary victims of colonial and chiefly politics, and, on the other, acculturated Fijians who did not know who they were triggered intense ambivalence after the 1987 coups d'état.

In the post-coup era, as part of the celebration of indigenous and commoner rights, a number of Fijian groups sought to reclaim land that had been alienated by high chiefs during the nineteenth century,[36] and, as a result, many conflicts between the government and high chiefs, on the one hand, and lesser chiefs and commoner Fijians, on the other, had arisen.[37] These claims provided a financial opportunity for a number of Fijian lawyers and so-called consultants in Suva who specialized in providing rural Fijians with legal advice on land disputes. These consultants' principal role was to prepare documents for submission to the government on their clients' behalf, in return for a portion of any resulting compensation.

During this period, Suvavou people also intensified their compensation campaign. The chief of Suvavou, the Tui Suva, Ratu Epeli Kanakana, began to make use of diverse styles of campaigning to advance Suvavou people's long-standing claim to Suva land. At my first meeting with the Tui Suva in November 1994, he compared the Suva land case with the cases of the Australian Aborigines and New Zealand Maoris, and he seemed very much inspired by the recent successes of indigenous peoples abroad in reclaiming their lands. In 1993, he published a full-page newspaper advertisement in the *Fiji Times* concerning his claim to the Suva land, entitled "To Commemorate the International Year for the Indigenous People."[38] He also publicly insisted that anyone who wished to avoid offending the spirits of Suva land should pay tribute to him before undertaking any major projects in the city.[39] In early 1994, the Tui Suva

even occupied a piece of reclaimed state foreshore land in Muani-
kau and settled his relatives from Rewa there in order to demonstrate his authority over the land.[40] Ratu Epeli also worked closely
with nationalist leaders and politicians, including a former president of the Methodist Church, Rev. Manasa Lasaro, and the Fiji
Nationalist Party leader Sakiusa Butadroka. During the period of
my research, the Tui Suva and his people also repeatedly visited the
residence of Prime Minister Sitiveni Rabuka to convey their desire
for compensation.

As part of this campaign, Suvavou people engaged Anare Matahau, principal of one of the more successful consulting firms in
Suva, Anare Matahau and Associates, to press their case. Matahau,
a former Ministry of Fijian Affairs official, had studied law and
land management in England before returning to Fiji to participate
in a review of the Fijian administrative system during the mid
1980s.[41] Matahau had become a controversial figure in the 1990s
after establishing the Foundation of the Indigenous People of Fiji,
commonly known among Fijians as Yavutu.[42] The organization's
principal demand was the return of all state land to its original
owners. Its establishment in 1993 coincided with the International
Year of the World's Indigenous People, when Matahau organized a
march through Suva that attracted a number of chiefs from western Viti Levu and from other lesser chiefdoms who were not content with the post-coup political situation.[43] The Tui Suva, Ratu
Epeli Kanakana, was deeply involved in Matahau's movement, and
even served as one of the Yavatu's directors.

Matahau collaborated with another former Ministry of Fijian
Affairs official, whom I shall call Inoke Vuki, to research the Suva
land case. Together they prepared a 222-page report entitled *Suva
State Land: "Land of My Fathers."* In July 1991, the Tui Suva,
Ratu Epeli Kanakana, signed and submitted this report to the gov-
ernment. The report claimed that all 2,000 acres of state land in the
Suva Peninsula should be returned to Suvavou people. The princi-
pal argument of the report was founded on a Ministry of Fijian
Affairs confidential file from 1963 that Vuki discovered at the min-

Figure 1. Tui Suva Ratu Epeli Kanakana signing a report prepared by
Anare Matahau at his residence in Suvavou on July 15, 1991. Courtesy
Fiji Times.

istry. In this file, the secretary for Fijian affairs speculated that the
government's acquisition of Suva land had been legally based on
Clause 4 of the Deed of Cession.[44] The clause in question reads:

> That the absolute proprietorship of all lands, not shown to be now
> alienated, so as to have become *bona fide* the property of Europeans or
> other Foreigners, or not now in the actual use or occupation of some
> Chief or tribe, or not actually required for the probable future support
> and maintenance of some Chief or tribe, shall be and is hereby declared
> to be vested in Her said Majesty, Her Heirs and Successors.[45]

Upon identifying Clause 4 of the Deed of Cession as the government's principal justification for the taking of Suva land, the report
claimed that Fiji's first governor, Sir Arthur Gordon,[46] had not regarded it as a workable clause.[47] If one took Gordon's view that
Clause 4 should not be implemented, the report argued, then that
clause did not provide a valid basis for the acquisition of Suva land,
as suggested in the secretary for Fijian affairs' interpretation in 1963.

The report also presented an alternative argument. It further noted that in a speech delivered to Fijian chiefs in 1908, Governor Im Thurn had suggested that the government should use Clause 4 to make Fijians' unused land available for European settlement. In that speech, Im Thurn had offered to pay Fijian owners two-thirds of the rent derived from land taken under Clause 4. Based on Im Thurn's interpretation of the uses of Clause 4, the report argued, then Suvavou people were owed two-thirds of the rent received by the government for properties in Suva since the founding of the capital. Under either interpretation of Clause 4, the report concluded, Suvavou people were entitled to compensation.[48]

Despite their support for Suvavou people, Vuki, Matahau, and many government officials believed that most of Suvavou people were uneducated and knew little of their own history. In his foreword to *Suva State Land: "Land of My Fathers,"* the Tui Suva admitted that he and his people did not know much about their own past. Vuki and Matahau believed that the truth could be found in the archives, but not in Suvavou, because Suvavou people lacked self-knowledge, and the purpose of their report was therefore to *restore* lost information about Suva land. There is a certain ironic continuity, in other words, between colonial and postcolonial government officials' conceptions of the reliability of Suvavou people's knowledge about their own past. From this point of view, the researchers' location of truth in the archives was emblematic of Fijians' wider alienation from knowledge about themselves.

The Hidden Document

As discussed in chapter 4, some Suvavou people, especially those who had conducted archival research on the Suva land case, opposed this view. Even critics of the consultants, however, shared their view that somewhere in the government archives, there was a document that would validate their claim once and for all. In discussing their research, they often complained that they had not been able to have access to crucial documents at government offices and in the archives. Both the consultants and Suvavou researchers explained to me that the government had hidden (*vunitaka*) crucial documents concerning the Suva land case and had closed (*sogo tiko*) all the files to protect its own interests. In an interview with me, Vuki's excitement about the discovery of the key confidential file was tempered by the fact that the crucial map of Suva land referred to in the letter was missing from the file.[49] One Suvavou researcher even sued the government for failing to release documentary evidence to her. This woman claimed that her mother was a descendant of the original chiefly line of Suva, which now was extinct, and that her mother's great-grandfather had signed a government document that promised his descendants a large amount of rent money for a portion of the Suva land. In the court pleadings, as in her conversations with me, she claimed that she once had seen this document at the Lands Department. While this woman's claims concerning her ancestry did not have many supporters in the village, other Suvavou researchers shared her view that crucial documents about Suva land were "locked up in a safe" at a government office. Another researcher told me of the Native Lands Commission: "They have another 'book' that is usually locked up in a safe. When we discussed our claim with them, they took the book out and checked our information by comparing it with the content of the book before putting it back again in the safe."

The question of Suvavou people's hope must therefore be contextualized, not only in colonial and postcolonial politics of recognition (see, e.g., Cohn 1987b; Dirks 2001; Rappaport 1994), as I have demonstrated to this point, but also in the epistemological consequences of archives more generally (cf. Axel 2002; Dirks 2002; S. Kaplan 2002; Steedman 1998; Stoler 2002a; see also Derrida 1995: 9–10; Foucault 1972: 6–7; Grafton 1997). At the time of my fieldwork, government records prior to 1960 were available to local researchers as well as to overseas research permit-holders at the discretion of the government archivist at the National Archives of Fiji. Yet Suvavou people believed that it was difficult for them to obtain access to even these "open" government records. Access to Native Lands Commission records was generally very difficult for both Fijian and non-Fijian researchers. At the time of my fieldwork, government officials as well as local researchers were under the impression that only chiefs or heads (*i liuilu*) of *vanua* (chiefdoms) could request these records from the Native Lands Commission (NLC). When I asked to see them, an NLC official instructed me to present a bundle of *yaqona* (kava, or *piper me-thysticum*) to the Tui Suva to obtain his written permission. The NLC official explained that the records belonged to chiefs and that one needed to seek their permission to examine them.

After several months of archival research, I also began to believe that crucial documents about the Suva land case must be hidden somewhere at the National Archives of Fiji.[50] Government records were classified into numerous separately indexed series, and none of the available indexes were complete. Many files had not been transferred to the archives from government offices and request slips for documents often were returned to me marked "Not avail-able" or "Missing." What is interesting in retrospect is that, as for Suvavou people, this experience only seemed to intensify my hope of locating "the lost or missing sheet." Even the government ar-chivist was concerned about the "sensitivity" of the Suva land case, because she also believed, she told me, that there might be a "polit-ical bomb" lying hidden somewhere in the archives.

We were not the only ones to become obsessed with the hidden document. What is clear from the archival record is that this obses-sion also afflicted generations of government officials. From the beginning of the conflict, the government confronted one problem-atic fact: despite the colonial government's meticulous documenta-tion of most transactions, no formal deed had been exchanged with respect to Suva land.[51] There was thus no written evidence to sub-stantiate the government's title. In 1907, Governor Im Thurn wrote frustratedly:

> Somewhere about 1882 we by arrangement with the then native occu-pants took over the land on which Government House stands and a good deal else—but, as I have said, I don't know what else.
>
> It is evident from C.S.O. 2908/07 that no title to the land or agree-ment with the Natives is in existence; and that even at that date it was proposed to remedy the defect by legislation; that this legislation was never carried into effect is certain; and that the Government has there-

fore still no title beyond what it may have acquired by the acquiescence of the natives in our possession of the land and by their acceptance of the rent since 1882.

No report on the arrangement made with the Natives was sent to the Secretary of State; and the only reference to the transaction to be found in despatches is in paragraph 9 of Sir G. W. Des Voeux'[s] Despatches No. 2 of 6th January 1882 in which, in commenting on the estimates for that year, he writes—"Item 9 rent charge on Suva Native Land, £200, is an amount which in the opinion of the Commissioner of Native Affairs is the least that will satisfy the Natives of the Suva peninsula, who in accordance with an arrangement made by Sir Arthur Gordon are to vacate these lands and to move the site of their principal town. . . ."

It appears probable that there never was any written agreement with the Natives as to our taking over the land, but that the arrangement, made in 1882, was a mere verbal one between the Native owners (as represented by Ratu Ambrose) and a Mr. Cocks[,] Clerk of the Provincial Office[,] and the Commissioner of Lands; that Mr Cocks at the time made some sort of a written memo as to the nature of the transaction but that this memo has long since been lost.[52]

Suvavou people could not have known at the time that precisely the point they were pressing in their letters to the government was sparking such intensive internal debate. In late 1907, Suvavou people approached a Suva legal firm, Crompton and Muspratt, which in turn requested that the government release any documentary evidence it might have that Suvavou people had "surrendered" their right to Suva land to the government.[53] In response, the Colonial Secretary, Arthur Mahaffy, confidently reiterated that: "Since the year 1882 your clients have accepted the sum of £200 as an 'annual amount due to the natives of Suva for their removal from all lands upon the Suva Peninsula and for their absolute surrender to the Crown of all right title and interest therein as taukeis or native owners of the said land' and have signed receipts in that form."[54]

Behind the scenes, however, Mahaffy expressed frustration at not being able to produce direct evidence for its position, writing: "The trouble is that we can produce no documentary proof of the transfer of these lands. The letter 'touches the spot.'"[55]

In light of the history I have recounted, Suvavou people's repeated failures in their quest for compensation can be attributed to the powerlessness of a marginal, displaced, and dispossessed people in both the colonial and postcolonial worlds. Their capacity to maintain hope in the validity of their claim could be understood from this perspective as a mere lack of appreciation of their own marginality, of the weakness of their position in the wider political economy of Fiji. It is also the case that their enduring effort in the face of their failure to find the hidden document in the archives is an effect of a wider regime of truth: the experience of the colonial government, of Fiji's government archivist, of the Suva consultants, and even myself clearly suggests the inherent capacity of archives to generate a sense of partiality and hence to defer the frontier of the truth.

However, I wish to return at this point to Suvavou people's repeated invocation of Ratu Sukuna's statement mentioned at the outset of this chapter and their ongoing search for something that would "prick the taro leaf." In contrast to the above explanations, their own explanations of their past failures focus on their failure to present themselves in an "effective" manner. Suvavou people often told me that the moment in which they finally obtained the promised money would be the moment in which, in their own words, "the truth manifests itself" ("basika mai na ka dina"). This mention of the "truth" was not accidental. As A. M. Hocart, Marshall Sahlins, and others have pointed out, in the Fijian context, what is effective or efficacious (*mana*) is truthful (*dina*) and vice versa (see Hocart 1914; Sahlins 1985: 37–38), and for Suvavou people, a search for an effective manner of request has become a search for the truth and vice versa. From this standpoint, Suvavou people's long-standing struggle for proper compensation for the loss of their land has been a quest for the truth, of which the promised money would serve as proof. It is in this nexus between money and self-knowledge that I wish to situate Suvavou people's hope. In the next chapter, I turn to this nexus of money and self-knowledge in the context of Suvavou's internal politics.

3 ⌒ A Politics of Self-Knowledge

As mentioned in the previous chapter, the post-coup coming to power of nationalist defenders of indigenous rights, together with the Tui Suva's own intensified campaign, had created an atmosphere of heightened anticipation among Suvavou people that their claim might this time finally be recognized. In anticipating the fulfillment of their long-standing hope, however, Suvavou people were sharply divided. This was evident from the earliest days of my fieldwork in Suvavou. Several weeks after I met the Tui Suva for the first time, I visited Suvavou, hoping to talk to him again. However, he was away attending a mortuary ceremony, and so I began to walk home. As I was leaving the village, a young man approached me and asked me what I was doing in the village. I explained that I was conducting research into the history of Suvavou, and that I had come to see the Tui Suva, but that no one was home. The young man interjected that there was no point in talking to the Tui Suva, because he did not know anything. Puzzled by this blatant criticism of the village chief, I listened to what this young man had to say. He suggested that I should meet his "uncle" instead, and gave me a telephone number to call. Several days later, I was taken by the man's younger brother in darkness to a small house in one of several settlements on village land. There, I met a middle-aged man, who recounted a very different version of Suvavou history. According to this man, who described himself as a "researcher," the Tui Suva was not a "true chief" (*turaga dina*). The researcher asserted that the Tui Suva's *mataqali,* whom I shall call Mataqali Kaiwai, had illegitimately assumed the chiefly title after the last surviving member of the original chiefly line, Mataqali Roko Tui

Suva, died in 1918. The researcher's *mataqali*, whom I shall call Mataqali Koromakawa, had produced a series of "reports" to prove its version of Suvavou history.

Mataqali Koromakawa's claim posed a significant challenge to the Tui Suva's campaign. The Mataqali Koromakawa researcher asserted to me that his kin would be able to stop any efforts to claim compensation for the loss of Suva land that did not have their endorsement. According to him, the village company, Nadonumai Holdings, was destined to fail because it was based on the wrong ordering of *vanua* ("chiefdom"). From the point of view of many of the Tui Suva's supporters, Mataqali Koromakawa's challenge was indeed well founded. They reasoned that the disunity in the village was to blame for the long delay in Nadonumai Holdings's acquisition of the title to a piece of land promised by the government for its business use. Some wondered if their hope would be thwarted once again, just like past hopes expressed in the petitions to the government discussed in chapter 2.

Mataqali Koromakawa's dissent from village efforts to gain compensation for their lands is part of a much longer history of disunity within the village.[1] Indeed, Suvavou people have been divided not only in their strategy for seeking compensation for Suva land but also as to the consequential details of their knowledge about who they are. The disunity among Suvavou people has manifested itself largely as disagreement about the method of distribution of shares of annuity and rent that villagers receive from the government (see chapter 2). Because of the way the government stipulates that it be distributed between different *mataqali* with particular ceremonial duties, the distribution of shares of the rent money immediately raises the question of how to allocate ceremonial duties, and vice versa. In order to resolve the question of how to distribute the rent, villagers must first agree on such questions as how many *mataqali* or *yavusa* (sets of *mataqali*) there are in a village, which *mataqali* is the legitimate holder of the chiefly title of a village, and so forth. The question of who gets what share of annuity and rent money, in other words, translates immediately into the question of knowledge about who one is in terms of the ritual order of a chiefdom or a village, and vice versa. The division of money arising from land therefore becomes the focus of the politics of self-knowledge.

In a series of writings on relations of parts and wholes, Marilyn Strathern contrasts the relationship between parts and wholes imagined in Euro-American knowledge with that of Melanesian knowledge (Strathern 1991b, 1992, 1997). According to Strathern, Euro-American knowledge focuses on the act of integrating parts into a coherent whole, while Melanesian knowledge focuses on the act of dividing a given whole. In Melanesian knowledge, she argues, parts are outcomes of the act of dividing a given whole, an act that aims to make division explicit. For Melanesians, parts therefore constitute the end point of analysis.[2] By drawing attention to the contrast between the direction of Euro-American knowledge and the direction of Melanesian knowledge in terms of the part-whole relationship, Strathern here points to the possibility of reorienting anthropological knowledge itself. In other words, the end point of Euro-American knowledge becomes the starting point of Melanesian knowledge and of Strathern's anthropological exploration, and this reorientation in turn makes available decomposition as an analytical aesthetic (see Strathern 1991b; see also Verran 2001).

What is particularly important for present purposes is Strathern's attention to the direction of knowledge. In this chapter, I seek to examine the interplay of two contrasting conceptions of the relationship between parts and wholes at work in Suvavou people's knowledge practices. My argument is that the politics of self-knowledge in Suvavou are also predicated on attention to its directionality. As we shall see in later chapters, this attention to the directionality of self-knowledge, and its associated temporal reorientation of knowing, are in turn central to the production of hope.

My focus is on disputes among different factions of the village over the method of distribution of shares of annuity and rent money. I first turn to anthropological debates about the nature of the Fijian *mataqali* as the unit of division, and in particular, as the unit of distribution of shares of money arising from land. The

mataqali surfaces as the ontological nexus of Suvavou people's pursuit of promised money and their effort to confirm their knowledge
of who they really are. My ultimate goal is to situate Suvavou people's hope in this politics of division.

The Logic of Division

For many Fijians, the question of who they are invokes a series of
questions regarding their *vanua* ("land," or a collective entity
under a titular head), *yavusa* (set of "clans"), *mataqali* ("clan"),
and *i tutu* ("standing," or ceremonial duty in the ritual order of the
vanua). This model of self-knowledge derives from the form of the
government's inquiry into Fijian social organization and landownership in the early twentieth century. In 1880, the Fiji government
established the Native Lands Commission (NLC) to register Fijian
titles to land according to an official model of Fijian social structure, in which Fijians were organized into *i tokatoka* (subdivisions
of *mataqali*), *mataqali*, and *yavusa*.[3] The NLC meticulously recorded the names and kinship of local landowning units, and as "evidence" of ownership, it also recorded each unit's narrative of
migration from its origin place to the land it now occupied. By the
end of the 1910s, the NLC had adopted a standardized form of evidence taking. At each hearing, NLC officials summoned representatives of each *yavusa* to give statements regarding their *yavusa*'s
migration to its present site of residence and to provide an account
of the current composition of the *yavusa*, including the ceremonial
duties or standing (*i tutu*) of each *mataqali* within the *yavusa*. Once
the NLC had obtained these statements, it summoned other representatives of each *mataqali* within the *yavusa*, asked them questions about each *mataqali*'s status within the *yavusa*, and finally
required them to swear to the validity of the statements given by
their *yavusa* representative. The main texts of the ensuing migration narratives were recorded in a book entitled *Ai tukutuku raraba* (literally, "general statements"), while the testimony of the col-
laborating witnesses was recorded in what the NLC called its
"Evidence Book." By the mid twentieth century, the NLC had reg-

istered all Fijian land ("Native Land") to particular owners, and wherever possible, it assigned ownership to *mataqali* according to the official model of Fijian social structure in which a Fijian village is segmented into *yavusa, mataqali,* and *i tokatoka* (see France 1969).

Since the completion of the NLC inquiries, anthropologists have repeatedly challenged the official focus on *mataqali* and its accompanying inalienable tie to land as the source of Fijian identity, contrasting the rigidity of the official model with the "flexible" nature of the reality of Fijian social organization. For example, the Fijian social anthropologist Rusiate Nayacakalou, who was trained at the London School of Economics, noted:

> [W]hile I have the highest regard for the records of the NLC and for the competence of the men who compiled them, I believe that the commission has erred in its conception of the basic structure of Fijian society. I believe that the compilation of these records was inspired by a conception of Fijian society which was too rigid, tying down the constitution of Fijian social groups to descent alone, thus robbing the system of much of its flexibility. (Nayacakalou 1965: 126)

After highlighting the fact that *mataqali* as landowning units were not known to the rural Fijians with whom he worked, Henry Rutz also argued that while "*mataqali* was a term employed unambiguously to refer to a division of the village . . . for purposes of ceremonial exchange, these units cross-cut *yavusa* and *tokatoka* [and were] terms used interchangeably to refer to political coalitions of unrelated (by descent) groups." Like Nayacakalou, Rutz aimed to demonstrate the flexible nature of Fijian social organization: "During the course of a year, the members of some of these groupings shifted several times, and informants would note the shift by saying that, *e.g.,* 'There were five *mataqali* but this year *mataqali veibatiki* split and now there are six.'"[4]

Likewise, Peter France, a colonial official turned historian, lamented: "Whilst in village life the [official] system is ignored or evaded wherever possible, it is, at the national level, lauded and defended as being the very foundation of Fijian social order" (France 1969: 174; see also Clammer 1973: 218–19).

The anthropologist A. M. Hocart, who conducted extensive ethnographic fieldwork in various parts of Fiji during the early twentieth century, took a somewhat different view. For him, *mataqali* were units that surfaced for the distribution of tasks and of shares in *veiqaravi* or presentation of feasts and gifts to the chief. As he put it: "The clan [*mataqali*] is partly artificial: it is a family cut and trimmed and adjusted to one particular purpose, the feast. . . . [T]he clan system is an organization for the purpose of levying contributions; and also for distributing them; for the fast [*sic*] is divided, it was collected, by clans."[5]

Hocart also pointed out the flexible nature of such units. Depending on the occasion, the units could be individual villagers, households, *mataqali, yavusa,* or chiefdoms:

> As the extent of the feast varies (it may embrace the whole state, or only part of a village), the units of assessment vary. Besides, a given unit is not fixed for all the time, like our provinces, districts, and parishes; the units are not territories, but families that multiply or die out, and so have to be split up, or fused with others. It thus may come to pass that such a unit may be a *matanggali* now, because it used to be one and yet not a *matanggali*, because it is too small to stand on its own, or has grown so big that it has had to be divided into several *matanggali*. (Hocart 1952: 22)

However, Hocart stressed that once units of division were determined, the difference in size between divisions was ignored: "[t]he *matanggali* is an assessment unit for feasts, that is to say that contributions in pigs, yams, fish, and so forth, are assessed by *matanggali*, not by heads" (1952: 22). For example, when *mataqali* were used as the units for division, although one *mataqali* might be bigger than the others, the *mataqali* each received an equal share of exchange items. In other words, while many systems might be available to divide the same whole, once a system was chosen, it was maintained throughout the entire operation of division. Different mechanisms of division were not to be used in a single operation such as the distribution of exchange goods.

Hocart's understanding of the nature of the Fijian *mataqali* derived from his recognition of what he termed Fijians' "passion for dichotomy" (1970 [1936]: 269). According to Hocart, this passion derived from the Fijian form of ritual order rooted in the "mutual ministration" (*veiqaravi*) between divisions (Hocart 1952: 52): "The ritual requires two sides which represent the spirits. Whatever the unit is that celebrates the feast, two sides there must be, and therefore every unit splits into two. In the words of a Lauan, 'In Fiji all things go in pairs, or the sharks will bite'" (ibid.: 57; cf. Toren 1994).[6]

Hocart's point was, therefore, that Fijians' interest in division that generates parts of a whole derived from this form of worship or "communion" (Hocart 1952: 53).[7] In other words, although the effect of the aesthetic of "mutual ministration" was a dichotomized world, the Fijian emphasis lay on the form of *veiqaravi* and not on the oppositions it engendered. Hocart noted that this form reappeared at every level of Fijian social life: "Every unit is divided into two, and again in two right down to the clan, which normally consists of two 'edges of the oven,' as they are called, a senior and a junior one. The subdivisions are to one another as the whole is to another whole" (Hocart 1970 [1936]: 269).

What I encountered in Suvavou during the mid 1990s was a proliferation of the official model of segmentation in all aspects of Suvavou social life. Suvavou people repeatedly used the officially registered model of three *yavusa* segmented into ten *mataqali* as a template for division of all kinds. Divisions into *yavusa* and *mataqali* remained the most important for the purposes of feasting, gift-giving, and the distribution of shares of rent money. Whenever gift-giving took place in the village, shares of valuables and feasts were redistributed according to these divisions. Suvavou people alternately chose *mataqali* or *yavusa* as units of distribution, depending on the occasion, and referred to each method of division as *wase vakamataqali* (division by *mataqali*) and *wase vakayavusa* (division by *yavusa*), respectively. For example, when the Seventh-Day Adventist Church in Fiji presented valuables and feasts to the Tui Suva to thank him for allowing the SDA Church to use a piece of village land for the mission-run secondary school, gifts consisting of a cow and drums of kerosene were distributed equally among the ten *mataqali*. Likewise, when I presented valuables and ritual food items to the Tui Suva upon my departure, I was advised to prepare three units of each item so that each *yavusa* might receive equal shares.

"[T[he term *mataqali* could be made unambiguous by narrowing the field of reference to dealings with administrators," Rutz noted in the 1970s (1978: 24). It is possible that Suvavou people's frequent use of the official model may have derived from the long-term intensive negotiations with the government described in the previous chapter. Indeed, partly because different village factions have repeatedly sought to enlist the government's support in their internal conflicts within the village, as I describe in this chapter, the authority of the government has always been present in Suvavou people's self-knowledge. Numerous letters written by Suvavou people to the government since the NLC inquiries attest to the way in which the official model became an important subject and basis for debate among themselves, as well as between the villagers and the government.

Alternatively, Suvavou people's strong interest in the operation of division according to the official model of segmentation may have resulted from what Hocart called Fijians' "passion" for division. With some irritation, Hocart noted Fijians' tendency to extend such operations of division to "secular" spheres of life: "[The] dichotomy was becoming so common as to be cheap. It was being extended to all occasions, and was no longer reserved for ritual ones. . . . Not only does too much use make stale, the multiplying of subdivisions was bound . . . to obscure the whole dualism."[8] The proliferation of the official model of segmentation in many aspects of Suvavou social life may be an example of the extension Hocart regarded as a sign of "decay" (Hocart 1952: 58).

The question I wish to address in the next section, however, concerns neither the effects of Suvavou people's long-term engagement with state power nor the effects of the excessive extension of Fijian symbolic order. I wish to focus, rather, on the competing conceptualizations of the relationship between parts and wholes entailed in different models of division that have emerged in dialogue with the official model of segmentation. Ultimately, my focus is on the different temporal relations involved in these competing part-whole relationships. I draw on disputes over the method of distribution of shares of rent in Suvavou since the 1920s.

The Division of Rent

Today, tourism is an increasingly significant part of Fiji's national economy. From the standpoint of ethnic Fijians, who own over 83 percent of the national territory, tourism is not only a major source of employment but also a major source of rental income arising from the leasing of their land to hotels and resorts. At the time of my fieldwork, the Native Land Trust Board (hereafter NLTB), the entity established in the 1940s to administer the leasing of Fijian land, divided money received from the leasing of Fijian lands into shares allocated to the head of *vanua*, the head of the *yavusa*, the head of the *mataqali* and members of the *mataqali*.[9] Officially, the NLTB scheme mandated that rent be allocated as follows:

NLTB (administrative costs)	25%
Landowners	75%
Turaga i Taukei (the head of *vanua*)	5%
Turaga ni Qali (heads of *yavusa*)	10%
Turaga ni Mataqali (heads of *mataqali*)	15%
Registered members of Mataqali	70%

(information from Ward 1995: 221)

Because of the way rent money is distributed, the process immediately involves questions of rank. As a result, the division of rent money has become one of the most sensitive and divisive issues in Fiji.

At the time of my fieldwork, there were no hotels or resorts on Suvavou land.[10] A large portion of Suvavou's 388 acres of land,[11] however, had been developed by the NLTB in the 1970s into a residential subdivision known as Delainavesi.[12] There were also several other tracts of land that were leased to outside parties under NLTB lease arrangements. In addition, the Seventh-Day Adventist Church had its headquarters and schools on Suvavou land. Suvavou people received rent for all of these pieces of land. At the time of my fieldwork, Suvavou people collectively received between F$9,000 and F$14,000 every six months as rent for village land leased through the NLTB. In addition, Suvavou people also collectively received F$9,400 per year from the government as an "annuity" for the Government House grounds where the Old Suva Village was located until 1882 (see chapter 2).[13]

These two kinds of money were paid to Suvavou people in different ways. The government divided the annuity money into shares allocated to the chief of the village, the heads of three *yavusa* of the village, the heads of ten *mataqali* of the village, and the ten *mataqali*. Rent money for Suvavou land, on the other hand, was paid to Suvavou people as an undivided lump sum.[14] This reflected the fact that, unlike in other Fijian villages, where land was registered to *mataqali*, Suvavou land was registered as the common property of the three *yavusa* of Suvavou. What makes the disputes over rent money in Suvavou unique, therefore, is the existence of two competing conceptions of the relationship between *mataqali* and land. Whereas the government's method of payment of the annuity money treated the *mataqali* as the unit of ownership, the government's method of payment of the rent money treated the village as a whole as the unit of ownership.

At the time of my fieldwork, following the standard manner of distribution of rent money elsewhere, Suvavou people informally divided the rent money they received into shares allocated to the heads of the three *yavusa* of the village, the heads of the ten *mataqali*, and the ten *mataqali*.[15] Since the 1920s, Suvavou people have had considerable disagreements about the proper method of division of rent and annuity money. In particular, several factions of Suvavou had challenged the NLC's registration of Suvavou land as the common property of the three *yavusa* and insisted that Suvavou land was owned with *mataqali* as units.

Judging from government records, however, prior to 1918, there was little disagreement about how to divide the village and the money. Suvavou people and government officials agreed that *mataqali* were the units of ownership. Before 1918, the government recognized the existence of nine *mataqali* in Suvavou. This was based on the NLC's first inquiry into land ownership among Suvavou people, completed in 1902. This inquiry found that Suvavou land was divided into pieces of land all of which had a name.[16] After that inquiry therefore, rent money for the leasing of a piece of Suvavou land was paid to the *mataqali* for which that particular piece was registered, after shares were paid to the Roko Tui Suva, as the head of *yavusa* as well as the head of *vanua*. This official allocation of land rights continued to provide a model for the informal allocation of land use rights. At the time of my fieldwork, each *mataqali* clearly claimed its own *kanakana* (planting ground) and *yavu* (foundations for houses) and enjoyed more or less exclusive rights to those pieces of land.[17] From time to time, *mataqali* granted land from their *kanakana* to immigrants under so-called *vaka-vanua* ("according to tradition"), or informally arranged settlements (see Rutz 1987). Such transactions did not involve any formal transfer of ownership or exchange of lease contracts but instead required the presentation of valuables such as *tabua* (whales' teeth) and kerosene, along with occasional contributions to the *mataqali* at the time of large gift exchange.[18] If these pieces of land were formally leased through the NLTB, however, rent would be paid to Suvavou people as a whole.

The disputes that have permeated the village originate from the death of the last member of Suvavou's chiefly *mataqali*, Mataqali Roko Tui Suva, in 1918.[19] This forced the government to confront the question of what to do with the shares of the annuity and rent money that the now "extinct" chiefly *mataqali* had received. Prior to 1918, the annuity money was divided into equal shares for the nine *mataqali*, after shares were distributed to the nine heads of *mataqali* and the holder of the chiefly title, the Roko Tui Suva. In 1907, for example, this money was divided as follows:

Buli Suva (government position in charge of
   the District of Suva)   £10/0/0
Turaga i Taukei (the head of *vanua*)   £10/0/0
Turaga ni Qali (the head of *yavusa*)   £20/0/0
Turaga ni Mataqali (heads of *mataqali*)   £30/0/0
   (divided by 9 turaga ni *mataqali*; each received £3/6/8)

Mataqali	£120/0/0
(divided by 9 clans; each clan received £13/6/8)	
Rewa Provincial Fund	£10/0/0

(CSO 4469/1907)

At that time, Ratu Avorosa Tuivuya collected the shares for the Turaga i Taukei, the Turaga ni Qali, and the head of his own *mataqali*, Mataqali Roko Tui Suva. In addition, a few pieces of land belonging to Mataqali Roko Tui Suva had been leased out, generating additional rent for that *mataqali*.

The government resolved the matter by keeping the *mataqali*'s shares of the annuity and rent money for itself.[20] The basis for this move was probably an official policy, first stipulated in the Deed of Cession, that land belonging to "extinct" *mataqali* should become the property of the Crown. As a result, in 1919, while the head of Mataqali Kaiwai received £10 as holder of the government position of Buli Suva, the government retained the shares of the annuity reserved for Mataqali Roko Tui Suva (£13/6/8), the head of Mataqali Roko Tui Suva (£3/6/8), the Turaga i Taukei (£10), and the Turaga ni Qali (£20).[21]

Suvavou people immediately objected to this arrangement.[22] A Native Lands Commission inquiry into Suvavou people was then under way. This NLC inquiry, completed in 1921, revised all previous NLC records regarding Suvavou that had served as the basis for the distribution of rent and annuity money until then. First, whereas in 1902 the NLC had found nine *mataqali* in Suvavou, the 1921 inquiry found ten. Second, where the earlier NLC report did not recognize any *yavusa* in Suvavou, the 1921 NLC report found three. Third, and most important, the NLC decreed that Suvavou land was owned in common by the three *yavusa*, because in 1892 Suvavou people had *purchased* their land from Lami people, the original owners of the Suvavou land, for £100, using a portion of the annuity money they had received for Suva land.[23] Given that the land had been purchased from Lami people with a portion of the money given to Suvavou people as a whole, the NLC reasoned, Suvavou land should be registered as the village's common property.

The significance of the 1921 NLC inquiry, therefore, is that it essentially denied to Suvavou people the notion, applied elsewhere in Fiji, that *mataqali* were the landowning units. Rent for any leased portion of Suvavou land should therefore be distributed in a lump sum to the village as a whole. As a result, the NLC mandated that the now "extinct" chiefly *mataqali*'s share of the annuity and rent money be distributed equally to the remaining ten *mataqali*.[24] The NLC also confirmed that Mataqali Kaiwai had succeeded to the chiefly title and therefore, as titleholder, was entitled to the shares previously allocated to the chief.[25]

However, this decision in turn led to further disputes. In 1923, men from a Suvavou *yavusa* that I shall call Yavusa Kaivanua contested Mataqali Kaiwai's collection of shares of rent money reserved for the chief. They claimed that because the original chiefly *mataqali* was a division of their *yavusa*, only their *yavusa* should receive these shares.[26] Stressing the divisions confirmed by the recent NLC inquiry, the head of this *yavusa* pointed out that the existing subdivisions within the *yavusa* constituted the proper and complete ritual order of the *vanua*, that is, that they constituted the proper arrangement of ceremonial divisions attending the chief: "All of us, the installer of the chief [*sauturaga*], the chief's spokesman [*matanivanua*], the chief's carpenter [*mataisau*] and the chief's fisherman [*gonedau*], are alive [*bula kece*]. . . . All shares of the Roko Tui Suva should be truly ours."[27] Here the head of the *yavusa* sought to show the existence of a self-contained system of division within the *yavusa* in order to argue that the *yavusa* as a whole fulfilled the conditions of an independent chiefdom. The implication was that all the *mataqali* that composed the other two *yavusa* were therefore external to the chiefdom of Suva.

In order to understand the significance of this complaint, we need to consider the directionality of the parts-whole relationship as set out in the official records. In 1921, after identifying three *yavusa* in Suvavou, the NLC proceeded to collect each of their three migration stories, or their stories of how they came to occupy the lands they now occupied, standard practice in all its inquiries. The NLC summoned three men representing each of the three *yavusa* for this purpose. The three men's accounts focused on how the separate *yavusa* gathered together at different points. For example, according to the representative of Yavusa Kaivanua, they had originally lived at a place called Nauluvatu and had been invited by Yavusa Vakalolo to join them at a place called Rairaiwaqa. Later, both *yavusa* joined Yavusa Kaiwai in Suva:

> Our ancestors were at Nauluvatu for a long time. Men of [Vakalolo] then came and offered Rairaiwaqa to our ancestors so that they might go and settle there. Our ancestors then joined them there. Our ancestors were at Rairaiwaqa for a long while before they became anxious about the possibility that the people of Lomaivuna might attack them, and so our ancestors held a meeting and decided to leave their settlement for Suva. They then left Nauluvatu and Rairaiwaqa for Suva to stay with the people of [Kaiwai]. Our ancestors were there for a long while before they were attacked by the people of Rewa.[28]

The witness detailed how the people of Suva had been dispersed after the Bau-Rewa war and how they were subsequently gathered together again. Both of the statements concerning the migration of Yavusa Vakalolo and Yavusa Kaiwai likewise narrate their journeys from their of origin places (*yavutu*) to Suva.[29] As the statement for Yavusa Vakalolo puts it, "Each of these *yavusa* left their origin place to gather together [*la'ki coko vata*] at Suva."[30]

These stories are predicated on a singular aesthetic of directionality.[31] The stories recorded by the NLC emphasize how three parts, the *yavusa*, joined together to form a singular whole, the chiefdom of Suva. There is thus a clear directionality to this historical narrative, from parts to a whole. At the same time, the official records also present each *yavusa* as a self-contained unit, a ritual whole of its own. In this conception of the whole, there are many coexisting wholes, and each is made up of further parts, *mataqali* with particular ceremonial duties. Within each whole, the parts-whole relations are not defined in temporal terms. It is a mutually defining relationship: parts are defined by the whole and the whole by the parts. In other words, the 1921 NLC record offers two competing conceptions of wholes—the whole as a historical entity, made up of different parts gathered together over time, and the whole defined by the distribution of ceremonial roles among its parts. The latter conception was subsumed in the NLC records, however, in the narrative of the former. The petition Yavusa Kaivanua sent to the government in 1923 sought to foreground the latter in order to challenge the foregrounding of the former in the official record.

What made these two contrasting images of the whole the locus of politics was the distribution of money. The definition of Suvavou land as the common property of the village as a whole mandated that annuity and rent were paid to the village as a whole. But this money in turn had to be divided, and thus a model of parts and wholes had to be agreed upon.[32] This rendered the dispute over the method of division of annuity and rent money a contest between two notions of a whole: the whole defined by the combination of parts, and the whole defined by and also defining its internal divisions.

These two competing conceptions of wholes in turn had different implications for what should be done with the rent money originally allocated to the now-extinct chiefly *mataqali*. If one conceptualized the money and the village as a whole as being made up of internal parts, one would accept that the money should be divided equally among the remaining parts (*mataqali*). If, conversely, one conceptualized the whole as the more particularized whole of the individual *yavusa*, defined by and defining particular internal parts with their own ritual duties, the money originally owed to the "extinct" *mataqali* should now be distributed only among the parts of that smaller whole, that is the *yavusa* of which that *mataqali* was a part.

At the heart of this issue was a contest over directionality. In the conception of the whole as constituted by the historical combination of parts, the act of dividing annuity and rent money reversed the direction of the original historical act of combination that defined the whole. In contrast, in the conception of the whole that took the multiple particular wholes (*yavusa*) as salient and focused on their mutual constitution by their parts, the division of annuity and rent money replicated the divisive logic that constituted the whole (*yavusa*). In the former, in other words, an act of division in the present reversed the act of combination in the past, while in the latter, an act of division was a replication of the act of division that defines the whole. At the nexus of money and self-knowledge, then, where each is a confirmation of the other, the politics of self-knowledge, mediated by disputes over the method of distribution of shares of annuity and rent, have continued to play on these contrasting directionalities. The concept of companies, and of shareholding, recently introduced in Suvavou, further complicated this politics.

The Company

At the time of my fieldwork (1994–96), Suvavou's internal politics revolved around a contest between two factions. One faction consisted of the Tui Suva, Ratu Epeli Kanakana, and his supporters, comprising eight *mataqali*, including two predominantly SDA *mataqali*. The other faction consisted of the dissident SDA *mataqali*, Mataqali Koromakawa, and another small SDA *mataqali* that supported Mataqali Koromakawa's challenge to the authority of Ratu Epeli. In more concrete terms, this contest manifested itself in disputes surrounding a company that Suvavou people incorporated in 1992 as the basis for distribution of shares of money recently promised by the government to arise from Suva land.

The company formed by Suvavou people was called Nadonumai Holdings. The idea of forming a company came from the government.[33] When Suvavou people first negotiated with Prime Minister Sitiveni Rabuka over compensation for Suva land, Rabuka made it clear that the government would not give Suvavou people money as long as it was to be divided into individual portions without being put to further productive use. Rabuka himself, I was told, requested that Suvavou form a company. In other words, the notion of the company was an explicit antidote to disputes about the logic of division. In the company, the operation of division was problematized as a hindrance to capitalist accumulation, and the solution was found in the new company form. In more concrete terms, the formation of the company coincided with Rabuka's offer to return Cruickshank Park, a piece of state land in downtown Suva, and to ensure that the village would receive a low-interest loan from the Fiji Development Bank to build an office building there. The company and its shareholders would dictate how profits from leasing office spaces in this building would be distributed.

It is important to note, however, that the company conflated two distinct logics. On the one hand, it was clearly intended to introduce capitalist practices. As reflected in the name of the company, Nadonumai, the ceremonial name of the Vanua ko Suva (chiefdom of Suva), however, the structure of the company made use of units of division already familiar to villagers. On the other hand, however, ownership of shares was limited to Suvavou *mataqali*, which raised funds and purchased "shares" (*sea*) in the company as individual units. Each *mataqali* contributed an equal amount of money and was represented on the board of directors by a *mataqali* member nominated as its representative and "shareholder." Care was taken that management responsibilities be distributed evenly among the three *yavusa*. The management team included the Tui Suva, Ratu Epeli Kanakana, as "leader of the *vanua*" (*i liuliu ni vanua*); an elder from Mataqali Koromakawa who held the administrative position of *turaga ni koro* (commonly translated as "village headman"); and three other directors, representing the three *yavusa* of Suvavou—Rev. Samuela Ratulevu, an elder from Yavusa Vakalolo who had served as the president of the SDA Church in Fiji; an elder from Yavusa Kaiwai; and an elder from Yavusa Kaivanua.[34] The most educated of all, Rev. Ratulevu, served as managing director responsible for day-to-day negotiations with the government. In its ownership and its leadership, therefore, the company thus replicated the chief, the three *yavusa*, and the ten *mataqali* of Suvavou.

In light of my discussion of part-whole relations, the company as a new whole stands in an interesting relationship to the competing concepts of the whole I have described. On the one hand, the company resembles the conception of a whole defined as a historical combination of parts. Just as each *mataqali* came together to form the whole in that conception, here, each *mataqali* purchased equal amounts of shares in the new whole. On the other hand, however, the notion of shareholdings adds a new dimension to this whole. In what follows, I wish to discuss how the novelty of this whole became evident to Suvavou people themselves.

At the company's inception, in a moment of renewed hope of receiving the long-awaited compensation for Suva land, Mataqali Koromakawa, the long-standing rival of the present chiefly *mataqali*, Mataqali Kaiwai, joined other *mataqali* in purchasing shares in Nadonumai Holdings. Within a few months of the company's formation, however, Mataqali Koromakawa declared that it would withdraw from the company to found its own company. It declared that its company would develop what the *mataqali* claimed to be its old village site in Suva. The logic behind this dissention was that the integrity of the company as a whole depended on the integrity of the village as a whole. Elders of Mataqali Koromakawa repeatedly told me in 1995 that Nadonumai Holdings would never succeed, because it was based on the wrong ordering of the *vanua*. The allocation of shares of ownership and responsibility in Nadonumai Holdings was based on a model of the *vanua* of Suvavou internally divided into three *yavusa* and ten *mataqali*. Mataqali Koromakawa, in contrast, insisted that the village consisted of only one *yavusa* and nine *mataqali*, following the pre–1921 NLC inquiry model. In their opinion, the artificial ordering of the chiefdom on which the company was based could not possibly be the basis for an effective "business" enterprise—it could never possibly serve as an effective form. Mataqali Koromakawa's reasoning derived precisely from the conflation of capitalist practices and ritual ordering described earlier.

What Mataqali Koromakawa did not take into account, however, was the fact that the company entailed a new conception of the relationship between parts and wholes. Although, like the village, the company as a whole resulted from an act of combination in the form of investment, the future act of division of the company's profits would not be bound by the original act of combination because this act of division would be defined by the ownership of shares at the time of the act of division. From this standpoint,

Mataqali Koromakawa's deployment of the old strategy of presenting a counter notion of a whole defined by an act of its division
as I have described in this chapter was not particularly effective.

Unlike in other cases where, in villagers' conception, the with-
drawal of one *mataqali* would threaten the efficacy of their collab-
orative ventures, by 1995, it would be fine if the company did not
have the participation of all village *mataqali*. The company, in their
view, had emerged as a construct based on the voluntary participation of a new category of entities, individual shareholders, and Mataqali Koromakawa's challenge would thus not pose a threat to its
integrity. As this view gained popularity and the success of the company seemed imminent, some members of Mataqali Koromakawa
and of one other dissident *mataqali* began to express their desire to
be part of the company. For their part, the elders of the two dissident *mataqali* in turn focused on their own companies and on pursuing their own business enterprises. The company as a new conception of a whole had begun to reorient the direction of Suvavou
people's self-knowledge.

4 ⌒ Setting Knowledge in Motion

As noted in chapter 2, over the past hundred years, the government of Fiji has repeatedly rejected Suvavou people's divergent claims to the Suva Peninsula as their ancestral land. Indeed, Suvavou people's history is a history of thwarted hopes. Yet Suvavou people have sustained their hope. In this chapter, I begin to address the simple question I posed at the outset: How have Suvavou people kept their hope alive for generation after generation, given that their self-knowledge has continued to fail them?

In his inaugural lecture at the University of Tübingen entitled "Can Hope Be Disappointed?" Ernst Bloch drew attention to the predication of hope on disappointment:

> hope must be unconditionally disappointable, *first*, because it is open in a forward direction, in a future-oriented direction; it does not address itself to that which already exists. For this reason, hope—while actually in a state of suspension—is committed to change rather than repetition, and what is more, incorporates the element of chance, without which there can be nothing new. (Bloch 1998: 341; emphasis in original)

In this lecture, Bloch situates hope in the realm of the not-yet and hence focuses on its radically indeterminate character. For Bloch, indeterminacy is the necessary precondition for hope:

> Hope's methodology . . . dwells in the region of the not-yet, a place where entrance and, above all, final content are marked by an enduring indeterminacy. In other words, referring directly to disappointability: hope holds *eo ipso* the condition of defeat precariously within itself: it is not confidence. It stands too close to the indeterminacy of the historical process, of the world-process that, indeed, has not yet been defeated, but likewise has not yet won. (Bloch 1998: 341)

For Bloch, therefore, disappointment is the engine of hope:

> [I]s it not the case that a thing, once it has become realized, whatever
> has been attained by its realization, so that it does not resemble what
> was previously hoped for, even though its content has passed, wholly
> undiminished, from the possible into the actual? And yet, a residue
> remains, in this instance only because of the still undiscovered (with
> respect to its content) "true and perfect being." But even such disap-
> pointment over realization's "minus" finally counts toward the credit of
> well-founded hope, and advances its existential as well as its essential
> demands. (Bloch 1998: 342–43)

Unlike classical metaphysics's conception of essence as already
given, but hidden from humans, in other words, what Bloch calls
the "true and perfect being" is radically underdetermined and surfaces only as "latency." The "essence of the matter" that hope
entails is "not-yet-being *par excellence,* something not already present and thus not available to be experienced, something that cannot be exhaustively determined—even so, its *direction*, in view of
its purposive content, which is that of genuine humanism, can be
determined as an invariant and at the same time as an indispens-
able factor" (Bloch 1998: 343; emphasis in original). Here Bloch
seeks to negotiate a delicate balance between future-oriented openness and anticipation of a moment in which hope is finally fulfilled.

If Bloch's solution to the problem of the disappointability of
hope focuses on his effort to situate hope in the realm of indeterminacy without undermining the possibility of its fulfillment, the
challenge for Suvavou people has focused on the question of how
to achieve such a condition of indeterminacy. For reasons to be discussed, the indeterminacy that Wittgenstein (1953) and other twentieth-century critics of metaphysics have taken as given (see
Bohman 1991) has not been a given condition for Fijians when it
comes to their knowledge about who they are. For them, rather, the
possibility of self-knowing is foreclosed precisely because self-
knowledge has already been fixed and made final. For Fijians, in
other words, self-knowledge belongs to the past and is not open to
reinterpretation from the standpoint of the present. This temporal
nature of the closure of Fijian self-knowledge in turn demands tem-

poral solutions. The focus of this chapter is Suvavou people's long-standing effort to set their self-knowledge in motion.

Ultimately, however, like Bloch, Suvavou people have striven to reconcile indeterminacy as a condition for the possibility of hope with their effort to render self-knowledge determinate once and for all. The question to which I now turn concerns a series of strategies specifically designed to situate hope in this delicate balance of openness and closure within the context of the particular colonial and postcolonial situation that Suvavou people have faced. These strategies have evolved through a series of petitions that Suvavou people sent to the government over a period of nearly one hundred years from 1898 to 1995, some of which are discussed in chapters 2 and 3. Here, however, my focus is on their form rather than their content (cf. Messick 1993; Riles 2000). The authenticity of the underlying claims is not my concern. Moreover, my interest lies in the hope and anticipation entailed in these petitions rather than in their unintended consequences.[1]

These petitions are quintessentially heterogeneous documents (cf. Hanks 2000: 13) that draw on diverse genres of knowledge practices, including bureaucratic, academic, and ritual practices. In many cases, the documents are also products of collaboration between the petitioners and their scribes, "researchers," "consultants," and lawyers (cf. Davis 1987: 5). Hence they cannot be reductively analyzed in terms of either their cultural specificity or their adherence to the technicalities of bureaucratic form.[2] Nevertheless, the documents deploy a variety of strategies deriving from, and in dialogue with, a genre of official documents produced by government officials to record Fijian social systems and migration narratives.[3] As mentioned earlier, these official documents, generated in the course the taking of evidence from Fijian witnesses by representatives of the colonial administration in the early twentieth century, have long been declared to be uncontestable. In this chapter, I seek to situate these petitions in a wider regime of document production, following Natalie Zemon Davis's analysis of letters of remission in sixteenth-century France (Davis 1987). I draw attention to specific strategies these petitioners deployed to challenge the finality of the knowledge about them contained in these official records.[4] I argue that although the strategies deployed in these petitions have changed over time in dialogue with the government's responses, one element has remained constant: the self-knowing effectuated by these petitions is overwhelmingly indeterminate, and yet it continues to anticipate the moment of the fulfillment of Suvavou people's hope as the confirmation of who they really are. Ultimately, I argue, Suvavou people have achieved this balance between indeterminacy and anticipation of closure by relocating self-knowledge from documents to an interactional and performative terrain.

Closed Knowledge

Marshall Sahlins recounts that a village elder once showed him a wooden chest, stored in the latter's bedroom, that contained Fijian valuables in the form of whales' teeth (*tabua*). The chest, known as the "basket of the clan" (*kato ni mataqali*), was inherited from one generation to the next: "Passing with the leadership of the clan, the chest was a palladium. So long as it is intact, [the elder] said, the *vanua*—the land, including the people—will be preserved" (Sahlins 1993: 23).

In Suvavou, there was no mention of such chests. Instead, I was repeatedly shown briefcases full of documents hidden in *mataqali* elders' bedrooms. The documents in the briefcase typically included a certified copy of a list of registered *mataqali* members, copies of other old government records concerning the Suva land case, and an old map of the Suva Peninsula. On occasion, elders opened their briefcases and took out the documents one by one as they narrated their version of stories about the history of the village.

The collection of documents was one of the major activities of those regarded by other villagers as "elders" (*qase*). Indeed, a document collection was one of the most significant marks of rank.[5] Like the "basket of the clan" that Sahlins mentions, the leaders of each *mataqali* had inherited these documents from their "father" (*tamaqu*) or "mother's brother" (*momo*), with an admonition to "take good care of" them (*maroroya vinaka*). Some Suvavou elders would not even allow me to take the documents (usually NLC lists of *i tokatoka* and *mataqali* membership) to a nearby store to photocopy them and insisted that I copy them by hand in front of them, as if the loss of the documents might have negative effects on their *mataqali*'s state of being. For Suvavou people, official records about themselves were objects to be enacted and displayed as proof (*i vakadinadina*) of their knowledge about who they were (cf. Rappaport 1994; Shryock 1997).

Suvavou people's approach to documents is a result of the government's conscious effort to instill in Fijians a sense of awe about official records concerning clans and their land rights. The NLC has not only restricted access to its records but also has sought to cultivate among Fijians a sense of the documents' finality and closure. For example, the NLC has repeatedly told Fijians that their ancestors' statements on oath are sacred texts (*i vola tabu*) (cf. M. Kaplan 2004: 168). Closure in this sense forecloses the possibility of going back to question the validity of statements made on oath in the past: Fijians are encouraged to accept their ancestors' testimonies as definitive statements about themselves. This has resulted in many contemporary Fijians experiencing a shared sense of alienation from knowledge about who they are. From the Fijian standpoint, official records about themselves are important not only because they constitute the legal basis for distribution of money arising from the land but also because they constitute the ontological foundation of their identity. For many Fijians, therefore, revising the official records entails a certain amount of risk, which has in turn shaped the form of their challenge to the official account of who they are. In what follows, I focus on a report submitted to the government in 1994 by Mataqali Koromakawa regarding its claim to the chiefly title. The report exhibits a variety of strategies that have evolved through petitions or "letters of request" (*i vola ni kerekere*) that Suvavou people, and Fijians more generally, have sent to the government over the past hundred years. These strategies derived from, and in dialogue with, official documents that they have treasured as sources of proof.

In 1994, Mataqali Koromakawa submitted a "report" to the NLC concerning its long-standing claim to the chiefly title of the village, Tui Suva. The title had been held by another *mataqali* of the village, Mataqali Kaiwai, for some time. Since the mid 1980s, Mataqali Koromakawa had repeatedly written to the NLC to challenge the legitimacy of the current chiefly *mataqali*. The NLC had rejected Mataqali Koromakawa's claim on the basis of NLC records showing Mataqali Kaiwai to be the legitimate holder of the chiefly title, and the fact that the NLC records were not open to revision. Soon after Ratu Epeli Kanakana of Mataqali Kaiwai became the new chief of the village in 1990, for example, the head of Mataqali Koromakawa wrote a letter of protest to the NLC. The chairman of the NLC replied by sharply reminding the head of Mataqali Koromakawa that their ancestors had given sworn (*bubului*) statements affirming Mataqali Kaiwai's claim to the chiefly title, and that it was the NLC's "duty" (*i tavi*) to "protect and preserve" (*taqomaka ka maroroya*) those statements. In other words, what their ancestors had confirmed could not be altered.

Mataqali Koromakawa's challenge to the NLC had not been entirely ineffective, however. In 1991, it had succeeded in obtaining a response from an NLC official that upheld a portion of its long-standing claim. The official migration narrative recorded by the NLC in 1921 listed Mataqali Koromakawa's standing (*i tutu*), or ceremonial duty in the chiefdom of Suva, as that of priest (*bete*). Yet the head of Mataqali Koromakawa pointed out in his 1991 letter to the NLC that when his grandfather had been asked by the NLC to swear to the validity of the migration narrative told by a representative of his *yavusa* in 1921, he had contested that portion of the narrative by claiming that his *mataqali*'s standing should be that of *sauturaga* (installer of the chief). In fact, this Mataqali Koromakawa man's objection had been recorded in the NLC's Evidence Book. The NLC responded by admitting the error and altering its records. Although the NLC's confirmation that the *mataqali*'s standing should be that of *sauturaga* did not seem to be endorsed by other *mataqali* in Suvavou, for Mataqali Koromakawa, it served as proof that the government would accept its claim to the chiefly title if it could support it with documentary evidence. In addition, this was an important step in the sense that as the installer of the chief, Mataqali Koromakawa would have the power to appoint any future chief. The report Mataqali Koromakawa submitted to the government in 1994 was, therefore, a product of its renewed hope.

Appendices

The Mataqali Koromakawa report consists of three parts. The first section is a narrative of the *mataqali*'s migration route from its origin place. The second section lists a series of questions regarding the details of NLC records concerning the three *yavusa* of Suvavou. The third section consists of appendices that contain copies of archival records. Each section draws on old and new strategies that have evolved as the dialogue with the government and its records has progressed over the past hundred years.

The appendices in the third section of the report reproduce archival records such as documents contained in files from the Colonial Secretary's Office (CSO) and NLC records. The practice of attaching copies of past government records as evidence seems to have emerged as common practice in Suvavou people's letters of request some time during the 1970s. In 1973, for example, when fifty Suvavou people objected to the NLC's registration of Suvavou land as the common property of the three *yavusa*, they enclosed with their letter a copy of a letter dated December 27, 1905, written in Fijian by Native Lands Commissioner David Wilkinson and detailing the locations of pieces of land held by each *mataqali* in Suvavou as evidence that in Suvavou, *mataqali* and not *yavusa* should be considered the landowning units.[6] This increase in the use of government records as documentary evidence since the 1970s was the result of the introduction of photocopying technology, on the one hand, and increased access to government records, on the other. The government's efforts to preserve administrative records and make them available to the public began in the mid 1950s (Crozier 1958, 1959; Diamond 1978), but I do not know

precisely when Fijians began to consult government records at the
National Archives of Fiji in order to prepare their letters of request.
By the 1970s, however, judging from Suvavou people's letters, a
fair number of government records seem to have been in villagers'
hands. In 1994, for example, a Suvavou elder showed me a copy of
Wilkinson's letter that he kept in his briefcase along with other old
government records. He told me that he had inherited these records
from his mother's brother. At the time of my fieldwork, many of
those who held leadership positions in *i tokatoka, mataqali,* or *yavusa* kept collections of government records concerning their own
i tokatoka, mataqali, or *yavusa.* These records usually consisted of
NLC lists of *i tokatoka* and *mataqali* membership (*i vola ni kawa
bula,* or native register).[7] Others kept copies of other kinds of government records, such as old maps of Suva, NLC records concerning the genealogy of Bauan chiefs to whom the original chiefly line
of Suva people was related, and other government records relevant
to their *mataqali's* specific claims.[8]

The appearance of appendices in Suvavou people's documents
coincided with the emergence of "researchers" in the village. Suvavou people repeatedly told me that they were not allowed to see all
the relevant government records about Suva people and their land
at the National Archives of Fiji and the NLC because the government wanted to hide the truth from them. At the time of my fieldwork, however, there were at least two people in Suvavou who had
conducted extensive research at the National Archives and other
government offices. One was the author of the Mataqali Koromakawa report and the other was the daughter of a Suvavou woman
who claimed to be a descendant of the original chiefly line. This
woman had conducted extensive research at government departments and had written numerous letters to the government regarding her mother's claim. Given their exposure to the style of bureaucratic writing at the archives, it is perhaps not surprising that both
researchers used appendices in their documents submitted to the
government. In 1989, for example, when the woman sent a letter
to the minister for Fijian Affairs regarding her claim to the chiefly
title of her clan, she attached, in chronological order, a series of

internal memoranda between government officials concerning her case, as well as all correspondence between herself and the government. The 1994 Mataqali Koromakawa report continued this use of appendices to demonstrate inconsistencies in the government records. This presentation of government records as appendices reflects a more general strategy, which an examination of the report's other two sections will make explicit.

Questions

In the second section of the 1994 Mataqali Koromakawa report, the author directs a number of questions at the government. Given that the NLC records the report challenges were their ancestors' responses, as witnesses, to government officials' questions, this strategy of asking questions of the government was an inherently subversive act. By asking the government questions, the Koromakawa report reversed the questioner-respondent relationship, the very context in which NLC records were created.

The reversal of the questioner-respondent relationship is one of the oldest strategies deployed by Suvavou people in their letters of request. Recall the first letter Suvavou people wrote to the government in 1898 expressing their discontent with arrangements regarding Suva Peninsula land.[9] This letter does not include a single question. The government in turn responded sharply with a series of questions: The chief of Suvavou and other Suvavou representatives who had signed the letter were summoned by Assistant Colonial Secretary W. L. Allardyce to his office. In their 1904 petition to the government, Suvavou people asked the government a number of questions and in so doing reversed the questioner-respondent relationship.

The author of the 1994 report, writing in the late twentieth century, was in a better position to ask questions. Unlike his ancestors, he had gained access to some of the government's own records. Questions in the 1994 Mataqali Koromakawa report therefore challenged technical details of the NLC records about Suva people and their land head-on. The report's questions focused on the in-

completeness and inconsistencies of information contained in the
NLC records. As mentioned in chapter 3, the NLC had conducted
two inquiries into the status of Suva people and their land. The first
was conducted by Native Lands Commissioner David Wilkinson in
1902, and the second took place between 1919 and 1921. At the
time of my fieldwork, the NLC regarded the result of the 1919–21
inquiry as the final record concerning Suva people and their land.
This was not unusual. By the 1920s, in response to the development of a standardized method of recording, the NLC had decided
that the work of Wilkinson's commission was inaccurate.[10]

The Mataqali Koromakawa report seized on apparent discrep-
ancies between the NLC's 1902 and 1919–21 findings, which it
offered as evidence of the findings' baselessness. The report notes,
for example, that whereas in 1902, the NLC found nine *mataqali*
in Suvavou, in 1919, it found four *yavusa* and twelve *mataqali*. The
report then asks: Why this difference? The report also points to the
incomplete nature of the information recorded by the NLC in
1921. In 1921, the NLC recorded three statements made by three
elders of Suvavou representing each of the three *yavusa* of the village. The Mataqali Koromakawa report points out, for example,
that none of the three narratives mentions the place of origin of the
witness's *yavusa*. Where, it asks, did these *yavusa* originate?
Furthermore, the report notes inconsistencies and contradictions
among the three *yavusa*'s narratives. For example, according to one
narrative, during a mid-nineteenth-century war between the powerful rival chiefdoms Bau and Rewa, the chief of Suva, Ratu
Ravulo, stayed in Rewa, while according to another narrative,
Ratu Ravulo stayed in Bau (see Sahlins 1991; Wall 1920). "Why do
these narratives disagree?" the report asks.

Of course, the NLC has never claimed that the basis for the finality of its records is their logical coherence. In fact, in some cases, the
NLC has abandoned the results of its earlier inquiries. Rather, the
finality of the NLC records is temporally defined: the NLC simply
denies the retroactive contestability of its records. In other words,
whether or not information given on oath at NLC hearings is logically incoherent or simply "wrong," it must be treated as final.

From this standpoint, it is probably not so much the act of pointing to the logical inconsistencies of the NLC records as the act of asking questions that is threatening to the integrity of the NLC records. The strategy of subversion in the questioner-respondent relationship seeks to engage the government in discussion and thus to reopen inquiries into landownership. Although access to government records in the 1980s opened up a new manner of engagement with the government for Fijians, namely, a substantive critique of government records, from their standpoint, the effectiveness of this new form of engagement depended on the old strategy of asking questions.

This strategy of asking questions invokes two aspects of the act of questioning. On the one hand, questions asked of the government are manifestations of a search for information and are designed to solicit a response (Goody 1978: 23). On the other hand, however, the questioners do not always expect a response, partly because there may be some doubt as to whether they will get one and partly because their main concern may not be to get answers to their questions but simply to "pose" them (Goldman 1993: 198). I suggest that these "open" and "closed" potentials of the act of questioning (ibid.: 199) can coexist in a single set of questions. The subversion of the questioner-respondent relationship, therefore, has the interesting effect of both openness and closure at once.

This is true from another perspective as well. Judging from the internal discussion within the government triggered by Suvavou people's questions, the strategy worked, and the government began to investigate Suvavou people's concerns. In 1904, for example, it prompted the government to investigate the legal grounds of its possession of the Suva land, although ultimately, the government's conclusion was that "[t]he question which was settled so long ago cannot now be reopened."[11] Nevertheless, Suvavou people's questions clearly had triggered an internal debate among government officials about the Suva land case. The strategy failed, however, in that Suvavou people did not succeed in reopening their case; the government almost always categorically denied the contestability of past government decisions concerning Suvavou people's land. In other words, for both sides, these questions opened and closed the possibility of self-knowledge for Suvavou people. In order to understand the full significance of the interplay between openness and closure embedded in the act of questioning, I now turn to another subversive strategy deployed by the report.

Migration Narratives

The first section of the 1994 Mataqali Koromakawa report presents an alternative migration narrative of Suva people that is more logically consistent and complete than the migration narratives recorded by the NLC in 1921, according to the author of the report. The first part of the narrative reads as follows:

> Ena i golegole mai Nakauvadra e ratou gole mai na noqu qase ena Yavusa Suva, Mataqali Suva ka nodratou Yavutu na Suva.

My ancestors, Yavusa Suva, Mataqali Suva, came down from Nakauvadra, and their origin place is Suva.

> Mai Nakauvadra e ratou gole sobu mai, vakamuria na tokaitua me yacova ni ratou sa mai yaco e na dua na vanua yacana ko Lutu, ena ulu ni wai na Wainimala.

They came down from Nakauvadra following a mountain range and finally reached a place called Lutu on the bank of the Wainimala River.

> Biu mai o Lutu e ratou gole sobu mai, me yacova ni ratou sa yacovi Delaitoga (Naitasiri). E Delaitoga e sa mai wase kina na Yavusa Suva. E sa mai toka yani kina e dua vei iratou na neitou qase ka se vakayavu tiko ga ni kua mai Delaitoga.

They left Lutu and came down until they reached Delaitoga (Naitasiri). At Delaitoga, they divided Yavusa Suva. One of our ancestors remained there and his descendants are still based at Delaitoga today.

According to this narrative, therefore, Suva people originated from Nakauvadra, a mythic origin place that many contemporary Fijians would identify as their ultimate origin place.[12] The mention of Suva people's origin place contrasts with the lack of such information in the migration narratives recorded by the NLC. The narrative ends in Suva with Suva people's allocation of ceremonial duties (i tavi) among three brothers who were Mataqali Koromakawa's ancestors:

> *Ena delana talega oqo e mai wasei kina na nodratou i tavi na noqu qase, ka mai buli kina nai matai ni Tui Suva. Me vaka ni ratou sa yaco mai ena vanua vou e ratou lewe tolu ka dua vei iratou e toka ga yani mai Delaitoga. E ratou sa mani vei lesi na lewe tolu na qase oqo.*
>
> On this hill, my ancestors divided ceremonial duties, and they installed the first Tui Suva. When they reached the new land, there were three people, and like before one had stayed at Delaitoga. Then these three were appointed [to different ceremonial positions].

According to the narrative, the eldest of the three brothers installed the youngest of the three as the chief of Suva. The eldest of the three installed himself as *sauturaga* (installer of the chief) and the other became *bete* (priest). This self-contained structure of the chiefdom of Suva as a whole contrasts sharply with the whole incorporating three different wholes as its parts in the 1921 NLC records.

This strategy of subverting the temporal direction of the relationship between parts and wholes embedded in migration narratives recorded in the 1921 NLC inquiry will be familiar from chapter 3. In those official accounts, the focus was on the present, in that they all point to how different parts gathered together to form the present whole. In other words, as one traces the migration stories back from the present toward the past, one finds the different places where different *yavusa* used to reside. In contrast, the narrative of the head of Mataqali Koromakawa quoted here focuses on how the original whole was divided at different points along the route. For example, when Suva people reached a place called Delaitoga, they divided themselves into two groups. One of them remained in Delaitoga, while the rest set out to sail down along a river and eventually reached Suva. In other words, where the migration stories recorded by the NLC seem to validate the composition of Suva people as a historically constituted whole at the time of the NLC inquiry, the story told by the head of Mataqali Koromakawa draws attention to the fragmentation of an original whole from which Suva people originated.

My focus here is on the implications of this reversal of the temporal relationship between parts and a whole for the question of indeterminacy. Like the subversion of the questioner-respondent relationship, the temporal subversion of the relationship between parts and whole in the migration narrative also creates a simultaneous effect of openness and closure. On the one hand, unlike the NLC's historically constituted and inclusive whole created by gathering disparate groups, Mataqali Koromakawa's whole defined by the act of division privileged formal closure and exclusivity. On the other hand, the subversion of the NLC's official migration narrative also revealed a new horizon of openness. If one traced back through the migration route presented in the Mataqali Koromakawa report, one would encounter other parts of the original whole of which Mataqali Koromakawa still considered itself a part.

This openness was defined by an interactional method of proof: Mataqali Koromakawa elders pointed out to me that they could prove the truthfulness of their story by going back to Delaitoga, where according to their migration story, their ancestors divided themselves into two groups. According to them, the descendants of the other half of the original whole still lived in Delaitoga and the stories of these two groups would "correspond" (*sota*), such that each would prove the other. This aspect of Mataqali Koromakawa's migration narrative equipped the report with the potential to trigger an ontologically based interactional closure of its own. The report, in other words, succeeded in situating Mataqali Koromakawa's hope in a delicate balance between future-oriented openness and anticipation of a moment at which their self-knowledge would be finally proven and closed.

Mataqali Koromakawa had a basis for their belief in this possibility. In December 1994, Mataqali Koromakawa organized a meeting for me at what they claimed to be their old village site in Suva. There, they showed me a clipping from a local Fijian-language newspaper entitled "A Song About Suva" ("Serekali kei Suva").[13] The song was composed by an elder from Serea, Naitasiri, a village on the route Mataqali Koromakawa elders believed their ancestors had taken, and exemplified what Mataqali Koro-makawa elders claim to constitute effective proof. While we sat on the floor, one of Mataqali Koromakawa elders read it aloud. In this song, the song-maker attempts to demonstrate that his *yavusa,* Yavusa Nadoloi, and Suva people share an origin. As evidence of this claim, the song traces the migration of Suva people and indicates the places where the original group divided itself and left parts along the route (at Lutu, Delaitoga, and Serea). Some details of the two narratives do not match. For example, the Mataqali Koromakawa narrative mentions the Wainimala River as the river along which their ancestors descended from Nakauvadra, instead of the Wainibuka River mentioned in the song. Moreover, the Mataqali Koromakawa narrative does not mention Lutu and Serea, two places where, according to the song, parts of Suva people were left. However, for Mataqali Koromakawa elders, the song's mention of Delaitoga was sufficient proof of their theory that stories told by people of the same origin would essentially match. For Mataqali Koromakawa elders, this in turn confirmed that if they went to Delaitoga, they would be able to prove their knowledge about who they were.

Spurred by this claim, I visited Delaitoga in January 1995 in the hope of learning what the people of Delaitoga knew about Suva people, and more specifically Mataqali Koromakawa. My trip generated great hope on the part of Mataqali Koromakawa elders. They asked me to tape-record all the stories the people of Delaitoga might have of Suva people. When I arrived, I discovered that there was indeed a *yavusa* called Yavusa Suva in Delaitoga, and I spoke with its head and other people there. However, during my short visit, over three days, I could not obtain much information about the Delaitoga perspective on Suva people.

Mataqali Koromakawa elders were disappointed when I returned to Suvavou without a substantial story, as they had been looking forward to the tape-recorded stories that would validate their self-knowledge. However, their disappointment soon turned into a kind of confirmation that only they could get such information. "If we go there to sit down with them and talk," they told me, "our stories will match." Naturally I could not gather the stories, they surmised, for to know the facts was not enough; the possibility of correspondence depended also on a particular form of ritual interaction (*veiqaravi*). Here closure was defined ontologically. The seemingly open character of the migration narrative was accompanied by a narrowly defined method for its own closure. The reemphasis on the performative dimension of the possibility of self-knowing reintroduced the kind of indeterminacy that sustained Mataqali Koromakawa's hope.

Delegating Closure

As far as knowledge about Fijian land is concerned, indeterminacy is not, therefore, a given condition, but a condition to be achieved.[14] In the petitions to the government I have described, the indeterminate character of self-knowledge is strategically created. As we have seen, the Mataqali Koromakawa report contains multiple devices for creating the effect of indeterminacy. These include the open-ended questions that appear in the second section of the report and the migration narrative presented in the report, the form of which suggests its own method of proof.

What these devices have in common is their dependence on acts of delegation or indirection (cf. Bauman 2001; Brenneis 1986; Keane 1997c). The subversion of both the questioner-respondent relationship and the form of the NLC's migration stories ultimately delegates closure to a third party. By asking questions of the government, the Mataqali Koromakawa report invites the government to answer the questions. The migration narrative likewise implicitly calls upon another *mataqali*, the part of the original whole that was left behind, to validate the narrative. The strategy of listing government records as appendices also reflects this delegation of the proof of self-knowledge.

Acts of delegation produce an effect of indeterminacy, because they situate self-knowing on an interactional and performative terrain. The indeterminate nature of interaction arises from the way it invokes a recursive relationship between an initiating act of interaction and its response. Whether questions will be answered, for example, depends not so much on their content as on the way they are posed. Likewise, whether stories will correspond and hence mutually prove their truthfulness depends on the character of the encounter between the parties involved. In the same way, whether access to documents will be granted at the National Archives and other government offices depends on the identity of the parties and the nature of the relations between bureaucrats and clients. Interaction is radically indeterminate, in other words, because one side's response depends upon the other's manner of attendance. It is this radical indeterminacy of self-knowledge achieved in the reports and petitions of Suvavou people to the government that has enabled them to maintain their hope in the face of the government's repeated rejection of their claims. In the following chapter, I further explore the predication of hope on performance in an analysis of church and gift-giving rituals.

5 ⤖ Intimating Fulfillment

In this chapter, I turn to church and gift-giving rituals that repeatedly engaged Suvavou people in successive moments of hope and its fulfillment. I argue that the ritual experience of hope and its fulfillment was instrumental in the production of hope. When adeptly performed, this ritual process entailed a temporally and spatially orchestrated discursive game of agency that redefined and reconfigured the relationship between humans and God, and that ultimately made ritual participants' hope of God's ultimate response an echo of the ritually fulfilled hope. In this understanding, I suggest, the problem of how to maintain a prospective orientation displaces the question of who or what is the ultimate source of hope.

In more general terms, my attention to ritual moments in which human agency is placed in abeyance marks a departure from social theorists' long-standing emphasis on human agency and strategy (cf. Bourdieu 1977; Giddens 1979; Ortner 1984). Moreover, it seeks to respond to the more recent attention paid by Dipesh Chakrabarty and others to actors' imaginings of nonhuman agents such as God and spirits making evident the limits of secular disciplines such as anthropology and history.[1] My argument is that Fijian rituals point to the fact that what makes rituals consequential are not the intentions of God, spirits, and other experientially inaccessible entities but the limits placed, at least temporarily, on ritual participants' capacity to control the effects of their action in the world.

Questions and Answers

In Suvavou, the Methodist and Seventh-Day Adventist (SDA) churches have coexisted for over a hundred years, ever since the chief of Suvavou, the Roko Tui Suva, Ratu Avorosa Tuivuya, and some villagers became Adventists in 1898. Subsequently, in 1918, this original chiefly line ceased to exist with the death of its last member, and a Methodist *mataqali,* Mataqali Kaiwai, assumed the chiefly title (see chapter 3). In 1995, the Suvavou Methodist Church had a membership of 314, while the Suvavou SDA Church had 270 members. A few belonged to the Catholic Church, Assemblies of God, and other churches, all of which were located outside the village. Although it was not unusual for a Fijian village to accommodate more than one Christian denomination, Suvavou's history of religious pluralism is unique in its scale.[2]

The two churches offered Suvavou people very different models of social life (cf. Thomas 1997: 50–51, 224): At the most obvious level, Methodists observed the Sabbath on Sunday, while the Adventist Sabbath began at sunset on Friday and ended at sunset on Saturday. Many Adventists abstained from cooking on the Sabbath and spent most of the day attending church services. In contrast, for Methodists, Sunday lunch was the most elaborate meal of the week. Adventists adhered to many food prohibitions, such as those against eating pork and shellfish, and were highly conscious of following a healthy diet. Methodists observed none of these prohibitions. *Yaqona (piper methysticum,* or kava) drinking was an integral part of Methodist gatherings, while Adventists did not drink *yaqona,* alcohol, or even tea (see Steley 1990: 209–11; cf. SDA General Conference 1988: 281–82).

The organizational structures of the two churches were very different also. The Methodist Church in Fiji and Rotuma was a self-contained national body separated into "divisions" (*i wasewase*) and "circuits" (*tabacakacaka*). In sermons and church activities, members of the Methodist Church were constantly reminded of being part of a national church structure with the president (*qase levu*, literally, "big elder") at its apex. In contrast, Adventists stressed their membership in a worldwide community of Sabbath keepers who every Saturday studied the same section of the same textbook produced at the world headquarters of the SDA Church in the United States. At the Suvavou Methodist Church, only Fijian preachers preached, and they did so in Fijian. At the Suvavou SDA Church, European, Tongan, and Samoan preachers, in addition to Fijians, gave sermons. Many non-Fijian preachers delivered their sermons in English, which Fijian Adventist schoolteachers translated into Fijian almost simultaneously. Finally, the Methodist leadership played a central role in nationalist politics, and church activities were steeped in commentary on Fijian cultural identity. In contrast, Adventists did not portray their church as exclusively and independently Fijian and did not regard the church as a forum for the explicit celebration of Fijian ethnicity and its relationship to Christian faith.

The doctrinal and organizational differences between the two churches were sometimes the subject of joking debates between cross-cousins (*tavale*) of the kind Andrew Arno has also observed in the Lau Islands (1990). For example, on New Year's Eve in 1995, following the annual joint church services held successively at the SDA and Methodist churches in the village, Ana, a Methodist, and her Adventist cross-cousin, Jo, held such a joking debate while Ana's husband and daughter and I chatted outside Ana's house. The debate began when Jo told of his experiences working as a cook at a resort hotel near the village. In the course of the story, he mentioned that he had served pork and shellfish to the passengers of a cruise ship. Ana jokingly challenged him to justify serving to other people what he himself was not allowed to eat. Jo responded that it was what tourists wanted. Ana's husband, Sikeli, joined in and repeated Jo's response. Ana then asked if it was a sin to serve food to others that he himself would not eat. Sikeli repeated Ana's question and asked Jo how he would respond. Jo quickly countered with a quotation from the Bible that one must give others what they need. This response provoked appreciative laughter from all of us. Jo also added that he had not touched the pork and shellfish, because non-SDA women had prepared those items. Ana's daughter then shouted, "You ate them too!" and we all burst into laughter.

Donald Brenneis's description of *pancayat*, or conflict resolution sessions among Indo-Fijians, as concerning "more than its topic, for aesthetic pleasure, or pleasure expressed in aesthetic terms, is central to it" (Brenneis 1990: 230) could apply equally well to Fijian joking debates. In the interchange described above, a conflict over religious doctrine provided the basis for a particular kind of social engagement. It was the quick rhythm of the engagement, the sequence of challenges in the form of questions, and responses in the form of answers, that captured our attention and entertained us (cf. Arno 1990: 264).

An exchange of questions and answers between two sides was also a predominant manner of religious learning at both Methodist and SDA churches. Every Sunday morning, for example, when Methodist villagers gathered together for their Sunday church service, a group of old women seated in the back pews of the church read aloud, in a rather monotonous tone, a set of questions and answers, an exercise known as *laga taro* (literally, "singing questions," meaning "catechism"). These questions and answers concerned Methodists' fundamental beliefs and were printed at the back of the Methodist Church hymnbook. With a measured cadence, the leader of the group read aloud a question, such as "Is it possible for the Holy Spirit to descend to us also?" and the rest of the group read aloud the answer: "It is possible as Peter said on Pentecost Sunday: 'Repent, and be baptized every one of you in the name of Jesus Christ for the remission of sins, and ye shall receive the gift of the Holy Ghost. For the promise is unto you, and to your children, and to all that are afar off, *even* as many as the Lord our God shall call' [Acts 2:38–39]" (Methodist Church in Fiji 1988 [1938]: 439; my translation).

Unlike the joking debate between cross cousins, this exchange scripted both the questions and the answers, and all that was required was to read them in unison as printed in the hymnbook. As church members arrived at church and took their seats, the

monotonous back and forth of question and answer served as a
kind of background music or rhythm, which filled the few minutes
before the opening of the worship. Even more than the joking
debate, Methodist women's practice of singing questions focused
not so much on the content of the question and answer pairs as on
the rhythm that these sets produced.

Although it was less predetermined than Methodist women's
singing questions, there was a similar pattern of questions and
answers in the Adventist religious service. Every Saturday morning,
Adventist villagers assembled at their church to attend "Sabbath
School."[3] Bible study groups, known as "classes" (*kalasi*), were
organized according to age and sex. Teachers were senior male
church members. In their classes, women and young people generally kept quiet and deferred to the group leader. In contrast, in the
male elders' classes, members took turns each week serving as
teacher, and the teacher's authority was limited to asking the first
question and directing the conversation at particular moments.
Male elders' classes often involved heated debate as participants
openly disagreed with one another's interpretations of the Bible.

One of the interesting features of these conversations was that
the teacher did not aim to demonstrate his authority (cf. Goody
1978: 42). Rather, members of the elders' class took turns leading
the discussion by asking a question. The interaction among male
elders consisted of sets of discussions, each focusing on a particular question; one elder asked a question of the others, and each of
the others attempted in turn to formulate an answer.

Consider the following discussion in one male elders' class about
the role working for the church plays in salvation.[4] Referring to a
passage from Luke (23:42–43), in which one of the two men crucified with Jesus cried out, "Remember me when thou comest into
thy kingdom," to which Jesus responded, "Verily I say unto thee,
To day shalt thou be with me in paradise," Sakeasi asked, how the
sinner could be saved simply by asking for salvation, without having done any work for God in his lifetime. The designated teacher
responded:

I think that he knew this was the end of his life. . . . He believed that this was Christ, the Savior. . . . So he believed. But this shows that God will accept us when we change. What do you think? If there is another "chance" [English word] for this man, I believe it is possible for him to take up that chance.

Disregarding the teacher's answer as irrelevant, Sakeasi repeated the question. After another member made a comment, which Sakeasi again rejected, he once again repeated his question, and the teacher again attempted to respond. Yet again, Sakeasi was not satisfied. He reminded members of the discussion group of the significance of the question and asked them to try to listen to what the Holy Spirit might say to them on this point: "This is a good question because sometimes we are not focused and suddenly someone asks us and we get confused. We should give some thought to its answer. The Holy Spirit can give us what we should talk about." Then, the teacher and another member of the class again responded. Both seized on Sakeasi's mention of the enlightenment of the Holy Spirit and projected this insight onto an understanding of the sinner's behavior. Dissatisfied with these answers, Sakeasi finally gave his own answer to his question:

> Now that we have come closer to the question regarding our study, I would like to present my own thoughts. . . . Who was nailed to the cross along with the sinner? Jesus. Only Jesus is deciding everything. . . . You believe in the Lord Jesus Christ. Whether you tithe and then die today or you don't tithe . . . and then die today, you believe [in God] and He knows that [you are] a sincere person, right? You are being sincere. God is watching you. You can be in trouble today and not tithe but [intend to] tithe next week. But if you die suddenly, God will know that you had difficulty and therefore did not give anything. . . . [Do you think that] He is waiting for you to tithe, and then [when you tithe, He will say,] "I will save him"? No. He says that [what matters is] your sincere heart. [As He says,] "If you want to follow me, I will save you."

This answer then prompted others to confirm Sakeasi's answer as correct by each reciting language from the Bible supporting his point. For example, one member of the class offered the following quotation from the Bible and the Sabbath School textbook: "'As ye

have therefore received Christ Jesus the LORD, *so* walk ye in him
[Col. 2:6].' It is interpreted as follows: 'To follow Jesus requires
wholehearted conversion at the start, and a repetition of this conversion every day'" (quoted in Gane 1995: 64, taken from Nichol
1978 [1953]: 1113).

Although rounds of questions and answers began as contests
among elders, as the above example illustrates, the person who
asked the question usually concluded the round of answers by providing his own answer. Once the proper answer was found, the
other participants then offered further *confirmation* of the correct-
ness and finality of that answer by citing Bible passages that supported it. If Methodist women's practice of catechism achieved a
sense of completion through the chanting of printed sets of questions and answers, Adventists' Sabbath School sessions achieved it
through an exchange of questions and answers between class members.

For Adventists, therefore, asking a question was extremely significant. For example, Sakeasi stated:

> We know that we believe in Jesus as God's son but very often we are
> too shy to show in a straight way, and to ask in a straight way, what
> troubles us. . . . Very often I am weak and I find it difficult to talk in a
> straight manner to a pastor or a lay preacher. . . . The Holy Spirit
> inspires . . . us to act with purpose. Let us not be too shy to ask in a
> straight manner following the path indicated by Jesus. . . . Shyness is
> the weapon of the Devil that makes one's mind small and that tells us
> not to show in a straight manner what worries us or what makes it pos-
> sible for us to obtain eternal life.

Although Bible study sessions always began with a prayer for
the Holy Spirit's guidance in their debate, and participants often
referred to the Holy Spirit's guidance during the course of the
debate, as Sakeasi did at one point in the above example, the issue
of the agency of the Holy Spirit in "speaking through" the participants (see Bauman 1983, 1989 [1974]; Harding 1987, 2000), that
is, the question of whether the Holy Spirit was actually directly
influencing the speakers, was secondary. In Sakeasi's theory of
questions and answers, what was crucial, rather, was one's attitude,

one's "straight manner." Shyness, evidenced by a reluctance to ask a question, prevented a person from being enlightened by the Holy Spirit. In other words, asking a question not only evidenced one's "straight manner" but also guaranteed one's capacity to reach the right answer.

Problems and Solutions

In Methodist and Adventist church sermons, there was a similar rhetorical pattern. Like questions and answers in Bible study sessions, the sermons of both Methodist and Adventist preachers consisted of a contingent set of paired problems and solutions. Through this pattern, the preacher urged the congregation to realize the problematic nature of their present method of worship and to seek a solution. In other words, the preacher sequentially formulated and then solved problems concerning the congregation's way of life.

Methodist and Adventist preachers thus used the same problem-and-solution technique for thinking about the proper method of worship, although stressing different conceptions of temporality. Methodist preachers constructed a problem and its solution out of the contrast between the past and present and emphasized the maintenance of the rituals of the past. In contrast, Adventists presented the state of an individual as a problem in need of a solution and showed greatest interest in the need for a change in the present and in the coming of the end of the world. The differing conceptions of temporality in Methodist and Adventist sermons evidenced disparate doctrinal positions and served as indexes of the contrasting forms of collectivity that the two churches strove to achieve. In other words, like joking debates, Methodist women's singing questions, and Adventist elders' Sabbath School sessions, Fijian sermons focused on the completion of a specific form. At this level of form, despite differences of content, striking similarities between Methodist and Adventist ways of preaching emerged.

The predominant theme of Methodist sermons concerned the

relationship of the present to the past. Methodist preachers frequently used stories about early Fijian chiefs' encounters with Christianity (cf. Thornley and Vulaono 1996) as vehicles for criticizing the congregation's sinful practices. In these sermons, early Fijians' conversion to Christianity and manner of worship was presented as a *model* for present-day Fijians, whose life had lost its strength and vigor. Preachers often pointed to social problems such as the increasing crime rate among Fijians and explained that these resulted from contemporary Fijians' improper manner of worship. For example, in a sermon delivered at the Suvavou Methodist Church during one Sunday service, a preacher from a nearby church pointed out that contemporary Fijians' manner of worship was not good enough:

> If you want Fiji and Fijians to be lively [*bula*], let Fiji restore the manner in which our ancestors "attended" [*qaravi*] God. Our ancestors accepted Christian clothing in 1835. Please forgive me, my relatives, for saying a word of criticism. The way God is worshipped today in Fiji is not proper . . . That is why we have more rape and more murder today and the prisons are full. This is not the custom of Fijians.[5]

The preacher went on to illustrate early Fijians' rigor in "seeking" (*vakasaqara*) God by describing their first encounter with European missionaries:

> My relatives, I would like to show you the way our ancestors attended God. European missionaries arrived in Tubou but did not respect anything that Fijians were doing at the time. Our ancestors then wondered: "Where does the missionaries' strength come from?" "Where is their power?" From sunrise, throughout the day and into the evening until midnight, they looked for it. They then finally found Christ!

The preacher then stopped and directly confronted the congregation: "If you say you have accepted Jesus today, I will ask you today if you have found him. How did you find him? I wish to point out to you the lesson of this story. If you search for him, you will find him."

This critical commentary on contemporary Fijians' manner of worship exemplifies the Methodist usage of conversion narratives and their emphasis on the relationship of the present to the past through the "maintenance" (*maroroya*) of the proper manner of worship (cf. Gewertz and Errington 1993; Jolly 1992, 1996: 252–53; White 1991). In this view, the truth about God and the attendance owed to Him by human beings was already entirely known and could be found in Fijians' past. Moreover, this theme of maintenance was explored through a particular rhetorical form: a sermon often portrayed some aspect of village life as a *problem* and then offered early Fijians' manner of worship as its *solution*. Like a question and its answer, the problems of the present were resolved through a return to the ritual forms of the past.

In contrast, Adventist sermons rarely mentioned mission history. I heard only one sermon in Suvavou that referred to the chief's conversion to Adventism and the village's long history of Adventist belief. In this sermon, the preacher actually alluded to the past only to negate its importance. He opened his account with the famous parable of the payment of laborers in the vineyard (Matt. 20:1–16), in which the landowner equally rewards the laborer employed from early in the morning and the laborer employed at the very end of the day. The preacher then noted that the people of Suvavou had been the first to become Adventists in Fiji:

> I believe about a hundred years have passed since we accepted the church. [The chief of Suvavou] has been remembered throughout Fiji for generations. Many of us were born into this church. There are many faithful families. Blessed are those who are called to help the church's activities. However, my relatives, I believe tonight that there is only one payment. Forget your beginning. Whether you start in the morning or at the end of the day, the Bible says that there is only one payment, that is, eternal life.[6]

Adventists' sermons focused on the present and the future—and, in particular, on church members' individual efforts to change themselves. In sermons and other religious conversation, Adventists repeatedly reminded themselves that people were sinful beings. Because the end of the world was approaching, each person needed to prepare him- or herself by rendering his or her life "sin-free," "clean," "straight," and "truthful." As the resident minister of Suvavou's SDA Church told the congregation in one sermon: "I know you all will stand up to say, 'I have done something.' God knows about it. There is something I have done and should tell Him. This year, God's words challenge us. You are expected to show Him something, something good, clean, straight, and holy in His eyes."[7]

Despite their different temporal orientations, however, both Methodists and Adventists stressed the importance of the proper manner of worship. Methodists portrayed the attitude to God of early Fijian converts as the ideal model. The Methodist preacher mentioned above emphasized that if contemporary Fijians revived this ideal manner of worship, everything would be better. Similarly, Adventists stressed the sinfulness of human life and the importance of consistent efforts to dedicate one's life to God and to cleanse one's body and mind, because these must evidence the proper attitude of worship. As demonstrated by ancestors' conversion stories or biblical parables, the preacher suggested that adopting the truthful manner of worship would ensure that one received God's response and guarantee that one's life generally would "move forward" (toso) (cf. Tomlinson 2002a). In other words, notwithstanding their different temporal orientations, the idealization in their sermons of the faith of early Fijian converts by Methodists and of sin-free cleanliness in the present by Adventists both made the future contingent on congregations' conforming to an ideal model.

This critical commentary on the congregations' manner of worship is somewhat surprising, however, given that before the sermon began, the worshippers had taken great care in their self-presentation. At both churches, members paid enormous attention to the propriety of their appearance, speech, and conduct. Both Methodists and Adventists wore their best dress to church. Men wore a tie, a *sulu vakataga* ("pocket *sulu*," or skirts with pockets), a shiny white shirt and a Western-style jacket.[8] Women wore a white or light-colored long dress over a black or dark colored *sulu* that covered their ankles, and a pair of leather shoes with heels. Choir groups devoted long hours during the week to practicing hymns. Both congregations strove to attain the ideal model of worship the preacher offered as a solution and a source of closure. Why, then, did the preacher devalue and even deny their efforts to present their best appearance through their attire, hymns, and speeches and stress instead the problematic nature of the present manner of worship, that is, the way in which it fell short of the ideal model?

This question recalls the SDA Sabbath School sessions, although the role of the questioner in those sessions was less rigidly defined than that of the preacher. Recall that Sabbath School class members' efforts to answer a given question almost always fell short of the questioner's expectations, and that the questioner ultimately answered his own question after dismissing the answers of other members as incomplete. In both cases, the preacher and the questioner temporarily negated the other side's effort to conform itself to an ideal model and subsequently completed the round of engagement by providing their own answers to questions they had originally posed.

Agency in Abeyance

Esther Goody points out that a question often "compels, requires, may even demand, a response," and she compares the question-answer form of conversation to gift exchange: "In the incomplete nature of the question there is a parallel with Malinowski's view of the gift—for the gift, like the question, demands a return. Both may be seen as social devices for compelling interaction—for forcing two partners to enter into a social exchange" (Goody 1978: 23). Other writers, however, have challenged the assumption in Goody's analogy that questions are coercive (see Brenneis 1990; Goldman 1993: 198; cf. Green 1975; Keenan et al. 1978; Mertz 1996).

The sequential form of questions and answers or problems and solutions that I have described in the context of Suvavou people's Christian worship does indeed bear a strong resemblance to Fijian gift-giving. For the Fijian case, however, the analogy of questioning and gift-giving would be more fruitful if it were to focus on the form of the exchange of gifts and speeches rather than on the character of the debts that reciprocity engenders. What I have in mind is the distinctively Fijian form of gift-giving predicated on the notion of *veiqaravi,* or "facing."[9] My focus here is on the temporal process of its completion rather than on "reciprocal duties" (Hocart 1970 [1936]: 270; cf. Bourdieu 1977: 5). *Veiqaravi,* I argue, is a form of interaction between two sides that sequentially completes itself.

Veiqaravi rests on an indigenous theory of attendance and response repeatedly observed by anthropologists in Fiji and in other Polynesian societies. According to this theory, although gods, chiefs, and kings exert influence over people, their own efficacy depends upon people's attention to them. Valerio Valeri has observed of nineteenth-century Hawaiians, for example, that the agency of gods and kings was activated by human belief in the efficacy of these entities: "On the one hand, the gods are conceived as the autonomous source of all *mana* 'power.' But on the other hand, it is believed that the gods' power does not exist independently from man's worship and, in particular, from sacrifice. . . . Thus quite paradoxically, gods are the source of power but at the same time their worshippers are said to be the source of their power" (Valeri 1985: 89).

"People attend on (*qarava,* lit. 'face') the Christian God, who is above all," Christina Toren says of contemporary Fiji. "The old gods and ancestors still exist but their power has waned for they are no longer the object of the people's sacrifices; so the Christian God is invoked not as 'the only god' but as 'the only god who is served'" (Toren 1995: 166). Fijians' devotion to the Christian God thus does not necessarily entail the complete banishment of other gods. Fijian Christians always, in fact, have their ancestors and the old gods in mind, Toren observes (see also Tomlinson 2002b). From the Fijians' perspective, however, they remain in the background as long as no attention is paid to them. Veneration of a chief or god, whether Christian or otherwise, is a matter of choice (cf. Hocart 1970 [1936]: 99; M. Kaplan 1995: 114; Kasuga 1994; Ravuvu 1987: 259; Sahlins 1985: 37–40).

The temporal aspect of this theory of attendance and response, however, has so far escaped anthropological attention. Fijian gift-giving, I suggest, entails a moment at which gift-givers place their own agency in abeyance and a subsequent moment in which gift-receivers recuperate the gift-givers' agency. A comparison between Christian rituals and gift-giving rituals will bring this temporal process into focus.

In comparing Christian rituals and gift-giving rituals, I do not mean to suggest that Fijian Christianity is an extension of the *vei-qaravi*-style of interaction and thus distinctively Fijian. Indeed, many aspects of Fijian Christian rituals, including the use of the problem and solution or question and answer sets described above, are not at all unique to Fijian rituals (see M. Kaplan 1990a; Tomlinson 2002a, 2002b, 2004; Toren 1988, 1990, 1995, 1999, 2003). Christian rituals and Fijian gift-giving rituals should rather be regarded as two *versions* (cf. Hollander 1959) of a single form, which unfolds in time (cf. Toren 1988).

This treatment of two realms of knowledge encountered in Fiji parallels Fijians' own discourse on *lotu* (church) and *vanua* (land) as separate "paths." This discourse does not use either of these categories to explain the other. At times, Fijians observe that these two paths are the same; at others, they claim that the paths are entirely different and therefore should not be mixed together or confused analytically. Anthropological observations that Fijian Christian churches have taken a distinctively Fijian form resonate with the former claim but contradict the latter. The latter already contains within itself, *and* rejects, the anthropological rendering of Fijian Christianity as a local manifestation. Instead of explaining one realm of knowledge as the outcome of the other, then, I aim to bring into view ritual participants' aesthetic experience (cf. Riles 2000) as the basis for the common Fijian assertion that the two ritual processes are at once the same and profoundly separate.

For Suvavou people, *veiqaravi* entailed a very particular "aesthetic" or "constraint of form" (Strathern 1988: 180–81). As two parties faced each other spatially and exchanged gifts and speeches, both the gift-givers and the gift-receivers *attended* to each other in a manner emphasizing "respect" (*veidokai*). In gift-giving, any expression of conflict was out of place and to be avoided. Thus, for example, when *mataqali* that competed for leadership in Suvavou exchanged gifts and speeches at one another's mortuary rites, neither raised issues of contention in their speeches. Rather, "the way of relationships" (*vakaveiwekani*) as a morally empowered practice required proper words to be uttered at such occasions. Gifts and speeches *confirmed* the respectful relationship between the two sides.

This does not mean that gift-giving was a mechanical act. The successful execution of gift-giving called for a spokesman's competent performance. Typically, the gift-givers assembled a group of men and women who represented their clan, church, or other entity. A senior male figure who was particularly skilled in making speeches acted as the group's spokesman.[10] The spokesman was usually a member of the *mataqali*, or the entity he represented, although in some cases, he had no direct connection with those he represented.[11] The spokesman did not consult with the delegation about what he was to say. The understanding was that he would know what was to be said on behalf of the delegation (see Arno 1976a: 82).

Ritual participants were well aware of the risks entailed in gift-giving, which included the possibility that the gift-receivers might reject the gift, although this was extremely rare. The spokesman or other members of the delegation might stray from the ideal model of mutual respect and express overt criticism of the gift-receivers during the course of the event. Participants' intentional or unintentional misgivings might ultimately lead to the failure of gift-giving: the gift-receivers might later comment on the spokesman's poor performance or on the inadequacy of the gifts, and they might speculate about the negative consequences that this poor performance might have on the gift-givers (see Arno 1976a: 82). Such "failure" could be made evident retrospectively when the spokesman or one of his clansman became sick or died following the gift-giving event).[12] In the rituals I observed in Suvavou, however, awareness of these risks did not overwhelm the participants' commitment to completion, a sense of which was created by an exchange of speeches between the two sides.

In every case of gift-giving, the gift-givers' designated spokesman moved forward, while their delegation sat quietly behind him, facing the gift-receivers. Sitting on his knees holding a *tabua* (whale's tooth), he delivered a speech after the gifts (mats, money, and food) had been piled beside him. The first task the spokesman faced was to define the two sides, that is, the participants, both present and absent.[13] The spokesman typically began with an acknowledgement of the various groups of people on the receiving side by addressing himself to their chiefs by their titular names. For example, the spokesman for a delegation from an outer island made the following speech on the occasion of a mortuary exchange for a Suvavou woman's death:[14]

> *Spokesman for the gift-givers:* In the chiefly manner, [I address myself] to Nadonumai [the ceremonial name used for Suvavou people], to the chief, the Tui Suva, Vasu ki Bau [the uterine nephew of Bau].
> *Gift-receivers in unison:* Wa oi oi u.
> *Spokesman for the gift-givers:* [I also address myself] to Mataqali Koromakawa [the gift-receivers], to the *turaga* [literally, "chiefs"], its *itaukei* ["owners," meaning "clansmen"].
> *Gift-receivers in unison:* Vinaka saka [literally, "Good, Sir," meaning "Thank you, Sir"].
> *Spokesman for the gift-givers:* [I also address myself to] the chiefly land of Nakorotubu [from which the deceased originated], to the chief, the Gonesau [the chiefly title of Nakorotubu].
> *Gift-receivers in unison:* Vinaka.
> *Spokesman for the gift-givers:* [I also address myself] to the chiefly relatives who have gathered together at your place tonight.
> *Gift-receivers in unison:* Vinaka.

The speaker then explained the reason for his delegation's visit. He usually apologized for the shameful inappropriateness of the gifts (cf. Hocart 1929: 71; Hooper 1982: 122) and the lateness of his *mataqali*'s arrival. In this case, for example, the spokesman for the gift-givers said,

> We thought we would come earlier but the travel was difficult. We crossed the sea so that we might join you on this important occasion

today. Valuables displayed here are only small *reguregu* [literally, "kissing with the nose," meaning death gifts] from [our chief].

Gift-receivers: Levu [Big!]

Spokesman for the gift-givers: We thought we would bring something good. Here is a small mat, tea, food and an envelope [referring to money] . . . but if it is not useful, please forgive us.

In his list of apologies, the spokesman usually noted how long and redundant his speech had been.

At the end of the speech, the spokesman emphasized the close blood ties between the two sides and requested that the gift-receiving side accept the gifts and his speech. The speech ended with the mention of the titular names of the gift-givers' and the gift-receivers' chiefs. In this case, for example, the spokesman concluded, "[These are] death gifts from Nabala, from the Tui Nakasa, to Nadonumai, to the chief, the Tui Suva, to Mataqali Koromakawa, to the gentlemen, its clansmen. To Nakorobutu, to the Gonesau, and to the descendants that follow." After finishing his speech, the spokesman for the gift-givers remained motionless holding a *tabua* in front of him until a spokesman for the gift-receivers took it away from him. The speaker then retired to join other members of his *mataqali*.

The *tabua* was then passed to the chief or the most senior member of the gift-receivers who kissed it and proclaimed that it was accepted. For example, in response to the speech above, the most senior member of the gift-receivers said, "I have touched the valuable, a good valuable, a valuable of relationships, togetherness, thickness of blood ties." This speech consisted of only one or two sentences (cf. Hooper 1982: 122) and often ended with a standard phrase referring to the Christian God, such as "May all of us [inclusive of both sides] be led only by God [*da liutaki tiko mada ga mai vua na Kalou*]."[15] After this, the *tabua* was passed to the spokesman for the gift-receivers, who gave a longer speech, in which he acknowledged the gift-givers' effort as "respectful" (*vakarokoroko*) and "chiefly" (*vakaturaga*) and denied that there was a need for gifts (cf. Hooper 1982: 122). For example, following the brief speech above, the gift-receivers' spokesman said, "You did not need to bring anything. You should have brought only yourselves. We could have just met in the manner of relatives [*sota ga vakaveiwekani*]. However, you came with a large whale's tooth, valuables, and food. I thank you very much." The speech of the gift-receivers' spokesman ended with a series of prayers and always referred to God. In this case, the speech was concluded in the following way:

> Your valuables have been offered to Heaven so that we all may be given Heavenly blessing. May the Tui Nabala [the gift-givers' chief] be blessed. May your descendants be blessed so that they may study well every day to grow up to be strong enough to attend on our God. . . . May God love us together and may our duties be possible. Our mutual love is the only valuable.

When the speaker finished his speech with this reference to "mutual love" (*veilomani*), all present responded, "Let it be effective and true! (*Mana ei dina!*)" (cf. Hocart 1929: 71; Hooper 1982: 122; Ravuvu 1987: 254). This was usually followed by the standard phrase: "I will lay my hands on the gift . . . the whale's tooth, valuables, and food . . . It is plenty! Things from the past, things from the past" (cf. Ravuvu 1987: 78, 82, 86). In response, clapping their hands, everyone shouted, "*A muduo, muduo, duo.*"[16] Then, in the same humble manner in which the gift-givers presented their gift, the receivers presented a whale's tooth as a return gift (*dirika*) and thanked the gift-givers for their effort, and the gift-givers in turn declared that the return gift was accepted.[17] Ritual participants often expressed a sense of accomplishment at the completion of gift-giving. Although *veiqaravi* was then complete, however, it was often followed by further rounds of *veiqaravi*. For example, the identical form of exchange of gifts and speeches was repeated between the hosting *mataqali* and different visiting *mataqali* during the course of mortuary rites, and it was understood to be part of a succession of other occasions for gift-giving.

As described here, there are remarkable similarities between gift-giving rituals and church services. As in sermons and Bible study sessions that sequentially presented problem and solution or question and answer, the spokesman for the gift-givers posed a problem for the gift-receivers to solve. For example, when the gift-givers' spokesman described their gift as problematic, "small" (*lailai*), "useless" (*sega ni yaga*), and so forth, the gift-receivers immediately shouted, "Big!" (*Levu!*), confirming its appropriateness. The gift-receivers' spokesman brushed aside the concern about their gifts that was repeatedly expressed by the gift-givers' spokesman by dwelling on their generosity and on the mutual respect and eternal blood ties between them and the gift-receivers. Finally, at the end of his speech, the gift-receivers' spokesman declared "mutual love" to be the ultimate gift, obviating any need for gift-giving. The gift-givers' spokesman's speech and the gift-receivers' spokesman's speech thus constituted a problem-and-solution set.

In both the Christian and gift-giving rituals, the spokesman (the Sabbath School questioner or preacher in the case of the former) was instrumental in completing these sets of problems and solutions, first rendering problematic the efforts of the other class members, the congregation, or the gift-givers to conform to an ideal and then offering a solution to the very problem he had raised. In the case of church rituals, the questioner or preacher solved the problem by confirming the ideal model to which the participants in the ritual had already striven to conform. Even though the participants' roles involved different degrees of rigidity and scriptedness, all were framed by questions and answers or problems and solutions organized sequentially.

Most important, this similarity between Christian and gift-giving rituals at the level of form is reiterated at the level of content. The completion of these sets of sequenced problems and solutions coincided with a moment at which speakers expressed a hope for a response from God or the Holy Spirit. Recall Sakeasi's mention in the Sabbath School class of God's response to one's sincerity and of the Holy Spirit's response to straightforward questions; recall also the Methodist and Adventist preachers' repeated emphasis that the congregation's proper attendance would elicit God's response. Likewise, in the gift-giving ritual, the spokesman for the gift-receivers concluded his speech by referring to a hope for a response from God in such prayers as "May all of us [the gift-givers as well as the gift-receivers] be led only by God" or "Your valuables have been offered up to Heaven so that we all may be given Heavenly blessing." The role of the questioner and the preacher in church rituals was similar to the role of the spokesman in gift-giving rituals in effectuating a moment of abeyance of agency—a moment at which all present ceased to emphasize their own or others' actions and instead looked to God for a response.

One way to understand such abeyance, ambiguation (Battaglia 1997) or indirection (Brenneis 1986) of agency is to view it as the ultimate strategic act of rhetorical manipulation (see also Marcus 1988). Based on his study of Cretan shepherds' use of oaths, Michael Herzfeld (1990, 1997) has, for example, called such moments "structural nostalgia," observing: "People generally ignore human agency when it suits them to do so. . . . [They] invent, refashion and exploit . . . [timeless] structures as moral alibis for their contingent actions" (1997: 113). Similarly, in his study of ritual speech in Anakalang, Eastern Indonesia, Webb Keane has likewise discussed the strategic abeyance of human agency as a tool for overcoming the risks that ritual itself makes explicit. According to Keane, "[t]o speak in couplets [according to the manner by which ancestors speak] is . . . to display a strategy of avoidance . . . [T]he indirection and distancing effects of ritual speech protect its users from the challenges each presents to the other—or rather, they allow its users to act *as if* such protection were necessary" (Keane 1994: 620; emphasis in original). Here, Keane suggests that the use of a particular style of speech renders participants aware of the risks involved in the exchange of gifts and defines the management of those risks as the task of exchange.[18] In this act of abeyance, exchange creates the possibility of experiencing the efficacy of ancestral agency itself.

The Fijian case, however, draws attention to ritual participants' commitment to completion rather than to their interest in strategies for controlling risks. For Fijians, the abeyance of agency entailed a three-step process, that is, an effort to conform to an ideal model, the problematization of that effort, and the presentation of the same ideal model as a solution. As exemplified most starkly by the utter stillness of the gift-givers' spokesman at the end of his speech while he awaited the gift-receivers' response, the exchange of problems and solutions in gift-giving, preaching, and Bible study entailed a temporary negation of the ritual participants' agency. When the gift-givers' spokesman fell silent, he laid the gift-givers open to the risk of rejection—he placed his hope in the hands of the gift-receivers. Likewise, when the questioner dismissed other class members' questions, and when the preacher dismissed the congregation's effort to conform to the ideal model of worship, the questioner and the preacher suspended the agency of the other class members and the congregation, respectively. Nothing the other class members and the congregation said or did was adequate, they were told. In turn, the solution that the questioner, the preacher, and the gift-receivers' spokesman provided always lay in the proper manner of attendance. Note that none of these moves to place agency in abeyance was completely open-ended. Both sides shared a commitment to closure. The moment of hope that emerged at the moment of abeyance of agency was, then, simultaneously open and closed.

Ultimately, however, successive moments of abeyance of agency and the subsequent recovery of agency preceding the ultimate moment of abeyance of human agency in these rituals enabled participants to anticipate another moment of fulfillment. In other words, the three-step process intimated an ultimate response. From this standpoint, it is clear that by repeatedly presenting sets of questions and answers or problems and solutions, Fijian ritual participants experienced intimations of fulfillment. It is through the appreciation of or "empathy" (Bateson 1979: 8) for the completeness of these sets, I claim, that Fijian ritual participants experienced the fulfillment of their hope as the capacity repeatedly to place their own agency in abeyance.[19] Thus, the hope produced in this process surfaced as the replication of a hope ritually fulfilled.

Note that in both genres of self-knowledge I have described, church and gift-giving rituals, this three-step process was repeated again and again. For example, in gift-giving, the form of each episode of gift-giving was almost identical, except that each involved a different delegation of gift-givers, with its own specific tie to the gift-receivers. From the gift-receivers' point of view, therefore, these episodes of gift-giving were experienced as successive moments of hope and its fulfillment, and these successive moments in turn generated one further moment of hope: after all of the gifts had been presented, the gift-receivers were required to present food for collective consumption. During their presentation speeches, many gift-givers alluded to this obligation, known as *i burua,* with statements such as "this is our assistance for tomorrow's work" (meaning the work of preparing the feast). For ritual participants, then, there was a homology between the temporal trajectory of the entire mortuary rite—from a moment of hope in an ultimate response that emerged as each delegation completed its presentation of death gifts to a moment of the completion of *i burua*—and the temporal trajectory experienced in the course of each individual episode of gift-giving. In other words, this larger and extended state of waiting for a response, which gradually became more and more immanent as successive delegations presented their death gifts and was ultimately completed with the preparation of the final feast, was a homological replication of all previous moments of hope and their fulfillment. In chapter 6, I turn to the effect of this repetition in Suvavou people's hope.

6 ⌒ Repeating Without Overlapping

In the previous chapter, I sought to demonstrate how hope is ritually produced as an effect of discursive play of agency, in particular, as an effect of what I have called the abeyance of agency. However, as mentioned in chapter 1, this kind of analysis in turn raises a further methodological problem. As noted at the outset, there is a certain incongruity between the retrospective orientation of my own analytical framework, which approached hope as the product of a ritual process, and the prospective orientation of its subject, hope itself. The retrospective rendering of hope, as a subject of analysis, foreclosed the possibility of describing the prospective momentum inherent in hope. As soon as hope is approached as the end point of a process, as in the previous chapter, the newness or freshness of the prospective moment that defines that moment as hopeful is lost. The solution to this methodological problem seemed to be to reorient the direction of my own analysis toward the future and render the analysis synchronous with its subject. Such synchronicity would be an illusion, however. Moreover, I came to understand that my retrospection was not the cause of the trouble I was confronting. Moving away from the illusion of achieving analytical synchronicity, I began to see that temporal incongruity was instrumental in the production of hope. In this chapter, I want to advance the argument framed in terms of agency in the previous chapters by examining the role of temporal incongruity in the production of hope. The objective now is not simply descriptive but also methodological. I return to the methodological problem of temporal incongruity between my analysis and its object as an opportunity.

Instead of explaining hope, would it be possible to anticipate it? Let me first take a step back and describe the argument to this point in light of the problem of temporal incongruity. In chapter 4, we saw that from Suvavou people's point of view, a state of synchronicity was not achievable. The official account of who they are, contained in government documents, belongs to the past. It is not open for reinterpretation from the point of view of the present. For them, temporal incongruity was therefore a given condition of their self-knowledge. Where the possibility of synchronicity was specifically foreclosed, Mataqali Koromakawa's report described in chapter 4 deployed a strategy of knowledge that resulted in the production of the official account. For example, the report reversed the questioner-respondent relationship in land inquiries and the parts-whole relationship in migration stories. These efforts aimed to create a realm of indeterminacy, in the context of this temporal incongruity, in which they sought to situate their hope. This entailed a strategy of delegating the act of closure to a third party, which in turn also deferred closure to a future moment.

With different degrees of scriptedness, the church and gift-giving rituals examined in chapter 5 also created moments of temporal incongruity. In criticizing his flock for failing to conform to the proper form of worship, a preacher countered the prospective orientation of the congregation, which had prepared itself by dressing up, studying the Bible, or practicing hymns, with the inherent retrospectivity of self-critique. In gift-giving, the prospective orientation of the gift-givers' prospective gesture of waiting for the gift-receivers' favorable response was countered by the gift-receivers' retrospective language of evaluation praising the gift-givers' manner of presentation as "respectful" (*vakarokoroko*) and "chiefly" (*vakaturaga*) and confirmation of the close ties between the two sides. In both cases, the moment of temporal incongruity thus created resulted in a renewed moment of prospectivity. The preacher suggested once again that the congregation conform to the form; the spokesman for the gift-receivers dedicated the gifts to God. In both petitions and rituals, in other words, the hope produced at the completion of a ritual was thus placed in a delicate balance between future-oriented openness and anticipation of a moment of ultimate fulfillment, effectuated as an echo of the moment of fulfillment just achieved in the ritual.

The interplay of retrospective and prospective perspectives in different genres of self-knowledge in Suvavou recalls Walter Benjamin's messianic historian discussed in chapter 1. I demonstrated that retrospective attention to what Benjamin calls "hope in the past" generates hope in the present, reimagined as moments of retrospection. My argument was that this hope is a product of the temporal incongruity between the prospective momentum of the past moment of hope that the historian sought to recapture and the retrospective perspective of the historian. What emerges at the intersection of Suvavou people's and Benjamin's hope, then, is their shared solution to my original problem of how to recapture (and maintain) hope. In both cases, hope in the past is extrapolated and replicated as hope in the present.

In what follows, I examine instances of such replication in a field of discourse beyond petitions and rituals. My goal is to understand the implications of Suvavou people's hope for the location of Fijians' hope in the multi-ethnic state.[1] I first examine a series of speech events surrounding the Suvavou village company Nadonumai Holdings's foundation-laying ceremony for its office building, whose chief guest was Prime Minister Sitiveni Rabuka. My focus is on the way a retrospective perspective constantly invaded the prospective moment of the ritual and how that retrospective turn was then countered by a further prospective turn. My larger claim here is that hope surfaced as an ontological condition that Fijians constantly strove to maintain. In the second half of the chapter, I turn to the case of Prime Minister Sitiveni Rabuka's 1996 apology for his past actions. This apology triggered a public debate in Fiji's national newspapers that engaged a variety of Fiji citizens, including Europeans, part-Europeans and Indo-Fijians. The case makes apparent the difficulty of extending Fijian hope to a wider discursive arena. My point is that hope cannot be argued for or explained; it can only be replicated. Hence the potential danger of hope transforming itself into self-aggrandizement and self-right-eous anger. This example both demonstrates the character of hope as a method and signals its limits.

The Invasion of Retrospection

EXCEPT the LORD build the house, they labour in vain that build it

[*Kevaka sa sega ni tara na vale ko Jiova, era sa oca wale ga ko ira era sa tara*].

Ps. 127:1

Quoting one of Fijian Christians' favorite Bible passages, Rev. Samuela Ratulevu, an SDA pastor from Suvavou, who had just been designated managing director of Nadonumai Holdings, pro-posed to hold a series of prayer meetings in the village. At the time of my fieldwork, Fijian Christians often quoted this passage when they insisted that they should pray for God's blessing and assistance before holding a meeting, embarking on a villagewide project, and so forth. For Fijian Christians, it was generally considered impera-tive to pray for God's blessing and assistance before embarking on any project. If one prayed for God's assistance, they reasoned, everything would go well. Psalms 127:1 thus constituted an effec-tive model for social and political action.

What interests me about Rev. Ratulevu's proposal is that he intended it to counter a certain retrospective perspective that per-meated Suvavou people at the inception of Nadonumai Holdings. Rev. Ratulevu knew that many Suvavou people were skeptical of Nadonumai Holdings because all past business enterprises initiat-ed by Suvavou individuals and *mataqali* had failed miserably. We might say that Suvavou people were haunted by their memory of the past. Seeking to counteract such negative memories, Rev. Ratulevu quoted Psalms 127:1 and told Suvavou people, "Unless God is with us, nothing will be possible." Rev. Ratulevu's choice of the passage, "EXCEPT the LORD build the house, they labour in vain that build it," seemed particularly appropriate for the occa-sion, because in this case the company's project was literally to build an office building in Suva City. His implication, however, was that all past Suvavou business enterprises had failed because they had not been founded on Christian truth and therefore had not received God's blessing and assistance. In other words, Rev. Ratulevu redefined Suvavou people's past failure as evidence of the truthfulness of Psalms 127:1 and argued that if they prayed for God's blessing and assistance in following the teaching of Psalms 127:1, they would always succeed. At his insistence, therefore, the two congregations in the village, Methodists and Seventh-Day Adventists, gathered together and held a week-long prayer meeting at the village green. By seeking God's blessing, Rev. Ratulevu sought to ground Suvavou's new business enterprise in Christian faith.

Note that Rev. Ratulevu's effort to turn a moment full of retrospection, that is, memory of past failure, into a moment of hope was predicated on a certain slippage in the conception of agency. Whereas Psalms 127:1 focuses on the importance of God's agency in the effectiveness of humans' work, Rev. Ratulevu's vision focused on the importance of the work of devout Christians like himself. Rev. Ratulevu explicitly told his fellow villagers that he wanted to use his long-term experience of ministry in the Seventh-Day Adventist Church as a basis for this business enterprise. In other words, Rev. Ratulevu sought to found Nadonumai Holdings on the truth that he himself embodied. This recentering of human agency in turn allowed Rev. Ratulevu to present a concrete solution to the problem of Suvavou people's past failures, that is, prayer for God's blessing. Hope that this would be the first successful business enterprise thus emerged in the ontologically defined gap between Suvavou people's past approach to life and their present effort to emulate a truthful Christian way of life.

Retrospection easily invades and thwarts a prospective moment, however. Despite having been launched with prayers, Rev. Ratulevu's business did not proceed smoothly. It took three years for Nadonumai Holdings to secure title to the necessary piece of state land in Suva and start construction, and villagers attributed the delay to their own disunity. During the three years, the company's integrity was threatened by disputes among village *mataqali*. Within a few months of the company's formation, Mataqali Koromakawa, a long-standing challenger of Mataqali Kaiwai's leadership, dropped out of the company. These disputes reminded the villagers of their long history of past feuds (see chapter 3). Then, in October 1995, the paramount chief of Rewa, Adi Lady Lala, the wife of Ratu Sir Kamisese Mara, who was president of Fiji at the time, announced that the Rewa Provincial Council planned to construct an office building on a lot directly adjacent to Cruickshank Park, Nadonumai Holdings's construction site. Many Suvavou people feared that the Rewa Provincial Council project would intentionally or unintentionally "spoil" their company's project. A Suvavou woman expressed this pervasive view when she told me that Rewa people were jealous of Suvavou people because of Prime Minister Rabuka's attention and favor.

This woman's comment is paradigmatic of a wider form of memory that is triggered by immanent failure. Her comment invoked a history. The famous war between Bau and Rewa, two competing chiefdoms in southeastern Viti Levu, in the 1840s is said to have begun, in part, over an incident that took place in Suva (see Sahlins 1991: 52–60). A. M. Hocart, who visited Suvavou in 1910, and Colman Wall, who also visited Suvavou early in the twentieth century, recorded Suvavou's traditional stories about the Bau-Rewa War. According to these stories, the war broke out as a result of an incident in which a high chief of Rewa, Ro Qaraniqio, attempted to capture a pig in Suva. The Roko Tui Suva, Ratu Ravulo, was angry about Ro Qaraniqio's behavior and chased him away from Suva. Angry about this, Ro Qaraniqio determined to destroy Suva. Suva people fought back successfully against Rewa's first attack but succumbed to the second attack, when a number of Suva people were killed. Survivors of this fight fled to various villages in neighboring regions, and Ratu Ravulo himself took refuge in Bau. Later, the most powerful chief of the time, the Vunivalu of Bau, Ratu Seru Cakobau, returned the remaining Suva people to Suva (Hocart n.d.a: 2507–12; Wall 1920).[2] Suvavou people I knew did not seem to be much interested in these war stories, although they were clearly aware that Rewa people had defeated Suva people in that war. The implication of the woman's comment, therefore, was that the actions of the Rewa Provincial Council were yet another manifestation of the long-standing tension between the two chiefdoms.

It is not simply memory that introduces a retrospective perspective to a present moment. A sense of achievement might also induce retrospection. In 1995, Nadonumai Holdings finally acquired the piece of state land in Suva City that it needed and received commitments from several government departments to occupy its office building once it was completed. On December 8, 1995, Nadonumai Holdings invited Prime Minister Rabuka, who had personally assisted Suvavou with this project, to its foundation-laying ceremony. Rev. Ratulevu's vision of a business enterprise founded on Christian faith permeated the ceremony, which began with a prayer by Rev. Ratulevu. This was followed by the presenting of a series of gifts to Rabuka. With the first of these, the spokesman for the chief and *mataqali* of Suvavou stressed the role of God's blessing and assistance in Nadonumai Holdings's accomplishment so far:

> This morning, I am holding a valuable in front of you to welcome you in a chiefly manner according to the expected manner and procedure and with such respect [*veidoka*] and humbleness [*veirokorokotaki*] as our parents and elders have always shown since the olden days. I wish to show you the joy of the people of Nadonumai in inviting you as a guest of honor in a respectful and humble manner to this foundation-laying ceremony for development of the people of Nadonumai. We wish to tell you that we are grateful for using your time of leadership to give us a blessing. A blessing for our now deceased parents who moved out from here. . . . For 113 years since we left this land, we have been at a crowded place in Suvavou. We have been at a difficult place. . . . We have prayed to God that the time will come when a government that will remember us will appear in the suffering that we are going through. Prime Minister, you are God's appointee. Sitting beside you are the president of the Methodist Church, the acting principal minister for the Suvavou Circuit, and others, including the minister of the SDA Church. They have prayed for [Suvavou people] many times. We believed that the time would come when God would give us His blessing. . . . We have cried for generations until today. Prime Minister, this

is a valuable for many thanks from the Tui Suva and the people under him. We are very grateful to you and are very pleased with your leadership.[3]

Here, the spokesman for Suvavou people situated this moment as the achievement of many years of prayer for God's blessing and assistance. In one of the speeches following the presentation of valuables, Rabuka took up the theme this Suvavou spokesman raised and acknowledged that this was a time of God's blessing for Suvavou people: "You have grumbled for years. Other people have gained millions of dollars in business on your land, the soil where you obtained your food in the past. Now is the beginning of your steps toward wealth as a result of development at the time of God's blessing for you." But Rabuka also elaborated the implications of Suvavou people's struggle for a more general Fijian aspiration for empowerment and stressed that Suvavou people's success proved that if Fijians were united, everything they wanted would come true. Later, in response to the final presentation of valuables, Rabuka concluded his speech by positing "unity" as a future necessity:

> I hope that we shall not forget that this land is not ours. We are only inhabiting it for those future owners of this land. . . . In everything we make happen, we are thinking of those future landowners. May our gathering be successful. May our development be successful. We all—*vanua, lotu,* and *matanitu*—hold hands together [*taurilinga,* meaning "collaborate"]. May God lead our land always.[4]

Note the way in which Rabuka's grand vision for Fijians' development projects introduced a future orientation to his response. Whereas the Suvavou spokesman's speech celebrated the efficacy of Suvavou people's prayer for God's blessing and assistance, Rabuka deployed a popular Fijian idea about the importance of the collaboration among *vanua, lotu,* and *matanitu* as the condition of Fijians' future success (cf. Jolly 1992; M. Kaplan 1988, 1990a; Rutz 1995). In Rabuka's vision, if Fijians brought their tradition and Christian faith together in the governance of the country, everything would be possible. Here, the case of Nadonumai Holdings served as proof of this fact. If the Suvavou spokesman celebrated the present moment as an effect of Suvavou people's past prayer, Rabuka's speech introduced a prospective momentum beyond Nadonumai Holdings's project.

There is a parallel between the way Rev. Ratulevu used Psalms 127:1 as an inspiration for his vision of a company founded on Christian faith and the way Rabuka presented a grand vision of Fijian unity. Both Rev. Ratulevu and Rabuka generated a prospective momentum for audiences among whom a retrospective perspective seemed to reign. This was accomplished by a shift from a focus on God's agency to a focus on humans' (further) work.

Following the presentation of valuables and the foundation-laying ceremony, the police band played music, and village women invited guests to dance (taralala). This dance, however, provided Mataqali Koromakawa, the dissident SDA clan that had withdrawn from the project of Nadonumai Holdings two years before, with an opportunity to disrupt the festive and hopeful mood of the rest of the village, because the SDA Church, to which a half of the village belonged, prohibited dancing.[5] At church the following Sabbath, Mataqali Koromakawa elders requested that all SDA church members who had danced at the foundation-laying ceremony be punished.

In response to Mataqali Koromakawa church members' request, the board of the Suvavou SDA Church decided to give the dancers an opportunity to confess their sin and seek forgiveness at the year's last communion ceremony, to be held four days later.[6] When no one who had danced at the ceremony confessed to wrongdoing,[7] Mataqali Koromakawa church members publicly named the villagers who had failed to seek forgiveness for their sin and demanded their formal punishment. A heated debate ensued, and church elders finally summoned Rev. Ratulevu, who reluctantly admitted that SDAs should not have participated in dancing.

To the surprise of many Methodist villagers, Mataqali Koromakawa church members' persistent emphasis on the importance

Figure 2. Prime Minister Sitiveni Rabuka at the foundation-laying ceremony for an office building to be owned by Suvavou people's company, Nadonumai Holdings. Courtesy *Fiji Times*.

of church law swayed other influential SDA church elders, including a handful of elders from other *mataqali* who backed Nadonumai Holdings and had attended the foundation-laying ceremony. Church elders ultimately decided to punish their cousins, daughters, and wives for their sinful behavior by prohibiting them from performing official duties at church for a period of three months.[8] Mataqali Koromakawa church elders' theological interjection thus was successful in dividing the other church elders who did not necessarily share Mataqali Koromakawa's stance on the company.

"Let us love one another [Me da veilomani]." With this statement, Ratu Epeli, the chief of the village, stood up to make a plea (*vosa ni vakadre*) at the beginning of the annual joint church service on New Year's Eve several days after this crisis. It was the first time Ratu Epeli, a Methodist, had attended an SDA church service since assuming the chiefly title in 1990. He was not a regular churchgoer at his own church, and perhaps this was part of the reason for his beginning in an apologetic and humble tone:

> Ladies and gentlemen who have duties at church, . . . I did not intend to come here to speak this evening. I have not entered this church for a long time. It occurred to me at the last minute. Ladies and gentlemen, I do not preach in my own church. I just go to church from time to time. If anything I say misses the point and is awkward, arrogant and wrong, ladies and gentlemen, please forgive me.[9]

To everyone's great surprise, he went on to quote Scripture:

> "For thus hath the LORD of hosts said, Hew ye down trees, and cast a mount against Jerusalem: this is the city to be visited; she is wholly oppression in the midst of her [Sa vakaoqo na vosa i Jiova ni lewe vuqa, Dou taya sobu na kau, ka viri suva kei Jerusalemi: oqo na koro me cudruvi; sa caka e loma ni koro nai valavala vakausausa (Jer. 6.6)]." I do not read the Bible too often. This is just what I happened to pick up.

It was clear to everyone that the speech was intended as a response to the recently intensified dispute between Mataqali Koromakawa and the rest of the village about Nadonumai Holdings. Ratu Epeli continued:

Those who have duties at church should [fence off a church com-
pound][10]. . . . They should tell the congregation not to gossip, not to
point to someone or not to speak behind someone's back. Then your
vanua will be good. . . . I have seen behavior among members of the
church that is not good. There are acts of deception. Young people,
both Methodists and SDAs, are fighting and do not follow the teaching
of the church. They fight from the Sabbath to Friday. There is no
Sabbath. Churches are lost. You should put a fence and tell them what
is right. . . . If they remain like this, they will be worse. Moreover, there
will be noisy behavior. Causing a lot of noise is a sin. . . . Let us love
one another [*Meda veilomani*]. . . . We should love one another and
everything will go well. . . . The first thing I strongly feel in my heart is
that our parents did not behave like this. This is a new thing that I have
seen happening for the last two weeks. I have been wondering when this
stops. . . . I hope we will love one another and will hold hands together and will put a fence, the fence of the church or the fence of the *vanua*.
This is important for our children.

Here, in response to Mataqali Koromakawa's theological interjection, Ratu Epeli invoked the effectiveness of love and the need
for a "fence" that would stop rivalries among *mataqali* from enter-
ing the church. Love would make everything possible, he stressed.
The notion of love as an effective form now made Mataqali Koromakawa's interjection fundamentally problematic (cf. Toren 1999:
131–32). After Ratu Epeli's speech, which once again gave a prospective momentum to the project, his supporters and those of
Nadonumai Holdings were triumphant. Ratu Epeli's turn to Jeremiah 6:6 was predicated on a slippage similar to the slippage from
God's agency to human agency in Rev. Ratulevu's use of Psalms
127:1. Ratu Epeli's focus was not on God's punishment of a corrupt city as described in Jeremiah but on the commitment of devout
Christians to erecting a fence and to loving one another.

The conceptual slippage entailed in the extension and translation of Psalms 127:1 into a discourse on the importance of prayer
in all aspects of Fijian social life is one manifestation of a pervasive
shift from an emphasis on God's agency to an emphasis on the
importance of human agency in Fijian Christian discourse. The
shift in turn allows Fijian Christians to present themselves with a
model to emulate in order to achieve a state where, as they say,

"everything [they want] is possible." Hope therefore follows self-aggrandizing proclamations of faith in humans' work. In other words, in Fijian Christian discourse, the production of hope is paradoxically predicated on the temporary backgrounding of God's agency. This process renders the truthfulness of biblical texts simultaneously both self-evident and emergent. The source of hope lies in extending the biblical example to social and political action and foregrounding human agency.

In this way, Fijian Christians repeatedly sought to introduce a prospective perspective to a present constantly invaded by retrospection. They reoriented the temporal direction of their knowledge by redefining and reconfiguring the relationship between humans and God. Suvavou people first devalued and even placed in abeyance the agency of humans by confirming the certainty of God's intention before presenting themselves with a concrete model for effective action. This two-step process of redefinition turned a present moment characterized by retrospective perspective into one filled with hope. My argument is that the maintenance of hope is predicated on this operation. Hope as a method, in other words, is an effort to preserve the prospective momentum of the present. The flip side is that hope cannot be preserved otherwise. I now turn to a demonstration of this latter point.

The Limits of Hope

At a church service broadcast throughout Fiji in November 1996, then Prime Minister Sitiveni Rabuka stood up to pray for the nation. Before beginning, however, Rabuka sought the forgiveness of the people of Fiji: "For those of you who are listening in, I don't know how many people I have wronged. . . . If you feel I have wronged you, forgive me first before I pray for this nation. . . . If I am forgiven, then I can pray for this nation."[11]

Rabuka later explained to a local newspaper that he had felt compelled to apologize to the nation after reading a certain Bible passage in preparation for the service: "[T]hat morning it came very very clearly to me that if you are at the altar to present your offerings and there you remember that your brother has something against you, go back and make your peace with your brother."[12]

In 1987, Rabuka had led two military coups that toppled the legitimately elected National Federation–Labour coalition government of Fiji. Rabuka described himself as a devout Christian and a lay preacher (Dean and Ritova 1988: 22), and he had always emphasized Christian themes in his public speeches. For example, soon after the coups, he characterized his role in the 1987 coups as "a mission that God has given me" (quoted in ibid.: 11; emphasis removed; cf. Garrett 1990: 88–89). As he understood it, the coalition government threatened ethnic Fijians' privileged right to their land, "the land that God has given them" (quoted in ibid.: 11, emphasis removed), because in his view the government was dominated by Indo-Fijians.[13] The following is a version of Rabuka's justification for the first military coup:

> There is only one reason for this coup, that is my apprehension that the time might come when the rule of our land and our soil might be taken and that in such future times our descendants might therefore be impoverished. We people of Fiji have been well off, because of the religion of our living God.
>
> If we welcome the enlightenment of this religion of God and we believe it, we must accept everything that comes to pass in his world.
>
> When first God's religion came to our land the chiefs of that time were strong and they were strong and successful in war then.
>
> God decreed that those true chiefs of the land of that time should convert to Christianity. These true chiefs welcomed the religion then, and it was fortunate that they did, [because] we nowadays have received its blessings. We are enlightened thereby, our land was developed thereby and we have learned much nowadays.
>
> If we approve of and welcome this, let us welcome the fact that these chiefs were the source of our blessedness. Their descendants who are leading nowadays, they are blessed because their ancestors who have passed on before them welcomed Christianity.
>
> The basis of our blessedness is their having accepted our God's religion, His name, His salvation, and His light. It is right thereby that we see everything that comes to us as something blessed, including development in the work we do, and the coming here of the Indians was a thing of blessedness to our land. Everything has happened because of the acceptance of the religion by our true chiefs who have led us from those days to the present.

It is thus right that we use all of these blessings, to employ them for our use, but let us not lose the paramountcy of [national political] leadership of the true chiefs of the land.
Let not our thoughts thereby be led astray so that we say to ourselves, since we have studied we can be chiefs. It's wrong, if we study we are wise, if we are chiefs, we are chiefs; they the chiefs are chiefs only from God, as the Apostle Paul says.[14]

Because Rabuka's 1996 apology appeared to contradict his 1987 justification of the coups, it triggered a public debate in the local press.[15] The *Fiji Times,* a national daily that tended to express views critical of the government, published an article on Rabuka's apology on the front page alongside a cartoon that portrayed Rabuka begging for the forgiveness of an uninterested audience. In its editorial that day, the newspaper portrayed Rabuka as "a mixed-up, guilt-ridden man who cannot draw the line between private prayer and leading a nation."[16] In a letter to the *Fiji Times,* Sir Len Usher, a long-time Suva resident and vocal critic of the Rabuka government, noted: "There is one puzzling thing about the Prime Minister's tearful plea for forgiveness for wrongs which . . . he has done to the people in Fiji. He has repeatedly told us that in all his public actions, from the 1987 coups on, he has been specifically chosen and directed by God."[17]

Imrana Jalal, a Suva lawyer and internationally recognized women's rights activist, also dismissed Rabuka's apology and declared that she would not forgive him. As she wrote in her weekly column in the *Fiji Times,* "Unfortunately Mr Prime Minister, not that it matters in the slightest to you what I think of you, at this moment I do not forgive you."[18] Jalal pointed out that Rabuka's apology was merely words, the antithesis of the "action" that she believed was needed to solve the political problems caused by the coups:

Actions speak louder than words, and words are cheap. I hold you and others of your ilk indirectly responsible for the loss of my family[,] the majority of whom departed for greener shores, for the loss of my friends of all races who[m] you have made unwelcome in this country that I love, for the suspicion and mistrust that now exists amongst childhood friends, for the disdain with which people abroad look upon Fiji, for the debacle of the National Bank of Fiji, for the loss of investors, for the downward spiral of our economy, for the racism and hatred now pervading our country, and for the fact that my two little boys may grow up not loving this country as I do. . . . Show us with your deeds, not with what you say that you are genuinely sorry. Make me feel that my children will have similar rights in this country as do your children Mr. Prime Minister then I will forgive you.[19]

In addition, Jalal criticized Rabuka for bringing his Christian agenda into politics: "Although you may have genuinely believed in your God-given right to act as you did[,] it was not right for you to sacrifice the prosperity of this country based simply on your belief."[20]

Following criticism of Rabuka's move by Jalal and others, letters from readers flooded the local press. Many defended Rabuka's apology. They did so, however, not by denouncing Jalal and others' political analysis of the coups, but by asserting that the critics had misunderstood the context of Rabuka's apology.[21] According to them, Rabuka's apology fell into the realm of faith, not that of politics, and the critics had invaded that realm with political discourse. In a letter to the *Fiji Times*, for example, Michael Ah Koy, a Suva businessman and a son of Rabuka's political ally, Jim Ah Koy, criticized the *Fiji Times*'s negative reportage of Rabuka's apology:

> For you to take that deeply spiritual moment and lampoon it in a cartoon on the front page of your paper is sacrilege.
>
> You may not like the Prime Minister's politics and you may not think much of his Government, but please do not demean his faith in Jehovah—our forgiving God.
>
> In doing so you demean my faith and the faith of every other Christian in Fiji—Fijian, Indian and others alike.[22]

One "S. V. Taka" noted in the same vein:

> Rabuka may have been apologising to the nation[,] but he was doing it within the sacred portals of the church.
>
> Every good Christian knows that one must humble himself before God and confess his sins, in order that one may be strengthened by the Holy Spirit.
>
> And that was the context in which Rabuka prayed before the congregation.
>
> However unpalatable his gross misconduct may have been during

the coup or during his present administration, he has proven to everyone that he can be human to admit his weakness.[23]

Taka interpreted Rabuka's apology as a moment at which he submitted himself to God's decision. Whether others forgave Rabuka
made no difference to God's decision to forgive, as long as Rabuka
had been humble enough to seek others' forgiveness. The apology
therefore was not a matter for human beings such as Jalal to comment upon:

> It was a moment of atonement in which Rabuka sought fellowship
> with God. And yet you [Jalal] and the media have portrayed it as if he
> was baring his soul to the nation.
> It was a private gesture turned public simply because he was Prime
> Minister.
> In that moment of reckoning Rabuka was not asking the nation to
> forgive him, he was asking God to do so. He was not asking your for-
> giveness for he knew very well you would publicly ridicule him as you
> have done.
> But as a good Christian Rabuka would know well the paradox of St.
> Paul "that from ridicule one is strengthened."[24]

Rabuka's defenders thus did not focus on his critics' political
views or on the substance of their critiques of Rabuka's past
actions. Rather, the issue for them was these critics' failure to
respond properly to Rabuka's humble display of himself. In light of
the argument of the previous chapters, one can understand that for
Rabuka's defenders, Rabuka's apology was a moment of hope
analogous to the moment of the gift-givers' spokesman's stillness
after his speech, as he waits for the other side's response (see chapter 5). In this interpretation, Jalal and others' questioning of the
sincerity of Rabuka's apology was out of place for that particular
moment, and thus inappropriate and disrespectful.[25] In an interview with the *Fiji Times*, Rabuka himself proclaimed: "Well, if the
people don't feel happy about [forgiveness], then it's their fault.
They just don't feel it, and we cannot explain, I cannot explain, it
is very difficult for anyone to explain."[26]

Erasure of his own agency figures in both Rabuka's 1996 apology and the theological justification he came up with after the first

1987 coup. In his 1987 justification, Rabuka claimed to have been on a God-given mission to restore the relationship that God had established between chiefs and people (land), and in his 1996 apology, he presented himself as a humble Christian pursuing forgiveness for his past sinful behavior and willing to submit to God's decision. This erasure of his own agency was exactly what bothered his critics, for whom his apology was simply an attempt to evade responsibility. "People generally ignore human agency when it suits them to do so," as Michael Herzfeld has pertinently observed (1997: 113).

Rather than address the question of whether Rabuka's apology was genuine or strategic, however, I wish to focus on what may seem a somewhat obvious aspect of the case—the way Rabuka's apology was politicized by his Christian sympathizers' defense. Notwithstanding their plea that politics be kept out of it, by asserting Rabuka's moral superiority vis-à-vis his critics, Ah Koy, Taka, and others inevitably politicized what they portrayed as a nonpolitical, nonstrategic act. Taka concluded:

> Your naive reaction to his lament proves you neither know nor care about what Christian churches do.
> We all pray for our sins—from a beggar in the street to a Prime Minister who leads people of different faiths.
> We all take the time to do what our faith requires of us, to humble ourselves before God.[27]

Likewise, the *Sunday Post,* the Sunday edition of a national daily generally sympathetic to the government, attacked the critics of Rabuka's apology, not only for being "culturally insensitive," but also for provoking hatred between ethnic groups:

> Being culturally insensitive in our mutually-complementary mixed society is tantamount to blatantly committing the unpardonable sin.
> Yet, that is the divisive path a vocal minority is openly flaunting in orchestrated efforts to discredit Prime Minister Sitiveni Rabuka and by association, bring disrepute to his government.
> Ungodly heathens including those swayed by acquisitive Western values can hardly be expected to fully appreciate the genuine value placed on spirituality and religious beliefs which are cornerstones of our island heritage.

Islanders in particular have the tremendous capacity to forgive and forget since that is part and parcel of values passed on to them generation-to-generation through the extended family system.

Symbolic presentation of the tabua (whale's tooth) and yaqona traditional beverage achieve solidarity and forgiveness far beyond that envisaged by any legal system.

Their transparency leads to mutually-beneficial weeping and putting themselves in the hands of the Creator for salvation.

To interpret instantaneous outpouring of tears as signs of weakness and hypocrisy is the unkindest cut of all.

Persistent needling reminders of past misdeeds will in the final analysis lead to a backlash when blood could flow.

Thus, in the name of whichever almighty power that breed of malcontents remotely believes in—back off.

Instead, grasp the window of opportunity which is available to take the beloved country to greater levels of achievement.

Either that, or if convinced that the nation is rotten to the core and run by corrupt leaders, why remain in this perceived den of iniquity?[28]

If, from the viewpoint of these Christian commentators, Jalal's plea for action to correct the negative consequences of the 1987 coups missed the point, it was also the case that these Christian commentators also failed to recapture what they described as a genuine moment of Christian hope. Even though Ah Koy and Taka characterized Rabuka's apology as a "deeply spiritual moment" and "a moment of atonement in which Rabuka sought fellowship with God," respectively, the tone of their interpretation was that of an accusation: Ah Koy called the *Fiji Times*'s treatment of Rabuka's apology "sacrilege," while Taka called Jalal and others' reaction to Rabuka's apology naïve. In other words, if it is true that from many Fijian Christians' point of view, politics stopped when Rabuka apologized, politics also resumed when Ah Koy, Taka, and others asserted Christians' moral superiority over Rabuka's critics.

My point here is not to demonstrate the inconsistencies or the latent politics in the Christians' rhetoric. On the contrary, I wish to argue here that Rabuka's defenders' failure to recover what they characterized as a nonpolitical, nonstrategic moment without subsuming it into the very "political" discourse they sought to rescue it from did not derive from the strategic nature of the original act of apology. Instead, I wish to suggest that the failure derived from the incongruity between the temporal direction of their interpretation and that of the subject of their interpretation, Rabuka's apology.

In the terms of this book's argument, Rabuka's apology was a forward-looking moment of hope in which Rabuka neither mentioned the 1987 coups nor explained the misconduct for which he apologized. He simply humbled himself and sought forgiveness for his unspecified past action as part of his preparation for his prayer for the nation. In other words, Rabuka's apology *reset* the relationship between the vaguely defined past and the present moment of prayer for that moment. According to Rabuka's sympathizers, in other words, what mattered to Christians was an acceptance of this display of humility for its own sake as a moment of temporal resetting. Rabuka's real intention behind his apology was not important to them—not because it was impossible to see that behind a moment of hope might lie a political strategy, but because the significance of that moment lay in its resetting quality. As one Lautoka resident said, "Whether it was genuinely [*sic*] or not only time will tell. Until then why not let's give him the benefit of the doubt."[29]

What seemed wrong to Rabuka's sympathizers about interpreting Rabuka's apology as an apology for the negative consequences of the 1987 coups and his subsequent political leadership was the fact that reading the event in this way reintroduced a retrospective perspective to this moment of temporal resetting. The irony, however, is that in pointing out the inappropriateness of such a retrospective interpretation, Rabuka's sympathizers also retrospectively interpreted the moment of apology. In other words, their efforts to counter a retrospective perspective produced a retrospective interpretation of its own, which in turn undermined the moment's hopeful content.

Repeating Without Overlapping

The debate surrounding Rabuka's apology may therefore point to the limits of hope as a method of self-knowing. But it ultimately also points to the predication of "hope as a method" on a strategy of replication rather than a strategy of critique. This returns to my initial problem of how to recapture hope, and to the series of

speech events surrounding the foundation-laying ceremony described in the first part of this chapter, in which actors repeatedly
reintroduced prospective momentum to a present moment continually invaded by retrospection of all kinds, such as memory, nostalgia, a sense of achievement, or critique. Hope is the only method
of recapturing hope. In those speech events, in contrast to the debates surrounding Rabuka's apology, actors succeeded in main-
taining a hopeful moment, although every time hope was recap-
tured, it appeared on a different terrain (hope for the success of Nadonumai Holdings was, for example, displaced in the gift-giving
ritual of the foundation-laying ceremony by Rabuka's hope for the
success of ethnic Fijians as a whole). In other words, hope was
replicated from one moment to the next. And this replication was
mediated by the recurring impulse to reintroduce a retrospective
perspective to the present. From this perspective, we can understand that the method of hope consists in replicating the (immediate or distant) past. The method of hope, in other words, is a performative inheritance of hope.

Repetition is therefore a logical consequence of what I have
called the method of hope, that is, the performative inheritance of
hope in the past. This is perhaps evident from the composition of
this book. In every chapter, the same operation—the effort to replicate hope on a new terrain—appears across different episodes and
different genres of self-knowledge. Strictly speaking, the operation
thus repeated and replicated in each episode and each genre was
not, of course, identical. As shown in chapter 5, for example,
church and gift-giving rituals rested on different degrees of scriptedness and each replication is different in itself. Therefore, the
process of replication as a method of hope did not simply generate
repetition. Suvavou people experienced every moment of hope
anew, not as something already experienced, at least for that
moment.

This returns us to Bloch. In *The Principle of Hope*, Bloch's analysis moves from daydreams to music, to science and technology,
and to religion. Bloch sees manifestations of hope in all of these
and observes: "An encyclopaedia of hopes often contains repeti-

tions, but never overlappings . . . the repetitions of the book ideal-
ly always occur on a new level, have therefore both learnt something in the meantime and may allow the identical thing they are
aiming at to be learned anew" (Bloch 1986: 17).

Here Bloch does not elaborate the implications of repetition as
his method of representing hope. He simply emphasizes the significance of repeating what is important: "[S]o far as [repetition] is
concerned, Voltaire's statement is valid here that he would repeat
himself as often as was necessary until he was understood" (Bloch
1986: 17).

In light of my discussion of Suvavou people's hope, however, I
wish to suggest that Bloch's notion of repetitions that do not over-
lap is not so much a methodological innovation as an effect of the
method of hope I see in his work. I wish to suggest that the paral-
lelism between the nature of repetitions contained in this book and
the repetitions contained in Bloch's "encyclopedia of hope" may
not be accidental. What the parallel, or rather the replication,
implies is that hope demands that its own method be replicated in
the method of its representation. The method of hope is the only
method of representing hope. This in turn suggests that the success
of an effort like mine depends on whether it generates a further
moment of hope. In the next, concluding chapter, I turn to my own
hope in anthropology.

7 ⌒ Inheriting Hope

In this book, I have aimed to demonstrate that hope is a common operative in knowledge formation, academic and otherwise. I have sought to achieve this by replicating what I have called the method of hope in the shape of my argument. My inquiry began with a methodological problem I encountered at certain moments of hope in Fijian gift-giving in which the temporal direction of my analysis and that of its object, hope, seemed incongruous. I juxtaposed this methodological problem with the methodological problem that served Ernst Bloch as the starting point of his philosophical inquiry into hope, that is, the temporal incongruity between hope and philosophical contemplation. In both cases, hope made explicit temporal incongruity between knowledge and its object and prompted radical temporal reorientation of knowledge to the future. I have argued, however, that the retrospective character of knowledge is not itself the cause of this analytical trouble. In retrospect, my (and Bloch's) analytical impulse toward temporal congruity was a replication of the hope that had prompted the analytical impulse at the outset. Hope was replicated on a new terrain, in other words. The method of hope therefore revolves around radical temporal reorientation of knowledge and its resulting replication of past hope in the present. Each chapter of this book has been an ethnographic explication of this method, as well as an instantiation of the method itself. The resulting zigzag trajectory of my investigation points to yet another possibility for replicating Fijian hope on a new terrain. In this final chapter, I wish to turn to hope as a method for apprehending the present of anthropological knowledge.

Since the mid 1980s, many anthropologists have been anxious about their discipline's loss of relevance, based on the broadly held assumption that the world has changed radically. How, in this context, can anthropologists recover their distinct intellectual space in the academy? In the introduction to *Recapturing Anthropology: Working in the Present,* a volume of which he was the editor, Richard Fox notes, for example:

> How can anthropologists work in and write about the world at present? . . . [We] took the world "at present" not simply to mean the contemporary but also to refer to the peculiar: that is, we understood that fundamental and widespread changes had happened fairly recently in the world. . . . Our "present" appears to be substantially different from the "present" that our predecessors confronted, even just a short time ago. (Fox 1991a: 1)

More recently, George Marcus has noted that anthropologists "seem to have reached consensus about the substantial changes that surround and have altered the nature of anthropology's objects of study" (Marcus 1999: 25).

In more concrete terms, since the early 1980s, anthropologists have confronted the problem of how to respond to the postcolonial politics of cultural identity in which indigenous populations such as Suvavou people deploy what, in light of criticism by Edward Said and others, anthropologists would deem "essentialist" and ahistorical notions such as *kastom,* tradition, and culture (Said 1978). In his introduction to the first collection of essays devoted to the politics of tradition in the Pacific (Keesing and Tonkinson 1982), for example, Roger Keesing noted: "[T]here is special anthropological interest in *kastom* because it is culture itself that serves as symbol. (Anthropologists themselves often spuriously reify and idealize cultures into abstract, cultural systems. That Melanesian ideologues construct an imaginary *kastom* out of messy realities should perhaps give us some discomfort" (Keesing 1982: 300).

The attraction of this new focus has consisted at least partially in its power to project a mirror image of anthropological analysis of indigenous forms of "objectification of tradition" (Thomas 1992) and self-reflexive knowledge (see Jolly and Thomas 1992;

Inheriting Hope

Otto and Thomas 1997; Thomas 1997, for cases from the Pacific). The analytical attention to indigenous debates on culture, tradition, and nationhood has placed a particular emphasis on indigenous creativity as manifested in the politics of knowledge production. In this view, anthropologists and indigenous populations engage in a similar kind of representational politics. In other words, anthropologists have attempted to bring into view "their versions" of what we used to do, to reformulate Marilyn Strathern's phrase (Strathern 1990: 28). Furthermore, for anthropologists, this indigenous identity politics exemplifies a broader shift in the place of anthropological knowledge, which is in turn associated with a shift in the character of global capitalism and the political economy of academic knowledge (see, e.g., Foster 1995; Kelly and Kaplan 2001; Munasinghe 2001).

More recently, such anxiety about and fascination with the closing of distance between the knowledge practices of anthropologists and their research subjects has manifested itself in more methodological terms. In recent debates on the anthropology of expert knowledge, Douglas Holmes, George Marcus, Annelise Riles, and others have identified the ethnographic condition in which there is no distance between anthropologists' analytical practices and those of their research subjects as a methodological opportunity (see Brenneis 1999; Holmes and Marcus, in press; Marcus 1998, 1999; Maurer 2002; Miyazaki and Riles, in press; Riles 2000; Riles n.d. a; Riles n.d. b; cf. M. Lynch 1993). As Bill Maurer has put it: "The convergence or indeed isomorphism of anthropological tools and the knowledge-generating techniques of those they study opens possibilities for a new kind of ethnographic sensibility" (Maurer 2003: 163).

The lack of analytical distance between anthropologists' knowledge practices and those of their research subjects resonates with another kind of lack of distance, of which anthropologists have increasingly been aware, that is, the closing of distance between anthropology and other disciplines, such as history (see Cohn 1987a; Comaroff and Comaroff 1992; Thomas 1989; Thomas 1997; see also Axel 2002), art criticism (Myers 1995: 57-58), and philosophy. Commenting on the narrowing of distance between anthropology and philosophy, Clifford Geertz has recently remarked, for example:

> [T]here has been . . . a major shift in the way in which philosophers, or the bulk of them anyway, conceive their vocation, and that shift has been in a direction particularly congenial to those, like myself, who believe that the answers to our most general questions—why? how? what? whither?—to the degree they have answers, are to be found in the fine detail of lived life. (Geertz 2000: xi)

In Geertz's view, the narrowing of the gap between the two disciplines has resulted from philosophers' critique of metaphysics. Here Geertz points to a wide range of philosophers from Wittgenstein to John Dewey who have sought to dislocate knowledge from the cerebral terrain and relocate it to the social terrain (see Geertz 2000: xii, 21–22).

What is interesting for present purposes is that Geertz locates this new place of anthropological knowledge in a wider intellectual terrain in connection with the character of changes in the world. For Geertz, in this narrowed disciplinary gap, anthropology and philosophy have emerged as parallel efforts to understand the emergent world of which both forms of knowing are part. Geertz's discussion of William James's *The Varieties of Religious Experience* is a case in point. Here I wish to draw attention to the distinctive way in which Geertz brings into view the contemporary relevance of James's well-known individualistic treatment of religious faith. The focus of my attention is on Geertz's apprehension of what constitutes the contemporary: "[W]hen we look back at [*The Varieties of Religious Experience*] from where it is we are now, . . . it seems at once almost ultra-contemporaneous . . . and quaintly remote" (Geertz 2000: 168).

Geertz attributes the "quaintly remote" character of James's ideas simply to the fact that the world has changed:

> We see religion in other terms than James did, not because we know more about it than he did (we don't), or because what he discovered no longer interests us or seems important (it does), or even because it itself has changed (it has and it hasn't). We see it in other terms because the

ground has shifted under our feet; we have other extremes to examine, other fates to forestall. (Geertz 2000: 168)

"It is not in solitude that faith is made," Geertz observes (ibid.: 184), listing many instances of politicized religious faith:

> In James's time it seemed that religion was becoming more and more subjectivized; that it was, in the very nature of the case, weakening as a social force to become a matter wholly of the heart's affections. . . . But that is not how things have in the event turned out. The developments of the century since James gave his lectures—two world wars, genocide, decolonization, the spread of populism, and the technological integration of the world—have done less to drive faith inward toward the commotions of the soul than they have to drive it outward toward those of the polity, the state, and that complex argument we call culture. (Ibid.: 170)

In Geertz's view, "we" do not have adequate analytical tools for understanding what is happening now:

> The problem . . . is that if the communal dimensions of religious change, the ones you can (sometimes) read about in the newspapers are underresearched, the personal ones, those you have (usually) to talk to living people in order to encounter, are barely researched at all. We simply don't know very much about what is going on right now in James's shadow world of immense wings and unfleeable storms. (Ibid.: 179)

Ultimately, however, it is precisely in the socially situated nature of James's individualistic view of religious experience, and James's own awareness of it, that Geertz finds contemporary relevance:

> [M]ajor thinkers, like major artists, are both completely engulfed in their time—deeply situated, as we now would say—and transcendent of those times, vividly alive in other times, and . . . these two facts are internally connected. Certainly this is true of James. The radically individualistic, subjectivistic, "brute perception" concept of religion and religiousness, which his location as heir to New England intuitionism and his own encounters with the pinch of destiny led him into, was complemented by the intense, marvelously observant, almost pathologically sensitive attention to the shades and subtleties of thought and emotion they also led him into.
>
> It is this last, circumstantial accounts of the personal inflections of religious engagement that reach far beyond the personal into the conflicts and dilemmas of our age, that we need now. (Ibid.: 185)

Here Geertz rediscovers what has always defined anthropological knowledge, that is, the analytical category of the social. More
specifically, James's awareness of the social construction of his own
theory of religion in the midst of his otherwise individualistic take
on religious faith is precisely what anthropologists have always
argued for in their studies of religion. In Geertz's reasoning, in
other words, anthropological insights into religious faith have
emerged as acutely relevant as a result of changes in the world.
Moreover, the narrowed gap between the two disciplines further
proves the relevance of anthropology for the present moment.

Anthropologists' apprehension of these new conditions of
knowledge production is thus predicated on a particular apprehension of the present moment of the world. As discussed throughout
this book, however, accessing the present is not an easy task.
Moreover, using a philosophical lens, the problem of lack of distance might be framed as a problem of how to access the present.
As noted in chapter 1, many philosophers, including Bloch, have
regarded the problem of the present as paradigmatic of the analytical problem arising from the lack of distance between knowledge
and its object. In particular, the elusive quality of the present has
served as a subject of contemplation for the purpose of gaining
insights into a more general problem of how to apprehend one's
own self. This book argues that the problem of how to access the
present is precisely the problem of hope as a method of self-knowledge.

Indeed, these new ethnographic projects prompted by a perception of the changed world are *hopeful* projects. In these projects,
anthropologists have not simply been critical of their own past
modes of knowledge production. They have also sought to introduce prospective momentum to the moment of self-critique and
reflection by proposing *new* research agendas and *new* modes of
ethnographic writing that are supposed to reflect new ethnographic
conditions. For some, this future-oriented exploration has focused
on an effort to "historicize" anthropology (e.g., Clifford 1988;
Comaroff and Comaroff 1992; Thomas 1989) or on a search for
new forms of ethnographic writing (see Clifford and Marcus

1986), while for others, it has concerned new subjects of ethnographic research that not only render obsolete many of anthropologists' theoretical constructs but also demand new research strategies (e.g., Appadurai 1996; Fischer 1999; Greenwood and Levin
2000; Gupta and Ferguson 1997; Marcus 1998; Rabinow 1996).
For still others, like Geertz, as discussed above, new phenomena
have rendered old anthropological insights relevant again. In their
view, as Bill Maurer recently has pointed out, it is time for anthropologists to go back to "business as usual" (Maurer 2003: 169).

What all these divergent efforts to reinvigorate anthropological
knowledge have in common is anthropologists' acute collective
awareness of their belatedness in relation to the *now* of the world
they seek to represent (see also Miyazaki 2003). In the terms
deployed in this book, in other words, in these divergent responses
to the newly found condition of anthropological knowledge production, anthropologists have recreated a productive gap for
anthropology on another terrain. If, in the past, the gap was
between anthropology and other disciplines, or between the West
and the non-West, now the gap is between knowledge, more generally, and its object, that is, an emergent world. Here both anthropologists and philosophers, or anthropologists and their research
subjects, now share a common ground from which to explore this
emergent world (see Marcus 1998). In other words, anthropologists have created prospective momentum in the now recreated
realm of the future unknown, which has in turn generated an anticipation of congruity between knowledge and its object, the emergent world. It is the pull of this anticipation, I wish to suggest, that
has animated anthropological debates over the past two decades.
Hope has, in other words, served as a method of anthropological
knowledge.

One consequence of these hopeful endeavors has been a kind of
temporal reorientation, an effort to reconfigure the temporal
strategies embedded in anthropological knowledge. The focus on
the problem of time is perhaps not surprising, given that, as
Johannes Fabian has noted, anthropologists have always deployed
various temporal strategies in their writing, of which the fictional

and frozen "ethnographic present" tense is the most renowned (Fabian 1983). However, I wish to argue that there is something peculiar about anthropologists' current concern with time and its consequences for the character of anthropological knowledge production. In particular, at the heart of anthropologists' impulse to reorient the temporality of their knowledge at the moment is an awareness that the world has not only changed but continues to be changing. The "novelty of the world" (R. G. Fox 1991a: 4) has therefore manifested itself to anthropologists as a subject, that is, as what Michael Fischer terms "emergent forms of life" (1999).

This widely held analytical aesthetic, which I wish to call an aesthetic of emergence, renders not only the world but also its analysis provisional, indeterminate, and open-ended. Anthropological analyses not only focus on provisional "assemblages" of the old and the new but also become assemblages on their own (see Ong and Collier, in press; Rabinow 1999). This analytical aesthetic is pervasive not only in anthropological studies of so-called new ethnographic subjects but also in historical anthropology. In advocating a dialogical perspective, John Kelly and Martha Kaplan recently have noted, for example:

> We support an anthropology more dialogical in the Bakhtinian sense. For Bakhtin and others, history as a dialogical process is an open series, with neither absolute priorities of level nor finite numbers of subjects and objects involved. In a dialogical account, even global history is a series of planned and lived responses to specific circumstances that were also irreducibly constituted by human subjects, creating not a single vast chain of "the subject" changed by "the object" and vice versa, but a dense complex network of individual and collective subjects continually responsive to one another. These constitutive, irreducibly subjective dialogics add enormous contingency and complexity to what dialectic there is between material relations and human societies. (Kelly and Kaplan 2001: 6–7)

This aesthetic of emergence reflects a broader and more general move in social theory to emphasize the provisional, indeterminate, and open-ended nature of reality. As the philosopher of social science James Bohman has suggested, the focus of social scientific explanation has shifted from the pursuit of analytical determinacy to the recognition of the indeterminacy of reality (see Bohman 1991: 6–7). According to Barbara Herrnstein Smith and Arkady Plotnitsky, likewise, the concern with emergence currently popular in social theory, "reflect[s] the increasing need to address and describe, without implications of purposive agency or simple unilinear ("mechanical") causality, the ongoing effects of exceedingly complex interactions"; in this framework, "forces that are classically represented as distinct and opposed—for example, the genetic and the environmental or the natural and the social—are seen as reciprocally interactive and mutually constituting" (Smith and Plotnitsky 1997: 8). The aesthetic of emergence therefore forecloses the possibility of pinpointing the end point of analysis (see Barber 2000: 7; Pickering 1995, 1997), and all knowledge remains provisional, contingent, and ongoing. It is no surprise that this emphasis on provisionality and indeterminacy has had a strong appeal to anthropologists whose immediate concern has been to come to terms with what they perceive as a rapidly changing and unpredictable world.

It is important to note, however, that in this aesthetic of emergence and its associated focus on provisionality, indeterminacy, and open-endedness, the possibility of achieving congruity between knowledge and its object is foreclosed. Rather, ironically it is precisely the *failure* (cf. Riles 2000) to achieve such congruity and synchronicity that is central to the aesthetic of emergence. In other words, temporal incongruity is now embedded in the shape of knowledge itself. The aesthetic of emergence would seem to enable anthropologists to maintain prospective momentum without changing the temporal orientation of their knowledge any more. In this scheme, anthropologists' task becomes simply to trace or track the world as it emerges. Here knowledge itself is rendered emergent in order to mirror an emergent world.

In light of the argument of this book, however, the temporal reorientation to the emergent achieved in many of these recent hopeful anthropological efforts to reinvigorate anthropological knowledge may not be hopeful as it sounds. In the previous chapters, I have argued that the production of a hopeful moment is predicated on an effort to replicate a past moment of hope. Recall how the intimation of fulfillment enables Fijian Christians to maintain a prospective momentum. Recall, also, Bloch and Benjamin's attention to unfulfilled hope in the past and a sense of "not-yet" following the fulfillment of a hope. For them, hope is inherited from the past, and the pull of hope in the present derives from anticipation of fulfillment contained in that past hope. For Fijian Christians, as for Bloch and Benjamin, the effort to maintain prospective momentum entails an effort to replicate a past unfulfilled hope on another terrain, I have argued. The method of hope, in other words, is predicated on the inheritance of a past hope and its performative replication in the present. In the five ethnographic chapters, I sought to replicate the method of hope in the structure of my account of Fijian hope by showing the homological operation of the performative replication of a prospective momentum in different genres of Fijian self-knowledge.

In contrast, the aesthetic of emergence that now dominates anthropological attempts to reintroduce prospective momentum to an inquiry forecloses the possibility of such replication. The kind of prospective momentum embedded in the aesthetic of emergence is that of anthropologists' belatedness relative to the emergent world rather than a conscious effort to reorient knowledge to the future. In the aesthetic of emergence, as currently practiced in anthropology, the world is rendered open-ended and indeterminate from beginning to end. Yet by its very open-ended nature, the pull for knowledge comes from the emergent world and it does not leave room for hope and its method, that is, radical reorientation of knowledge. What worries me most about the aesthetic of emergence, in other words, is the way this analytical strategy seems to have taken away the driving force of knowledge from hope by giving too much credit to the so-called emergent world. Where knowledge does not seek its own radical reorientation, hope ceases to be the engine of knowledge.

In light of my discussion of the method of hope, reclaiming a place for hope in anthropology and social theory, however, demands more than a strategy of delayed provisional engagement with an emergent world. Instead of seeking to follow the world in a belated manner, I propose that one should make explicit one's own hope retrospectively via replication of others' hope on a new terrain. As I have demonstrated in the last six chapters, this retrospective perspective is anticipated in the method of hope.

The task of reigniting the "spark of hope" (Benjamin 1992 [1968]: 247; see chapter 1) in anthropological knowledge demands an effort to bring into view the possibility of radical reorientation of knowledge once again, rather than emergent (albeit belated) congruity between the temporality of knowledge and that of its object. This effort in turn will demand an effort to *inherit* and *replicate* the hope contained in anthropology's past hopes, that is, the task of anticipating a new kind of anthropology on another terrain. My hope is that in the incongruity between the temporality of the current anthropological aesthetic of emergence and that of this turn to my own hope, such anticipation of the new will indeed arise.

Notes

☞ Notes

Chapter 1. Hope as a Method

1. In his "panoramic" exploration of the category of hope, Vincent Crapanzano repeatedly points to the "uneasy relationship" between the two categories (2003: 4, 19): "Hope is . . . intimately related to desire. It is its passive counterpart, though it is sometimes used as an equivalent to desire. Desire is effective. It presupposes human agency. One acts on desire—even if that act is not to act on desire because one has judged it impossible or prefers the desire to its fulfillment" (6). In contrast, according to Crapanzano, "hope depends on some other agency—a god, fate, chance, an other—for its fulfillment" (6). Ultimately, however, in discussing Kenelm Burridge's classic work on Melanesian cargo cultists, *Mambu: A Melanesian Millennium* (1995 [1960]) Crapanzano points to the entanglement between desire and hope as categories of analysis, on the one hand, and desire and hope as what prompts the analysis itself, on the other: "Yes, the hope and desire of the cultists cannot easily be distinguished from those of the anthropologists. They are both caught. Though we place them insistently in the individual, neither desire nor hope can be removed from social engagement and implication. We are all, I suppose, caught" (25).

2. The three volumes of *Das Prinzip Hoffnung* were originally published between 1954 and 1959. The 1986 English translation (Bloch 1986) is based on the 1959 edition of the book.

3. Moltmann distanced himself from Bloch in his later works (Moltmann 1993b [1974]: 5). See Bentley 1982 for a discussion of German theologians' reception of Bloch's work.

4. Other commentaries on Bloch in the English language include Jones 1995 and T. H. West 1991, in addition to some fine introductory essays for English translations of Bloch's books.

5. Bloch's first major work, *The Spirit of Utopia* (2000), originally published as *Geist der Utopie* in 1918, is said to have inspired a number of German intellectuals, including Theodor Adorno, Walter Benjamin, and Herbert Marcuse (see, e.g., Geoghegan 1996: 15–16, 162).

6. Although Bloch's analysis of fascism through the concept of "non-synchronicity" (1991) has been often discussed (e.g. Harootunian 2000: 216; Jameson 1991: 307), his numerous books rarely draw substantial attention today. Bloch's biographer Vincent Geoghegan cites his strong commitment to Marxism and his active approval of Stalin during the 1930s as the primary reason for his exclusion from the influential circle of other German émigrés such as Adorno and Horkheimer (Geoghegan 1996: 19). Jack Zipes speculates that Bloch's distinctive writing style, influenced by expressionism and German idealism, has made his work look somewhat old-fashioned and inaccessible (Zipes 1988: xxix; cf. Kaufmann 1997).

7. Susan Buck-Morss has noted that the focus of Bloch's philosophy on reforming academic knowledge "left social reality untouched" (Buck-Morss 1977: 4). One of the goals of my current ethnographic inquiry into hope is to obviate this divide between the ideational and the social by drawing attention to a parallel in the way hope is generated in knowledge formation, academic and otherwise.

8. Here I limit my discussion to some philosophical reflections on hope. There is also an extensive body of literature on hope in psychology that largely focuses on the function of hope (e.g. Breznitz 1999; Lazarus 1999). As one of the three Christian theological virtues (see, e.g., Saint Augustine 1961), hope obviously also has theological implications, and there have been many theological writings on hope (see, e.g., W. F. Lynch 1965; Moltmann 1993a [1967]; Otto 1991; cf. Godfrey 1987; Marcel 1962.)

9. Bloch, who spent a little over ten years in exile in the United States, from 1938 until 1949, strongly disliked American culture (Geoghegan 1996: 18–19), and his work has little in common with that of Rorty, whose proposal that we set "hope in place of knowledge" (1999) largely rests on his own faith in America (see Rorty 1998).

10. Richard Roberts has noted that the ultimate goal of Bloch's grand project on hope was "the positive recovery of the divine in the human, rather than the negative (and orthodox Marxist) exclusion of God as illusory projection," arguing that Bloch's project aimed at "the religious assimilation of atheism" (Roberts 1990: 12).

11. My effort to approach hope in terms of the problem of the present resonates with Andrew Benjamin's approach to hope in his project, *Present Hope: Philosophy, Architecture, Judaism* (A. Benjamin 1997).

12. As Peter Szondi points out, Walter Benjamin's hope is not the same as Theodor Adorno's solution to despair. Szondi quotes the well-known final paragraph of Adorno's *Minima Moralia*: "In the face of despair, the only way philosophy can still be justified is as an attempt to consider all things as they look from the standpoint of salvation. Knowledge has no

light other than that which shines down on the world from salvation: everything else spends itself in reconstruction and remains a merely technical matter. Perspectives must be established in which the world comes apart, alienates itself, and reveals its cracks and fissures, as it will be one day when it lies poor and disfigured in the Messianic light" (Adorno 1974, quoted in Szondi 1986: 156). Adorno's hope lies in a retrospective perspective from the end of the world.

13. After completing a final draft of this book, I encountered the recent work of Nigel Rapport, which in my understanding is a similar effort to mine to take philosophy (in his case Friedrich Nietzsche's philosophy) as an ethnographic subject (see Rapport 2003). Other anthropologists have sought to apply modernist and postmodernist philosophical insights to specific ethnographic situations. For example, in his work on Indonesia, James Siegel has drawn on the work of and the writing style of Jacques Derrida. Siegel notes, "the path of thought [Derrida] has opened . . . has yet to be exploited by anthropologists and historians in the way it might be. It is in the first place because he shows the impossibility of our disciplines, precisely their lack of foundation. To continue after him means to accept this impossibility. But we must respond all the same, taking up in a context never imagined by him issues he has raised" (Siegel 1997: x). Siegel's conscious adoption of the Derridian style of inquiry makes his work more than a simple application of philosophy.

14. See, e.g., Wayne Hudson's discussion of Bloch in light of Marxism (1982) and Martin Jay's excellent discussion of Bloch's conception of totality (1984).

15. It is interesting to note how German political theologians such as Jürgen Moltmann and Johannes Baptist Metz responded to Ernst Bloch's atheist commitment. Although Bloch's influence permeates these theologians' early work (see, e.g., Moltmann 1993 [1967]; Metz 1969), both Moltmann and Metz subsequently distanced themselves from Bloch. Their problem with Bloch was grounded in Bloch's atheism and "militant optimism" (Bloch 1972: 247; emphasis removed), which they found incapable of dealing with the problem of suffering and death. In *The Crucified God*, for example, Moltmann shifted his original focus, as expressed in his much celebrated *Theology of Hope*, on "the remembrance of Christ in the form of the *hope* of his future" to a new focus on "hope in the form of the *remembrance* of his death," saying that "[u]nless it apprehends the pain of the negative, Christian hope cannot be realistic and liberating" (Moltmann 1993b [1974]: 5). In confronting this suffering and death, only God could emerge as the source of hope, these theologians insisted. As Moltmann put it, "For Ernst Bloch, atheism was the presupposition of active hope. . . . But for me, the God of promise and exodus, the God who has raised Christ and who lets the power of the resurrection dwell in us, is the ground for

active and for passive hope" (1993a [1967]: 9). My effort to juxtapose
Fijian Christians' hope with Bloch's atheist philosophy of hope may seem
destined to encounter the same problem faced by Moltmann and Metz as
they sought to deploy Bloch's insights in a Christian context. For Suvavou
people, as for many other Fijians I knew, God's presence was overwhelmingly self-evident. Even so, I wish to argue, it would be a mistake to assume
that for Suvavou people, God was the ultimate source of hope. Rather,
hope in God's efficacy needed to be ritually produced. As discussed in
chapter 5, what was instrumental in the ritual production of hope was
ironically the backgrounding of God's agency. From this perspective, the
insights of Bloch's atheist philosophy of hope are indeed apposite.

16. Anthropologists have often framed theoretical problems in terms of
incongruity between different temporal modes, such as cyclical versus linear time, myth versus history (see Obeyesekere 1992, 1997; Sahlins 1981,
1985, 1995), and the epistemological stasis characterized by the device of
the ethnographic present versus cultural and strategic innovation (Thomas
1989; cf. Fabian 1983; Wagner 1981 [1975]). Some have focused on positing the complementary nature of these modes. For example, Terence Turner has noted that "'mythic' and 'historical' consciousness are not mutually exclusive but are complementary ways of framing the same events,
which can, and usually do, coexist in the same culture, indeed in the same
utterance by the same person" (Turner 1988: 212–13). Others have drawn
attention to other ways temporality can be experienced, using metaphors
such as "rhythm" (Guyer 1988) and notions such as "everyday millenarianism" (Robbins 2001). Meanwhile, Carol Greenhouse has drawn attention to the centrality of "temporal improvisation" in political legitimation
(Greenhouse 1996: 10). In contrast to these studies, the present study seeks
to bring into view temporal incongruity as an *engine* of knowledge formation itself (see also Miyazaki 2003).

Chapter 2. A History of Thwarted Hope

1. In the 1960s, the government had no hesitation in turning a large
portion of Suvavou land into residential developments. There is also a
large rubbish dump for the city of Suva on the seashore near the village.

2. A typical household consisted of three generations: a couple, their
sons and daughters and their spouses, and the latter's children. On aver-
age, therefore, seven people might share a three-room house. Most households depended on two cash incomes. Men worked as occasional manual
laborers, called "cash-holders," or security guards, while women worked
in clothing factories, stores, and restaurants, or as so-called house girls in
Lami and Suva. At the time of my fieldwork (1994–96), a wage for such

work was F$10 per day, and the average household weekly expenditure for food was F$60. Many households also received remittances from their overseas relatives. There were a number of registered members of Suvavou *mataqali* (clans) living in Sydney and other Australian and New Zealand cities who contributed regularly to village mortuary exchanges and church activities. In most cases, these members had originally moved overseas in search of employment, and many sent contributions to individual households on a monthly basis. They also returned regularly for ceremonies, married in the village, and sponsored *mataqali* members for extended visits in search of temporary employment or medical attention.

3. Bau is an island off the eastern coast of Viti Levu. Since the mid nineteenth century, Bau's paramount chief, the Vunivalu, has been regarded as the highest-ranking chief of Fiji.

4. Agreement of Polynesia Company with United States Consul in Fiji, July 24, 1868, in United States n.d., Appendix, exhibit 45, p. 255.

5. Apparently, Cakobau offered to sell more than 200,000 acres of land (Charter of Polynesia Company, July 23, 1868, in United States n.d., Appendix, exhibit 46, p. 257–59). Acting British Consul John B. Thurston persuaded Cakobau to reduce the area for sale (France 1969: 81–82).

6. The mother of the Roko Tui Suva of the time, Ratu Avorosa Tuivuya, was one of Cakobau's daughters, and Ratu Avorosa's father, Ratu Ravulo Tabakaucoro, was also the son of a Bauan lady, a daughter of Tanoa, Cakobau's father (Cargill 1977: 179). Customarily, uterine nephews (*vasu*) could demand anything from their mother's brother (see Hocart 1915). However, it was usual for Bauan chiefs to use this tie to make demands on their own *vasu* (see Thomas 1986: 46).

7. See, e.g., LCC reports nos. 435 and 444, National Archives of Fiji, Suva. See also Scarr 1984: 42.

8. This was in accordance with Lord Carnarvon's instruction to Governor Arthur Gordon that "as the readiest mode of settling this claim, and with a view of preventing annoyance to the native occupiers, an offer should be made to the company, without prejudice to repay them the £9,000 advanced to the American Government, and to leave them in possession of 400 or 500 acres now in the occupation of the tenants of the company in the Suva district, and actually under cultivation; the remainder of the 90,000 acres, and all further claims under the charter, being surrendered to the colonial government" (C. 1337, August 6, 1875, quoted in "The Case of Benson Robert Henry," in United States n.d., p. 36). A 1963 confidential report on Suva land confirms the government's payment of £9,000 to the Polynesia Company. A Lands Department official told me in 1994 that this payment was one of the legal bases for the government's title to Suva land.

9. Derrick 1953: 207; Whitelaw 1966: 37, 42–43. See also "The Case of Benson Robert Henry," in United States n.d., pp. 34–51, which exhibits all relevant records concerning the sale of the Suva land.

10. "Report of George H. Scidmore, U.S. Special Agent," July 3, 1893, in United States n.d., Appendix, exhibit 60, p. 321. The site of the colonial capital was hotly debated in Fiji soon after the establishment of the colony in 1874. As early as 1876, Governor Gordon was inclined to choose Suva and confidently stated that "the land on which the town would be built at Suva can be obtained without difficulty and without expense" (Despatch No. 185/1876, "Report of Commission on Savu-savu, as Site for a Capital," November 18, 1876, National Archives of Fiji, Suva; see also Derrick 1953: 205–8; Whitelaw 1966: 42).

11. "Report of George H. Scidmore, U.S. Special Agent" and "The Case of Benson Robert Henry," in United States n.d., p. 37.

12. The public auction took place on November 22, 1880. See John B. Thurston, acting commissioner for lands, "Sale of Land, Suva," August 16, 1880, in Colonial Secretary's Office [henceforth cited as CSO] 2607/1887, enclosure in CSO 2599/1888, National Archives of Fiji, Suva.

13. Narikoso originally belonged to Lami people, who live on a hill located on the other side of Queens Road. According to the Native Lands Commission record, the government originally had planned to relocate the inhabitants of the Suva Peninsula to Kiuva, in Tailevu. However, Suva people desired to remain near Suva. While Suva people suggested Samabula (today a suburb of Suva) as an alternative site, John B. Thurston instead selected Narikoso, in Lami (see *Ai tukutuku raraba kei na yalayala ni vei Tikina ko: Suva, Raviravi, Sawau,* Native Lands and Fisheries Commission, Suva). In a Native Lands Commission report, Lami people are described as having "a far lower social rank" than Suva people (Basil Thomson and Marika Toroca's report on the dispute between Suva people and Lami people, September 22, 1893, in CSO 3221/1893, National Archives of Fiji, Suva). A. M. Hocart, who visited Suvavou in 1910, noted that Lami people constituted a border state (*bati*) for Suva people and had a duty to provide food for the chief of Suva (Hocart n.d. a: 2508). According to the Native Lands Commission records concerning Lami people, Lami was subject to the chief of Suva (see *Ai tukutuku raraba kei na yalayala ni vei Tikina ko: Suva, Raviravi, Sawau*).

14. Here I have in mind Carol Greenhouse and Laura Nader's attention to the link between religious and secular pursuits of justice (see Greenhouse 1986; Nader 1990: 291–308).

15. The Wesleyan missionaries David Cargill and William Cross, with the help of Josua Mateinaniu, who had converted to Christianity in Tonga, successfully converted the Tui Nayau, the chief of Lau Islands, in 1835 (see Garette 1982: 102). Following the conversion of Cakobau, the paramount

chief of Bau, in 1854, more Fijians followed (see Garette 1982: 114–5, 284).

16. Upon Ratu Avorosa's request, the pioneering SDA missionary John Fulton established the mission base in Suvavou. From Suvavou, Fulton expanded mission activities to other parts of Fiji. Pauliasi Bunoa, a Methodist minister married to a Suvavou woman, became the first Fijian SDA ordained minister in 1906 and served as a missionary to outer islands (Hare 1985 [1969]: 105–17; see also Krause 1986). According to a letter written by Ratu Avorosa and his SDA followers in 1900, there were twenty-nine members of the SDA church in the village at that time (Avorosa Tuivuya et al. to governor, September 21, 1900, in CSO 606/1900, enclosure in CSO 2256/1902, National Archives of Fiji, Suva).

17. Avorosa Tuivuya et al. to native commissioner, November 19, 1898, in CSO 4655/1898, National Archives of Fiji, Suva.

18. Assistant Colonial Secretary William L. Allardyce's minute, December 15, 1898, in CSO 4655/1898.

19. Ibid..

20. Letter to commissioner for Rewa, August 18, 1903, in CSO 3820/1903, National Archives of Fiji, Suva.

21. Native commissioner to colonial secretary, August 27, 1903, in CSO 3820/1903.

22. Letter to native commissioner, January 25, 1904, in CSO 562/1904, National Archives of Fiji, Suva.

23. Commissioner of works to native commissioner, January 29, 1904, in CSO 562/1904; emphasis in original.

24. Governor Henry Jackson to colonial secretary, February 18, 1904, in CSO 562/1904.

25. Native commissioner's letter to Suvavou, February 19, 1904, in CSO 384/1904.

26. Avorosa Tuivuya et al. to native commissioner, August 21, 1907, in CSO 4469/1907, National Archives of Fiji, Suva.

27. In 1905, Governor Im Thurn removed restrictions to the alienation of further Fijian land and enabled non-Fijians to acquire land for settlement (see France 1969: 149–54; Scarr 1984: 112).

28. Im Thurn to colonial secretary, September 16, 1907, in CSO 4469/1907.

29. Richard Rankine, clerk to the Executive Council, to colonial secretary, September 20, 1907, in CSO 4469/1907.

30. At the time of my fieldwork, Suvavou people described the money they received as the government's "ex gratia compensation," or *loloma* (literally, "love" or "charity").

31. According to Sir Francis Winter, "quit rent" meant "the rent that is paid by a tenant to the lord of the manor," and, in his opinion, this should

not be used in Fiji. "Lands are some times granted in fee simple subject to the payment of an annual rent properly called a 'fee farm rent,'" he noted, and he therefore interpreted the money granted to Suvavou people annually as an "annuity" (CSO 2908/1887, quoted in Acting Attorney General Gilchrist Alexander to colonial secretary, October 8, 1907, in CSO 4469/1907).

32. Gilchrist Alexander to colonial secretary, October 8, 1907, in CSO 4469/1907.

33. Ibid.

34. The first military coup took place on May 14, 1987, only one month after the formation of the National Federation–Labour coalition government led by Dr. Timoci Bavadra, a commoner Fijian from western Viti Levu. The Bavadra government came into being when a coalition of the National Federation Party largely supported by Indo-Fijians and the multi-ethnic Fiji Labour Party defeated the Alliance Party government led by the paramount chief of Lau Islands, Ratu Sir Kamisese Mara, who had been prime minister since Fiji's independence in 1970. As a lieutenant colonel of the Royal Fiji Military Forces and a commoner Fijian from Cakaudrove, northern Fiji, Rabuka led soldiers into the Parliament House to topple the Bavadra government. Following the first coup, Rabuka let his chief, the Tui Cakau, the paramount chief of Cakaudrove, and Governor-General Ratu Sir Penaia Ganilau lead negotiations between the Alliance Party and the National Federation–Labour coalition. However, dissatisfied with the process of Ganilau's negotiations, Rabuka led the second military coup on September 25, 1987, to seize leadership of the country himself (see Dean and Ritova 1988; Lal 1988).

35. The Suvavou people I knew did not share these views. Instead, their perception of themselves often focused on the positive differences between their lifestyle and that of other Fijian villagers because of their familiarity with Suva's city life. A Suvavou woman observed to me, for example, that Suvavou people were more "individualistic," meaning that their daily activities focused more on each family (*matavuvale*) than on the village, and that village women tended to be more vocal than other women. Suvavou people's perception of the language that they spoke also marked a difference from other Fijians. They described their language (*na vosa vaka Suvavou*) as "pidgin," meaning that they used English words in Fijian sentences.

36. By 1994, the Department of Lands had received 83 applications for funding to acquire 120 titles in total from Fijian groups who claimed to be the original landowners of freehold and state land (interview with Samu Levu, permanent secretary to the minister for lands, October 3, 1994). Contention surrounding the rights of commoners to land alienated by their chiefs had become so great that the 1987 coup leader and subsequent

Prime Minister Sitiveni Rabuka even called into question the security of freehold property during the election campaign in early 1994, when, as leader of the Soqosoqo ni Vakavulewa ni Taukei (SVT) Party, he promised to "review" the validity of the original transactions of all freehold land. See Sireli Korovulavula, "PM to Review Freehold Land," *Fiji Times*, February 8, 1994. This statement was made at a meeting with Suvavou people. The Rewa provincial constituency, of which Suvavou is a part, had elected a non-SVT candidate in the 1992 election, and in promising such a review, Rabuka urged Suvavou people to vote for SVT candidates in the coming election. However, as a result of criticism from other political parties, Rabuka was forced to retract the statement a few days later and assure voters that the government would not put freehold property owners in danger. See Sireli Korovulavula, "Freehold Land Worries Tora: Review Can Cause Instability, Says ANC," *Fiji Times*, February 9, 1994; and "Freehold Titles Secure, Says PM," ibid., February 10, 1994.

37. For example, in 1991, when the island of Kanacea in northern Fiji, which the paramount chief of Cakaudrove, the Tui Cakau, had originally sold to a European settler in 1868, was sold by an Australian company, Carpenters (Fiji) Ltd., to an American company, the government persuaded Carpenters to pay compensation to the island's original landowners, Kanacea people, who had been relocated to the island of Taveuni at the time of the original sale. However, to the outrage of both the chief of Kanacea and the Tui Cakau, a number of Kanacea commoners demanded that the island be returned to its original landowners because the original sale by the Tui Cakau had been invalid. See "Group Hits Kanacea Sale," *Fiji Times*, February 14, 1991; "Sale of Kanacea Is Legal: Minister," editorial, ibid., February 17, 1991; "Kanacea Question," ibid., February 18, 1991; "US Firm Buys Kanacea," ibid., May 18, 1991. In response to the populist attack of Kanacea people's consultant Francis Waqa Sokonibogi on the Tui Cakau for having sold his people's land, the government and chiefs of Cakaudrove pressured the chiefs and people of Kanacea to distance themselves from Sokonibogi (see Francis Waqa Sokonibogi, "The Kudru na Vanua: A Review of the Issues, 1989–1994," pp. 8–9; on file with the author). As reported in the *Fiji Times*, the Bauan chief Ratu William Toganivalu, who was minister for lands in the interim government, said that the Tui Cakau, Ratu Golea, had sold the island of Kanacea because Kanacea people had sided with Tongans in a war between the people of Cakaudrove and Tonga. "The Tui Cakau at that time owned all the land because he was the 'Head Chief' and for that reason he did not need the permission from anybody to sell the land," Ratu William reportedly said ("Sale of Kanacea Is Legal: Minister," *Fiji Times*, February 17, 1991; see also Sayes 1982, 1984; LCC reports nos. 3–4, National Archives of Fiji, Suva; *Ai tukutuku raraba*, *Cakaudrove*, Native Lands and Fisheries

Commission, Suva). The government rejected Waqa's demand, and the government, chiefs of Kanacea, and Carpenters agreed that out of the F$6,000,000 for which the island was sold, Carpenters would pay the sum of F$1,000,000 as compensation to the people of Kanacea.

38. Epeli Kanakana, "To Commemorate the International Year for the Indigenous People: Suva Land," *Fiji Times*, June 4, 1993.

39. For example, when three Public Works Department workers were killed in the course of a reclamation project at Walu Bay in Suva in the early 1990s, Suva City Council officials concluded that the accidents might have resulted from their failure to seek the Tui Suva's permission for the project. They visited the Tui Suva and presented valuables, but the Tui Suva refused to accept the gifts and instead pointed out that he himself needed to perform a special and very public ceremony to seek the forgiveness of the spirits residing at the bay. Shortly thereafter, he performed the elaborate ceremony before members of the local press (see "Tui Suva Performs Bridge Ceremony," *Fiji Times*, March 19, 1991). Similarly, when the Australian government proposed to use the site of an old house in Nauluvatu, Suva, for its new embassy, it first engaged the Tui Suva to perform a ceremony at the site ("Tui Suva Exorcises Aust Govt Property," ibid., May 9, 1991).

40. "Squatter Told to Leave Park Land," *Fiji Times*, February 26, 1994; Rusiate Mataika, "It's State Land, Says Govt," ibid., March 1, 1994; "Suva Land Furore," ibid., April 16, 1994.

41. See "Team to Review Chiefs' Proposal," *Fiji Times*, May 18, 1984; Rodney V. Cole, Stephen I. Levine, and Anare V. Matahau, "The Fijian Provincial Administration: A Review," Parliament of Fiji, Parliamentary Paper No. 55 of 1985, National Archives of Fiji, Suva.

42. The full Fijian name of the foundation is Yavutu ni Taukei ni Vanua ko Viti (literally, "Foundation of the Owners of Land in Fiji"). The word *yavutu* means "foundation" in the sense of one's origin place and is thus very different in connotation from the English equivalent.

43. See Wainikiti Waqa, "Fijian Watchdog Group Formed," *Fiji Times*, August 7, 1993. I visited Matahau's office on occasion in October and November 1994, but I did not observe the subsequent development of his movement firsthand. Suvavou people had distanced themselves from Matahau by the end of 1994, because Prime Minister Sitiveni Rabuka did not like Matahau's involvement in Suvavou people's negotiations with the government. Although Matahau continued to claim a portion of compensation that Suvavou people might receive in the future as payment for his services in producing the report, Matahau's own interest in the Suva land case seemed to have faded when we met again in late 1995. At the time, he was busy with another controversial dispute concerning Namoli villagers, Lautoka Town's original landowners.

In 1994, Matahau had begun to elaborate a religious character for his movement. At his office, was a curtained space where Yavutu members prayed each day for one particular *vanua* (chiefdom) in Fiji. Matahau had also begun to claim that his movement and company were successors of Apolosi Nawai's Viti Kabani, which had attracted a large number of followers in the early twentieth century (see Kasuga 2001; Macnaught 1979, 1982). According to his associates, Matahau's father was the police officer who had been assigned to throw Apolosi into the ocean. When Matahau's father later encountered Apolosi in Suva and apologized to him for what he had done, Apolosi told him that his son would become his successor. In 1995, Anare Matahau conducted archival research on Apolosi to locate the reportedly hidden bank accounts of the Viti Kabani. He held a widely publicized meeting with the governor of the Fiji Reserve Bank, who explained that the Reserve Bank did not handle private accounts and suggested that he try the National Bank of Fiji instead (Robert Matau, "Getting Back a Heritage," *Fiji's Daily Post*, July 8, 1995). From late 1994 to early 1995, Matahau also teamed up with Apolosi's son to provide traditional medicinal treatments at Matahau's office, which was packed with patients.

Yavutu's evolution into a quasi-religious movement was probably partly because its original purpose was completely satisfied in late 1994 by the government's announcement that it would return state land to its original owners.

44. Anare Matahau and Associates 1991: 206.

45. *Fiji Government Gazette,* no. 1, October 10, 1874, National Archives of Fiji, Suva.

46. Governor Arthur Gordon laid the foundations for Fiji's land policies. His policies aimed at protecting the Fijian population and preserving and making use of what he understood to be Fijian chiefly custom (France 1969: 102–28).

47. Anare Matahau and Associates 1991: 207.

48. Ibid., 208–14.

49. According to the file, reviewed by me, forty-five copies of this map were produced and distributed to various sections of the Department of Lands. It thus seems unusual that no copy of the map has survived.

50. Ann Stoler has drawn attention to archives' power to seduce researchers into uncovering "state secrets" as their objective (Stoler 2002a: 98–99). What underlies this observation is Stoler's impulse to reestablish a more critical perspective. In contrast, here I seek to use the seductive power of archives as a tool to bring into view what Suvavou researchers, government officials, and anthropologists like myself share.

51. "Apparently no formal Deed was ever executed . . . but there is substantial evidence to show that the whole transaction had been carefully

arranged," the colonial secretary wrote the governor concerning the Suva land case on February 17, 1904 (in CSO 562/1904, National Archives of Fiji, Suva).

52. Im Thurn to colonial secretary, September 16, 1907, in CSO 4469/1907, National Archives of Fiji, Suva.

53. Colonial Secretary Arthur Mahaffy to Crompton and Muspratt, November 12, 1907, in CSO 4469/1907.

54. Colonial Secretary Arthur Mahaffy to Crompton and Muspratt, December 4, 1907, in CSO 4469/1907.

55. Colonial Secretary Arthur Mahaffy to acting attorney general, November 30, 1907, in CSO 4469/1907.

Chapter 3. A Politics of Self-Knowledge

1. Such disputes about chiefship are very common in Fijian polities. Christina Toren has demonstrated that these disputes constitute an intrinsic feature of Fijian sociality, predicated on a tension between equality and hierarchy (see Toren 1990, 1998, 1999).

2. The relationship between parts and wholes in ethnographic writing has been the subject of considerable scrutiny in the past two decades as the image of a coherent social whole that neatly integrates social parts such as economics, religion, and law has been rendered fictional. The resulting effect is that an aesthetics of partiality dominates current ethnographic writing. This notion of partiality emphasizes the impossibility of defining a whole. From Strathern's point of view, this aesthetics of partiality is simply a natural outcome of the direction of the parts/wholes relationship entailed in Euro-American knowledge.

3. The titling work of the NLC continued until the mid 1960s (see France 1969: 181, n. 34; Nayacakalou 1971: 208).

4. Rutz 1978: 23; emphasis in original. However, Rutz also acknowledged that villagers had begun to stress officially registered boundaries of *mataqali* land instead of rights to "fallow lands" (*veimada*) deriving from actual use, reasoning that they had begun to use *mataqali* as landowning units because of their need to "secure more permanent rights" (ibid.: 31) owing to their entry into commercial farming.

5. Hocart 1970 [1936]: 104. It is interesting, in this respect, that when Hocart visited Suvavou in 1910, instead of attempting to identify actual groups or landowning units, he recorded villagers' methods for dividing exchange items, feasts, and tasks. Hocart recorded the existence of nine *mataqali* for these purposes and detailed each *mataqali*'s duties and shares of food in feasting within Suvavou (Hocart n.d. a: 2513–15, 2588–91; Hocart n.d. b: 374D). Hocart further noted that Suvavou divided into two

for the purpose of preparing feasts: the people of the land (*kai vanua*) and the people of the sea (*kai wai*). He noted that Mataqali Roko Tui Suva, as the chiefly *mataqali*, was neither *kai wai* nor *kai vanua* (Hocart n.d. b: 373C).

6. Hocart's use of the term "mutual" is somewhat misleading, in that the term *veiqaravi* itself does not connote equality. My conceptualization of the *veiqaravi* form follows Hocart's insight about the importance of having two sides in Fijian rituals rather than the idea of equality between the two sides that the term "mutual" may imply. I thank Marshall Sahlins for requesting clarification on this matter.

7. Hocart also observed that division focused on the distribution of ceremonial duties in collectively performed rituals: "In Fiji the chieftains are not the heads of rituals which can be carried out separately, but office-bearers in a great common ritual. The herald cannot carry out alone the duties he carried out in that state ritual. The clans are not distinguished by having different cults, but by having different functions in the common cult" (Hocart 1970 [1936]: 107). By "common cult," Hocart meant the offering of feasts to the chief and to the god the chief represented.

8. Hocart 1952: 58. As a result of the repeated operation of division, which produced dichotomies at every level of social life, Hocart noted, a new version of these divisions had surfaced: "A new and more solemn interest seems to have already encroached upon the old dualism weakened by excess. That newer enthusiasm was the service of the chief. He and his family were exalted so far above the rest as to upset the old balance of paired groups. . . . The two sides that used to face each other, equal except in precedence, have begun to break up into units which all face the chief, like planets round the sun" (ibid.).

9. The NLTB is a body established by, but independent of, the government and under the authority of the high chiefs of Fiji (see Nayacakalou 1971).

10. There was a hotel on Suvavou land until it was closed after a fire in the 1980s. The Seventh-Day Adventist Church took over the hotel site and turned it into a secondary school.

11. This included not only approximately twenty-two acres of village land reserved for the exclusive use of villagers but also villagers' planting ground (*kanakana*) and many tracts of leased land outside the village proper.

12. The Eastern Ward, in which Delainavesi is located, had a population of 5,097 in 1996 (Bureau of Statistics, 1996 Fiji Census).

13. The original sum of £200 was increased to F$4,000 in 1972 and again to F$9,400 following the 1987 coup. See "Annuity Payments for Crown Land at Suva Peninsula (The Domain Site)," Cabinet Decision 128

of 1972, August 2, 1972, in Cabinet Paper (72) 121, in Ministry of Fijian Affairs 36/92/7, National Archives of Fiji, Suva; and "Suvavou to Get More for Domain," *Fiji Times*, March 23, 1988.

14. Every June and December, when NLTB officials, accompanied by a police officer, came to the village to distribute rent money to representatives of each *mataqali* of the Tikina ko Suva (the Fijian District of Suva), assembled at the residence of the Tui Suva, Suvavou people received the "Turaga ni Qali," "Turaga ni Mataqali," and "Mataqali members" portions as one undivided sum. A representative of Suvavou received the money from the NLTB officials and then took it from the Tui Suva's house into a house across the village green, where representatives of each *mataqali* were assembled. There, they divided the rent. Household shares of rent were minimal, although some *mataqali* pooled them and used them for purchasing necessary exchange items.

15. One significant innovation Suvavou people made in the convention was to classify their *mataqali* into three categories: large, medium-sized, and small. After the Tui Suva, the three *yavusa* heads, and the ten *mataqali* heads had each taken their shares in 1995, for example, the remainder was divided as follows:

Large Mataqali (*mataqali levu*)	F$2,368.74
Medium-sized Mataqali (*mataqali veimama*)	F$1,036.28
Small Mataqali (*mataqali lailai*)	F$814.22

Suvavou people called this "percentage" (*pasede*).

16. David Wilkinson to Buli Suva, December 27, 1905, in Ministry of Fijian Affairs 36/92/7.

17. These rights were usually passed on from a parent to his or her children. They were not exclusive to *mataqali* members but rather might leave the *mataqali* with a woman: When a village woman married a village man, a piece of her *mataqali*'s planting ground or house foundation was often transferred to her husband's *mataqali*, leading to disputes in later generations. The original landholding *mataqali* might claim such land, but it rarely reverted to its original owners at the death of a woman.

18. The population of these settlements also consisted of members of the *mataqali* that owned the land and other Suvavou residents who had marital ties with that *mataqali*.

19. The chiefly *mataqali*'s last male member and holder of the title of the Roko Tui Suva, Ratu Ravulo, died on April 21, 1916 (SNA 1367/1916, National Archives of Fiji, Suva). He had been married to a part-European woman from Nukuwatu, Lami, but they did not have any children. The last survivor of the *mataqali*, Adi Salote, who had married into the *mataqali* that held the chiefly title of the Ka Levu in Cuvu, Nadroga, died in August 1918 (A. J. Small to J. B. Suckling, August 30, 1918, in Meth-

odist Church Record F/1/1918, National Archives of Fiji, Suva; provincial commissioner, Rewa to acting secretary for native affairs, September 30, 1918, in CSO 8318/1918, National Archives of Fiji, Suva). Following the death of Adi Salote, Suvavou people attempted to bring her son, Ratu Orisi, from Cuvu to Suvavou to be installed as the Roko Tui Suva (see SNA 2935/1918, National Archives of Fiji, Suva). However, the government did not allow this, because Ratu Orisi was not registered in the *i vola ni kawa bula* (landowners' register) for Suvavou.

20. CSO 8313/1918.

21. Ibid.

22. CSO 7210/1920, National Archives of Fiji, Suva. Subsequently, a number of Bauan chiefs requested that the rent money reserved for Mataqali Roko Tui Suva be paid to them, on the theory that Bau ruled Suva (Ratu Edward Wainiu et al. to Roko Tui Tailevu, July 20, 1921, in SNA 1500/1921, National Archives of Fiji, Suva). See Ratu Popi Seniloli to secretary for native affairs, August 29, 1929, in SNA 1743/1929, National Archives of Fiji, Suva.

23. See CSO 3221/1893, National Archives of Fiji, Suva. At the time of the resettlement of Suva people in 1882, a piece of Lami people's land was given to Suva people as a gift. Later, however, a conflict between the two groups arose and the government proposed this solution.

24. Robert Boyd to secretary for native affairs, May 10, 1921, in CSO 2132/1923, National Archives of Fiji, Suva.

25. Ibid.

26. Letter to provincial commissioner, Rewa, June 15, 1923, NLC 109/23, in SNA 786/1923, National Archives of Fiji, Suva.

27. Ibid.; my translation.

28. *Ai tukutuku raraba kei nai yalayala ni vei Tikina ko: Suva, Ravi-ravi, Sawau*, Native Lands and Fisheries Commission, Suva, p. 19; my translation.

29. Ibid.

30. Ibid., p. 23; my translation.

31. Cf. Lederman 1986; Verdery 1999: 117–24. My focus on the aesthetics of Suvavou people's narratives of the past also resonates with Arjun Appadurai's attention to the formal constraints in the representation of the past (Appadurai 1981).

32. At the time of my fieldwork, however, Suvavou people recalled that the government had not distributed shares of rent money for leased portions of the village land in this manner until the 1960s. According to them, each *mataqali* had received rent for its own *kanakana*, or planting ground. Indeed, according to government records, some time in the 1950s, a section of the village petitioned the government to make the method of division of rent conform to the method of village land registration in the NLC

158 Notes

records. In response, the chairman of the Native Lands Commission wrote to Suvavou people in 1962:

The three *yavusa* of Suvavou own the village land in common. As far as rent money for [leased portions of land] is concerned, it belongs to all members of the three *yavusa* as they own the land in common. While the Turaga i Taukei of the Vanua ko Suva receives the usual portion of the rent money allocated to the holder of that title, there are no shares for the Turaga ni Qali or Turaga ni Mataqali because the land is owned in common. Shares that the Turaga ni Qali and the Turaga ni Mataqali have usually received are put together with money for the *mataqali* in the three *yavusa*. Members of *mataqali* in these *yavusa* must select their representative who will come and collect the money. It is an important duty for this representative to take the money on behalf of the members of the *mataqali* in the three *yavusa* and to divide it in a proper way among all *mataqali* members. [The method of division] is entirely up to you and the Native Lands Commission has no further decision to make. (J. S. Thomson, chairman of the Native Lands and Fisheries Commission, "Nai lavo ni lisi ni veivanua ni vei yavusa ena koro ko Suvavou [Rent money for *yavusa* land in Suvavou village]," February 18, 1962, in possession of a resident of Suvavou; my translation)

Villagers called this new method Tu Levu from the expression *taukeni levu tu* (owned as a whole), referring to the fact that the village land is owned in common in its entirety as an undivided whole. The introduction of this system intensified disagreement among villagers over the correct method of distribution of rent shares during the 1960s. This was also a period when a large tract of village land on a hill known as Delainavesi was developed by the NLTB into a residential area. As a result of this development, the amount of rent money collected dramatically increased. Some villagers felt that the Tu Levu system was unfair. They clearly recognized their own clan's planting ground (*kanakana*) as separate and wished to receive the entire amount of rent deriving from that portion of the land. The subsequent development of the percentage system further intensified these villagers' dissatisfaction with the Tu Levu system. *Mataqali* such as the Tui Suva's had already given away almost all of their own *kanakana* to outsiders on a *vakavanua* basis but still received shares of rent arising from the *kanakana* of other *mataqali*. Furthermore, critics pointed out that the percentage system allowed the Tui Suva's *mataqali*, as a large *mataqali*, to receive greater shares than others.

33. At the time of my fieldwork, there were at least three companies (*kabani*) in Suvavou. One of them was a company formed by an *i tokato-ka* within Mataqali Vakalolo in 1991 to develop the *i tokatoka*'s own planting ground (*kanakana*) into a residential development. The company

heads negotiated with the leaders of the three *yavusa* to allow the *i toka-toka* to develop its own separate *kanakana*. Endorsement was needed from the three *yavusa*, because Suvavou land was officially owned by the three *yavusa* of the village as common property. The company approached the NLTB and received permission to attempt a new form of development in which the company would market its own land rather than handing it over to the NLTB for development. The *i tokatoka* company mentioned above also invested in Fijian Holdings, a company established by the Great Council of Chiefs, which invested in successful local companies with the help of loans at favorable rates from the government. Fijian Holdings sold its own shares to companies owned by provincial councils (*yasana*), to village-based companies such as the Suvavou *i tokatoka* company, and to individual Fijians. Fijian Holdings was typical of a new post-coup form of development aimed at increasing the wealth of indigenous Fijians by combining corporate and traditional forms.

34. The consultant Anare Matahau acted as the "adviser" to the company and the office of the firm of Anare Matahau and Associates was registered as the company's official address.

Chapter 4. Setting Knowledge in Motion

1. Cf. Merry 2000. I have in mind the striking shift in focus from Bernard Cohn's attention to the unintended consequences of colonial policies such as the objectification of castes in the census in South Asia to Ann Stoler's attention to the failed schemes of Dutch colonial officials (Cohn 1987b; Stoler 2002b).

2. Joanne Rappaport and others have drawn attention to instances of local appropriation of bureaucratic means such as land registration (see, e.g., Rappaport 1994). For example, David Holmberg and Kathryn March have observed the significance of land records for Tamang in Nepal: "The meaning of writing . . . is different for nonliterate Tamang villagers than literate administrative officers. In the perspective of administrative or judicial officers of the state, written documents have a legal force in reference primarily to what is written. In village contexts, the social and discursive context of the production of written documents plays an essential part to their meaning. The production of a local document is a ritualized event in which the document symbolizes the understanding reached orally and gives an authority as much to the context as to the words set down on paper. Documents have metaphoric value for Tamang villagers that is not recorded in the written word as read" (Holmberg and March 1999: 13). These observations are certainly pertinent to my discussion of Suvavou people's approach to land records. However, in the present study, I seek to demonstrate that there is as much commonality and resonance as disjunc-

ture between knowledge practice of Suvavou researchers and government officials. My general claim is that careful ethnographic attention must be paid to seemingly bureaucratic techniques as well as seemingly local and distinctive practices entailed in the production of documents (see also Riles, n.d. a).

3. My present attention to what some may characterize as the "dialogical" character of Suvavou petitions resonates, for example, with the general orientation of Michael Silverstein's careful analysis of Edward Sapir's recounting of a Kiksht (Wasco-Wishram Chinookan) narrative (Silverstein 1996). Silverstein draws attention to "an earlier otherwise secret discursive life of the text(s)" seen in its dialogicality (Silverstein 1996: 81–82).

4. I thank Jane Collier for drawing my attention to Natalie Zemon Davis's work.

5. Suvavou people's interest in documents reflects a local articulation of literacy as a system of authority (cf. Shryock 1997). Literacy and in particular, the ability to conduct archival research has generated a complex interrelationship between education and rank. Suvavou people repeatedly told me that educated people such as schoolteachers, church ministers, lawyers, and consultants were more capable of conducting archival research but, at the same time, the very possession of archival records also influenced their evaluation of the truthfulness of a story. Therefore, people in Suvavou tended to regard those village elders capable of demonstrating the correspondence between their stories and archival records in their possession as knowledgeable (*kila vinaka*) regardless of their educational background.

6. Letter to minister for Fijian affairs, May 24, 1973, in Ministry of Fijian Affairs 36/92/7, National Archives of Fiji, Suva.

7. All heads of *mataqali* within two *yavusa* of Suvavou possessed NLC lists of *i tokatoka* and *mataqali* members, but none of the *mataqali* heads in the other *yavusa* had NLC records of their own *mataqali* membership. Not even Mataqali Koromakawa had a list of its own members. This might have resulted from the reluctance on the part of Mataqali Kaiwai, the present chiefly and leading *mataqali* of this *yavusa,* to distribute these NLC records within the *yavusa.* At the time of my fieldwork, both government officials and villagers were under the impression that only the chief or leader (*i liuilu*) of the *vanua* (chiefdom) could request these records from the NLC.

8. For example, the head of a Suvavou *mataqali* kept a record prepared by Native Lands Commissioner David Wilkinson in 1899 showing that his *mataqali* was registered as a landowning unit in another peri-urban village near Suva. He had kept the record as evidence of his *mataqali*'s entitlement to shares of rent arising from leased properties in that village.

9. Avorosa Tuivuya et al. to native commissioner, November 19, 1898, in CSO 4655/1898, National Archives of Fiji, Suva.
10. See, e.g., CSO 2690/1923, CSO 2689/1923, National Archives of Fiji, Suva.
11. Governor Henry Jackson to colonial secretary, February 18, 1904, in CSO 562/1904, National Archives of Fiji, Suva.
12. Nakauvadra is also the name of an actual mountain range. Many studies have drawn attention to the importance of topographic knowledge in making claims to ritual precedence and land rights in the Pacific (see, e.g., J. J. Fox 1979; Fox and Sather 1996; Kahn 1990; Lederman 1986; Parmentier 1987).
13. Osea Kaibale Rokosele, "Serekali kei Suva," clipping from *Nailalakai* (in possession of a resident of Suvavou).
14. My argument echoes Elizabeth Povinelli's claim that Australian Aboriginal women strategically invoke the "language of indeterminacy" in their efforts to "negotiate and interrelate" different domains of knowledge (Povinelli 1993: 680).

Chapter 5. Intimating Fulfillment

1. Chakrabarty 1997: 35; and see also Douglas 1989; Herzfeld 1990; Keane 1997a, 1997b. My discussion of Fijian Christians' uses of language builds on Richard Bauman, William Hanks, Susan Harding, Webb Keane, and others' pioneering work on religious language (see Bauman 1983, 1989 [1975]; Hanks 1996a; Harding 1987, 2000; Keane 1997a, 1997b; and see also Tomlinson 2000a, 2000b, 2004). These scholars have drawn particular attention to religious practitioners' own conceptions of the limits and possibilities of language in accessing experientially inaccessible entities.
2. According to the 1986 census, the vast majority of Fiji's ethnic Fijian population (74.2 percent) belongs to the Methodist Church, while Seventh-Day Adventists constitute only 4 percent of the ethnic Fijian population (Fiji Government 1989: 17; cf. Ernst 1994: 202).
3. Sabbath School classes followed a booklet entitled *The Adult Sabbath School Lessons*, produced at the SDA Church's international headquarters. Classes usually focused on a particular section of Scripture, such as the Book of Joshua (April–June 1995), on a particular subject, such as the Holy Spirit (July–September 1995), or on the proper method of Bible study (January–March 1996).
4. The Sabbath School discussion took place at the Suvavou Seventh-Day Church on July 29, 1995. All translations are mine unless otherwise indicated.
5. Sermon at the Suvavou Methodist Church, June 18, 1995; my translation.

6. Sermon at the Suvavou SDA Church, February 3, 1996; my translation.

7. Sermon at the Suvavou SDA Church, January 13, 1996; my translation.

8. Although some Adventist men, especially young members of the church, preferred to wear trousers instead of a *sulu* skirt, especially in the winter, SDA elders in Suvavou usually wore *sulu vakataga*.

9. Cf. Hocart 1952: 51–52, 57; 1970 [1936]: 270. The *veiqaravi* form is used in every kind of gift-giving, ranging from marriage ceremonies and mortuary rites to apology (see Arno 1976b; Hickson 1979; Hocart 1970 [1936]; Ravuvu 1987; Toren 1990; Williksen Bakker 1986).

10. The role of the spokesman in Fijian gift-giving may have derived from a more institutionalized role of the high chief's spokesman (*matanivanua*, literally, "face of the land"). Unlike that of the influential Samoan *tulāfale* (orator) (see Duranti 1994; Shore 1982; cf. Yankah 1995), the political role of the *matanivanua* is limited to the proper arrangement of ritual attendance (Hocart 1970 [1936]: 191).

11. For example, when a delegation consisted of women or young men, a man from the gift-receiving side might speak on behalf of the delegation.

12. For Fijian conceptions of the causes of illness and death more generally, see Becker 1995: 112–23; de Marzan 1987: 58; Spencer 1941. See also Belshaw 1964: 144–45.

13. The identity of the "side" was ambiguous and opened up to interpretation at infinitely receding levels of generality. The group of men and women assembled for the ceremony was a "delegation" representing multiple entities, which might or might not be present. A gift-giving event was located at the end of a longer chain of numerous gift-giving events on the gift-givers' side in that the delegation had accumulated gifts from among a wider range of people than the gift-giving group specifically represented in their spokesman's speech. Each smaller gift-giving event took a less elaborated but similar *veiqaravi* form. At each level, the gift-receivers' side assumed full responsibility for the use of the gifts they received. As the Fijians I knew stressed, the gift-givers had no say over the way the gift-receivers distributed the gifts at the next stage of exchange. In other words, at the time of exchange of gifts and speeches, the question of who actually contributed to this event behind the scenes or who would receive a portion of the gifts was not important. That was a question each side contemplated independently before and after the event.

14. All ceremonial speeches discussed in this section were recorded in Suvavou on September 27, 1995. All translations are mine.

15. Cf. Ravuvu 1987: 254–60. The Fijian language distinguishes between the first person plural "inclusive" pronouns *daru*, *datou*, and *da*, by

which the speaker refers to both him- or herself and those to whom he or she is speaking, and the first person plural "exclusive" pronouns *keirau,* *keitou,* and *keimami,* by which the speaker excludes those to whom he or she is speaking.

16. The meaning of this phrase is not clear. Capell 1941 focuses on the meaning of the word *mudu* (to cut or cease) and translates the phrase as "It is over!" Ravuvu 1987 translates it as "Accepted with deep reverence!" Hocart 1929 (71) does not provide a translation.

17. When the relationship between the gift-givers and the gift-receivers was very close, the gift-receivers' offer to make a return gift was often turned down by the gift-givers.

18. In focusing on strategic devices entailed in ritual form, Keane has extended the work of Judith Irvine and others (e.g., Irvine 1979; Myers and Brenneis 1984) aimed at correcting a simplistic view of form in ritual and ritual speech as limiting the possibility of challenging the preexisting power relations (see Keane 1997b: 54; Keane 1997c: 6, 144; cf. M. Bloch 1975).

19. In discussing the relationship between hermeneutics and faith, Paul Ricoeur proposes going beyond the study of faith "through its linguistic and literary expressions":

> Faith is the attitude of one who accepts being interpreted at the same time that he or she interprets the world of the text. . . . This is not to say that faith is not authentically an *act* that cannot be reduced to linguistic treatment. In this sense, faith is the limit of all hermeneutics and the nonhermeneutical origin of all interpretation. The ceaseless movement of interpretation begins and ends in the risk of a response that is neither engendered nor exhausted by commentary. (Ricoeur 1995: 46; original emphasis)

As implied in Ricoeur's definition, faith involves taking a risk, that is, exposing oneself to what is beyond interpretive control. We overcome this risk, Ricoeur implies, by keeping hope alive: "[Faith] could be called 'unconditional trust' to say that it is inseparable from a movement of hope that makes its way in spite of the contradictions of experience and that turns reasons for despair into reasons for hope" (Ricoeur 1995: 47).

Chapter 6. Repeating Without Overlapping

1. The present study draws on an ethnographic and archival project focusing on a historically significant Fijian village, and in that sense, it inherits the ethnically divided character of the anthropology of Fiji (see Kelly and Kaplan 2001; Norton 1990; Riles 2000 for notable exceptions).

This chapter represents my effort to remedy this aspect of my ethnography by drawing attention to the implications of my discussion of hope for issues surrounding the politics of multiculturalism in Fiji.

2. The Native Lands Commission recorded a similar story concerning Suvavou people (see *Ai tukutuku raraba kei nai yalayala ni vei Tikina ko: Suva, Raviravi, Sawau*, pp. 19–20). Present-day villagers knew little about the war, however.

3. My translation.

4. My translation.

5. "Adventists also teach that gambling, card playing, theater going, and dancing are to be avoided (1 John 2: 15–17). . . . Any activity that weakens our relationship with our Lord and causes us to lose sight of eternal interests helps to bind Satan's chains about our souls" (SDA General Conference 1988: 284).

6. Minutes of the Church Board, Suvavou SDA Church, December 26, 1996.

7. Although a village elder stood up to confess his sin of drinking *yaqona* when he was with his guests, others who stood up simply expressed thanks to God for the year.

8. Minutes of the Church Board, Suvavou SDA Church, December 30, 1996.

9. Ratu Epeli Kanakana's speech, Suvavou Seventh-Day Adventist Church, December 31, 1995; my translation.

10. The reference to a fence here derives from a common Fijian expression, *loma ni bai* (literally, "inside a fence"), meaning a church compound. In the past, missionary compounds were fenced. I thank Matt Tomlinson for reminding me of this.

11. Dharmend Prasad, "Please Forgive Me, Cries Rabuka," *Fiji Times,* November 26, 1996; see also "PM Begs for Forgiveness at Church Service," *Fiji's Daily Post,* November 26, 1996. The church service was held at the National Gymnasium in Suva on November 24, 1996, on the occasion of the opening of a new radio station devoted to Christian themes, and was attended by approximately 4,000 people. Rabuka and his party, Soqosoqo Vakatulewa ni Taukei, went on to lose the 1999 general election to the Fiji Labour Party.

12. Prasad, "Please Forgive Me, Cries Rabuka."

13. This perception has been challenged by sympathizers of the National Federation–Labour coalition government, who have emphasized a wider basis of support for the coalition (see Lal 1988, 1990).

14. Sitiveni Rabuka, speech delivered at a meeting with Fijians in Nadroga, *Nailalakai,* June 16, 1987, trans. Martha Kaplan in M. Kaplan 1990a: 140–41.

15. Apart from articles cited below, see Butch Grant, "A Crying Shame," *Fiji Times*, November 29, 1996; Prudence A. Rouse, "Action Not Words," ibid.

16. "Cry the Beloved Country," *Fiji Times*, November 27, 1996, editorial.

17. Sir Len Usher, "Acts of God," *Fiji Times*, November 27, 1996. See also Vinay Kumar Singh, "Reason for the Coups," ibid., December 12, 1996, for a similar view.

18. Imrana Jalal, "Action, Not Words: To Forgive or Not to Forgive," *Fiji Times*, November 28, 1996.

19. Ibid.

20. Ibid.

21. A number of Rabuka's Christian sympathizers wrote in to the local press and expressed support for Rabuka's apology. See "Sequel to PM's Confession, 'We Weep with You,'" *Fiji's Sunday Post*, December 1, 1996; Mere Bulivuata, "A Case of Forgiveness," *Fiji Times*, November 30, 1996; Losalini Mavoa, "Cartoon Not Funny," ibid., November 30, 1996; Michael Ah Koy, "Offensive Caricature," ibid., November 30, 1996; V. Delaimatuku, "Begin at Jerusalem," ibid., December 5, 1996; Emelita W. Wilson, "Time to Reconcile," ibid., December 5, 1996; and id., "PM's Apology" (the same content as the letter published in the *Fiji Times*), *Fiji's Daily Post*, December 4, 1996. See also Jerry B. McClun, "A Cheap Shot," *Fiji Times*, November 29, 1996, and Anil K. Sharma, "To Err Is Human," ibid., December 6, 1996.

22. Michael Ah Koy, "Offensive Caricature," *Fiji Times*, November 30, 1996.

23. S. V. Taka, "Rabuka's Lament," *Fiji Times*, December 2, 1996. The then ruling party of Fiji, the Soqosoqo ni Vakavulewa ni Taukei (Fijian Political Party) led by Rabuka, was known by the initials "S.V.T." Given that many letters to the editor are written under pseudonyms, this letter may have been a disguised statement by the party.

24. Taka, "Rabuka's Lament."

25. To some extent, all Fijian gift-giving entails elements of apology and expression of humbleness about the inadequacy of gifts and speeches (cf. Arno 1976b; Hickson 1979). For example, the spokesman for the gift-giving side apologizes for the insufficiency (*lailai*) of the gifts and people on the gift-receiving side respond immediately by saying that the gifts are plenty (*levu*). In this interchange, the question of whether this is false politeness is overshadowed by the immediate concern with the repeated and rhythmic completion of the exchange of words. Here the intention and strategy behind the gifts and speeches do not constitute guiding principles for immediate action (see Miyazaki 2000a).

26. Prasad, "Please Forgive Me, Cries Rabuka," *Fiji Times*, November 26, 1996.

27. Taka, "Rabuka's Lament."

28. "Time to Back Off," *Fiji's Sunday Post*, December 1, 1996.

29. Dennis Simpson, "Only Time Will Tell," *Fiji Times*, December 3, 1996.

⌒ References

Adams, Robert Merrihew
  1987   *The Virtue of Faith and Other Essays in Philosophical Theology.* New York: Oxford University Press.
  1998   Introduction. In Immanuel Kant, *Religion Within the Boundaries of Mere Reason and Other Writings.* Allen Wood and George di Giovanni, trans. and eds. Pp. vii–xxxvii. Cambridge: Cambridge University Press.

Adorno, Theodor
  1974   *Minima Moralia: Reflections from Damaged Life.* E. F. N. Jephcott, trans. London: NLB.

Allison, Anne
  2000   *Permitted and Prohibited Desires: Mothers, Comics, and Censorship in Japan.* Berkeley: University of California Press.

Anare Matahau and Associates
  1991   *Suva State Land: "Land of My Fathers."* Suva: Anare Matahau and Associates.

Appadurai, Arjun
  1981   The Past as a Scarce Resource. *Man,* n.s., 16(2): 201–19.
  1996   *Modernity at Large: Cultural Dimensions of Globalization.* Minneapolis: University of Minnesota Press.

Arno, Andrew
  1976a   Joking, Avoidance, and Authority: Verbal Performance as an Object of Exchange in Fiji. *Journal of the Polynesian Society* 85(1): 71–86.
  1976b   Ritual of Reconciliation and Village Conflict Management in Fiji. *Oceania* 47(1): 49–65.
  1990   Disentangling Indirectly: The Joking Debate in Fijian Social Control. In *Disentangling: Conflict Discourse in Pacific Societies.* Karen A. Watson-Gegeo and Geoffrey M. White, eds. Pp. 241–89. Stanford: Stanford University Press.
  2003   Aesthetics, Intuition, and Reference in Fijian Ritual Communication: Modularity in and out of Language. *American Anthropologist* 105(4): 807–19.

Asad, Talal, ed.
   1973   *Anthropology and the Colonial Encounter.* London: Ithaca
          Press.
Augustine, Saint
   1961   *The Enchiridion on Faith, Hope, and Love.* Washington, D.C.:
          Regnery Publishing.
Axel, Brian Keith
   2002   Introduction: Historical Anthropology and Its Vicissitudes. In
          From the Margins: Historical Anthropology and Its Futures. Pp.
          1–44. Durham, N.C.: Duke University Press.
Barber, Karin
   2000   *The Generation of Plays: Yorùbá Popular Life in Theater.*
          Bloomington: Indiana University Press.
Bateson, Gregory
   1979   *Mind and Nature: A Necessary Unity.* New York: Dutton.
Battaglia, Debbora
   1997   Ambiguating Agency: The Case of Malinowski's Ghost. *American Anthropologist* 99(3): 505–10.
Bauman, Richard
   1983   *Let Your Words Be Few: Symbolism of Speaking and Silence
          Among Seventeenth-Century Quakers.* Cambridge: Cambridge
          University Press.
   1989 [1975]   Speaking in the Light: The Role of the Quaker Minister.
          In *Explorations in the Ethnography of Speaking.* Richard Bauman and Joel Sherzer, eds. Pp. 144–60. Cambridge: Cambridge
          University Press.
   2001   Mediational Performance, Traditionalization, and the Authorization of Discourse. In *Verbal Art Across Cultures: The Aesthetics and Proto-Aesthetics of Communication.* Hubert Knoblauch and Helga Kotthoff, eds. Pp. 91–117. Tübingen: Gunter
          Narr Verlag.
Becker, Anne
   1995   *Body, Self, and Society: The View from Fiji.* Philadelphia: University of Pennsylvania Press.
Belshaw, Cyril S.
   1964   *Under the Ivi Tree: Society and Economic Growth in Rural Fiji.*
          London: Routledge & Kegan Paul.
Benjamin, Andrew
   1997   *Present Hope: Philosophy, Architecture, Judaism.* London:
          Routledge.
Benjamin, Walter
   1980   *Gesammelte Schriften.* Rolf Tiedemann and Hermann Schweppenhäuser, eds. 12 vols. Frankfurt a/M: Suhrkamp.

1992 [1968] *Illuminations*. Hannah Arendt, ed. Harry Zohn, trans. London: Fontana.

Bentley, James
1982 *Between Marx and Christ: The Dialogue in German-Speaking Europe, 1870–1970*. London: Verso Editions and NLB.

Bloch, Ernst
1972 *Atheism in Christianity: The Religion of the Exodus and the Kingdom*. J. T. Swann, trans. New York: Herder & Herder.
1986 *The Principle of Hope*. 3 vols. Neville Plaice, Stephen Plaice, and Paul Knight, trans. Cambridge, Mass.: MIT Press. Originally published as *Das Prinzip Hoffnung* (Frankfurt a/M: Suhrkamp, 1959).
1988 *The Utopian Function of Art and Literature: Selected Essays*. Jack Zipes and Frank Mecklenburg, trans. Cambridge, Mass.: MIT Press.
1991 *Heritage of Our Times*. Neville Plaice and Stephen Plaice, trans. Berkeley: University of California Press.
1998 *Literary Essays*. Werner Hamacher and David E. Wellbery, eds. Andrew Joron et al., trans. Stanford: Stanford University Press.
2000 *The Spirit of Utopia*. Anthony A. Nassar, trans. Stanford: Stanford University Press. Originally published as *Geist der Utopie* (Munich: Duncker & Humblot, 1918).

Bloch, Maurice
1975 Introduction. In *Political Language and Oratory in Traditional Society*. Maurice Bloch, ed. Pp. 1–28. New York: Academic Press.

Bohman, James
1991 *New Philosophy of Social Science: Problems of Indeterminacy*. Cambridge: Polity Press.

Bourdieu, Pierre
1977 *Outline of a Theory of Practice*. Richard Nice, trans. Cambridge: Cambridge University Press.

Boyer, Dominic
2001 On the Sedimentation and Accreditation of Social Knowledges of Difference: Mass Media, Journalism, and the Reproduction of East/West Alterities in Unified Germany. *Cultural Anthropology* 15(4): 459–91.

Brenneis, Donald
1986 Shared Territory: Audience, Indirection and Meaning. *Text* 6(3): 339–47.
1990 Dramatic Gestures: The Fiji Indian *Pancayat* as Therapeutic Event. In *Disentangling: Conflict Discourse in Pacific Societies*. Karen A. Watson-Gegeo and Geoffrey M. White, eds. Pp. 214–38. Stanford: Stanford University Press.

170 References

1999 New Lexicon, Old Language: Negotiating the "Global" at the National Science Foundation. In *Critical Anthropology Now: Unexpected Contexts, Shifting Constituencies, Changing Agendas*. George E. Marcus, ed. Pp. 123–46. Santa Fe: School of American Research Press.

Breznitz, Shlomo
1999 The Effect of Hope and Pain Tolerance. *Social Research* 66(2): 629–52.

Buck-Morss, Susan
1977 *The Origin of Negative Dialectics: Theodor W. Adorno, Walter Benjamin, and the Frankfurt Institute*. New York: Free Press.

Bultmann, Rudolf
1957 *History and Eschatology*. Edinburgh: Edinburgh University Press.

Burridge, Kenelm
1995 [1960] *Mambu: A Melanesian Millennium*. Princeton, N.J.: Princeton University Press.

Butler, Jonathan M.
1993 The Making of a New Order: Millerism and the Origins of Seventh-Day Adventism. In *The Disappointed: Millerism and Millenarianism in the Nineteenth Century*. Ronald L. Numbers and Jonathan M. Butler, eds. Pp. 189–208. Knoxville: University of Tennessee Press.

Capell, A.
1941 *A New Fijian Dictionary*. Suva, Fiji: Government Printer.

Cargill, David
1977 *The Diaries and Correspondence of David Cargill, 1832–1843*. A. J. Schütz, ed. Canberra: Australian National University Press.

Chakrabarty, Dipesh
1997 The Time of History and the Times of Gods. In *The Politics of Culture in the Shadow of Capital*. Lisa Lowe and David Lloyd, eds. Pp. 35–60. Durham, N.C.: Duke University Press.

Clammer, John
1973 Colonialism and the Perception of Tradition in Fiji. In *Anthropology and the Colonial Encounter*. Talal Asad, ed. London: Ithaca Press.

Clifford, James
1988 *The Predicament of Culture: Twentieth-Century Ethnography, Literature, and Art*. Cambridge, Mass.: Harvard University Press.

Clifford, James, and George Marcus
1986 *Writing Culture: The Poetics and Politics of Ethnography*. Berkeley: University of California Press.

Cohn, Bernard
   1987a *An Anthropologist Among the Historians and Other Essays.*
         New Delhi: Oxford University Press.
   1987b The Census, Social Structure and Objectification in South Asia.
         In *An Anthropologist Among the Historians and Other Essays.*
         Pp. 224–54. New Delhi: Oxford University Press.
Collins, Harry
   1985 *Changing Order: Replication and Induction in Scientific Prac-
        tice.* London: Sage.
Comaroff, John, and Jean Comaroff
   1992 *Ethnography and the Historical Imagination.* Boulder, Colo.:
        Westview Press.
Crapanzano, Vincent
   2003 Reflections on Hope as a Category of Social and Psychological
        Analysis. *Cultural Anthropology* 18(1): 3–32.
Crook, Tony
   In press *Kim Kurukuru: An Anthropological Exchange with Bolivip,
           Papua New Guinea.* Oxford: Oxford University Press.
Crozier, D.
   1958 The Establishment of the Central Archives of Fiji and the West-
        ern Pacific High Commission. *Transactions and Proceedings of
        the Fiji Society* 5: 91–106.
   1959 Archives and Administrative Efficiency. *Transactions and Pro-
        ceedings of the Fiji Society* 6: 144–52.
Damsteegt, P. Gerard
   1977 *Foundations of the Seventh-Day Adventist Message and Mis-
        sion.* Grand Rapids, Mich.: Eerdmans.
Daniel, E. Valentine
   1984 *Fluid Signs: Being a Person the Tamil Way.* Berkeley: University
        of California Press.
   1996 *Charred Lullabies: Chapters in an Anthropography of Violence.*
        Princeton, N.J.: Princeton University Press.
Daniel, Jamie Owen, and Tom Moylan eds.
   1997 *Not Yet: Reconsidering Ernst Bloch.* London: Verso.
Das, Veena
   1998 Wittgenstein and Anthropology. *Annual Review of Anthropol-
        ogy* 27: 171–95.
Davis, Natalie Zemon
   1987 *Fiction in the Archives: Pardon Tales and Their Tellers in Six-
        teenth-Century France.* Stanford: Stanford University Press.
Dean, Eddie, and Stan Ritova
   1988 *Rabuka: No Other Way.* Suva, Fiji: Marketing Team Interna-
        tional.

Dear, Peter
   1995   *Discipline and Experience: The Mathematical Way in the Scientific Revolution.* Chicago: University of Chicago Press.
de Marzan, Jean
   1987   Custom and Beliefs in Upland Vitilevu: Papers from Anthropos, 1907–1913. Nicholas Thomas, trans. *Domodomo* (Fiji Museum) 5(3–4): 28–62.
Deneen, Patrick J.
   1999   The Politics of Hope and Optimism: Rorty, Havel, and the Democratic Faith of John Dewey. *Social Research* 66(2): 577–609.
Derrick, R. A.
   1953   The Removal of the Capital to Suva. *Transactions and Proceedings of the Fiji Society of Science and Industry* 2: 203–9.
Derrida, Jacques
   1995   Archives Fever: A Freudian Impression. *Diacritics* 25(2): 9–63.
Diamond, A. I.
   1978   The Development of the Central Archives of Fiji and the Western Pacific High Commission. *Transactions and Proceedings of the Fiji Society* 12: 69–78.
Didi-Huberman, Georges
   2000   *Devant le temps: Histoire de l'art et anachronisme des images.* Paris: Minuit.
Dirks, Nicholas B.
   2001   *Castes of Mind: Colonialism and the Making of Modern India.* Princeton, N.J.: Princeton University Press.
   2002   Annals of the Archive: Ethnographic Notes on the Sources of History. In *From the Margins: Historical Anthropology and Its Futures.* Brian Keith Axel, ed. Pp. 47–65. Durham, N.C.: Duke University Press.
Douglas, Bronwen
   1989   Autonomous and Controlled Spirits: Traditional Ritual and Early Interpretations of Christianity on Tanna, Aneityum and the Isle of Pines in Comparative Perspective. *Journal of the Polynesian Society* 98(1): 7–48.
Duranti, Alessandro
   1994   *From Grammar to Politics: Linguistic Anthropology in a Western Samoan Village.* Berkeley: University of California Press.
Ernst, Manfred
   1994   *Winds of Change: Rapidly Growing Religious Groups in the Pacific Islands.* Suva, Fiji: Pacific Conference of Churches.
Errington, Frederick
   1974   Indigenous Ideas of Order, Time, and Transition in a New

Guinea Cargo Movement. *American Ethnologist* 1(2): 255–67.

Fabian, Johannes
    1983   *Time and the Other: How Anthropology Makes Its Object.*
            New York: Columbia University Press.

Fajans, Jane
    1997   *They Make Themselves: Work and Play Among the Baining of
            Papua New Guinea.* Chicago: University of Chicago Press.

Ferch, Arthur J., ed.
    1986   *Symposium on Adventist History in the South Pacific: 1885–
            1918.* Wahroonga, NSW, Australia: South Pacific Division of
            Seventh-Day Adventists.

Fiji Government
    1989   *Report on Fiji Population Census, 1986: Analytical Report on
            the Demographic, Social and Economic Characteristics of the
            Population.* Suva, Fiji: Bureau of Statistics.

Fischer, Michael M. J.
    1999   Emergent Forms of Life: Anthropologies of Late or Postmoder-
            nities. *Annual Review of Anthropology* 28: 455–78.

Foster, Robert J., ed.
    1995   *Nation Making: Emergent Identities in Postcolonial Melanesia.*
            Ann Arbor: University of Michigan Press.

Foucault, Michel
    1972   *The Archaeology of Knowledge.* A. M. Sheridan Smith, trans.
            New York: Pantheon Books.

Fox, James J.
    1979   "Standing" in Time and Place: The Structure of Rotinese His-
            torical Narratives. In *Perceptions of the Past in Southeast Asia.*
            Anthony Ried and David Marr, eds. Pp. 10–25. Singapore:
            Heinemann.

Fox, James J., and Clifford Sather, eds.
    1996   *Origins, Ancestry and Alliance: Explorations in Austronesian
            Ethnography.* Canberra: Department of Anthropology, Aus-
            tralian National University.

Fox, Richard G.
    1991a   Introduction: Working in the Present. In *Recapturing Anthro-
            pology: Working in the Present.* Richard G. Fox, ed. Pp. 1–16.
            Santa Fe, N.M.: School of American Research Press.

Fox, Richard G., ed.
    1991b   *Recapturing Anthropology: Working in the Present.* Santa Fe,
            N.M.: School of American Research Press.

France, Peter
   1969   *The Charter of the Land: Custom and Colonization in Fiji*. Mel-
          bourne: Oxford University Press.
Franklin, Sarah
   1997   *Embodied Progress: A Cultural Account of Assisted Concep-
          tion*. London: Routledge.
Gane, Erwin R., ed.
   1995   *Adult Sabbath School Lessons: Enlightened by the Spirit*. Teach-
          er's Edition. July, August, September 1995. Warburton, Victoria,
          Australia: Signs Publishing.
Garrett, John
   1982   *To Live among the Stars: Christian Origins in Oceania*. Suva,
          Fiji: Institute of Pacific Studies, University of the South Pa-
          cific.
   1990   Uncertain Sequel: The Social and Religious Scene in Fiji Since
          the Coups. In *As the Dust Settles: Impact and Implications of
          the Fiji Coups*. Brij V. Lal, ed. *The Contemporary Pacific* 2, spe-
          cial issue (1): 87–111.
Geertz, Clifford
   2000   *Available Light: Anthropological Reflections on Philosophical
          Topics*. Princeton, N.J.: Princeton University Press.
Gell, Alfred
   1992   *The Anthropology of Time: Cultural Constructions of Temporal
          Maps and Images*. Oxford: Berg.
Geoghegan, Vincent
   1996   *Ernst Bloch*. London: Routledge.
Gewertz, Deborah, and Frederick Errington
   1993   First Contact with God: Individualism, Agency, and Revivalism in
          the Duke of York Islands. *Cultural Anthropology* 8(3): 279–305.
Giddens, Anthony
   1979   *Central Problems in Social Theory: Action, Structure and Con-
          tradiction in Social Analysis*. Berkeley: University of California
          Press.
Godelier, Maurice
   1999   *The Enigma of the Gift*. Nora Scott, trans. Chicago: University
          of Chicago Press.
Godfrey, Joseph J.
   1987   *A Philosophy of Human Hope*. Dordrecht, Netherlands: Nijhoff.
Goldman, Laurence
   1993   *The Culture of Coincidence: Accident and Absolute Liability in
          Huli*. Oxford: Clarendon Press.

Good, Mary-Jo Del Vecchio, Byron J. Good, Cynthia Schaffer, and Stuart
        E. Lind
    1990   American Oncology and the Discourse on Hope. *Culture, Med-
            icine, and Psychiatry* 14(1): 59–79.
Gooding, David, Trevor Pinch, and Simon Schaffer, eds.
    1989   *The Uses of Experiment: Studies in the Natural Sciences.* Cam-
            bridge: Cambridge University Press.
Goody, Esther
    1978   Towards a Theory of Questions. In *Questions and Politeness:
            Strategies in Social Interaction.* Esther Goody, ed. Pp. 17–43.
            Cambridge: Cambridge University Press.
Grafton, Anthony
    1997   *The Footnote: A Curious History.* Cambridge, Mass.: Harvard
            University Press.
Green, Georgia M.
    1975   How to Get People to Do Things with Words: The Whimpera-
            tive Question. In *Syntax and Semantics.* Vol. 3. *Speech Acts.* Pe-
            ter Cole and Jerry L. Morgan, eds. Pp. 107–41. New York: Aca-
            demic Press.
Greenhouse, Carol J.
    1986   *Praying for Justice: Faith, Order, and Community in an Ameri-
            can Town.* Ithaca, N.Y.: Cornell University Press.
    1996   *A Moment's Notice: Time Politics Across Cultures.* Ithaca, N.Y.:
            Cornell University Press.
Greenwood, Davydd, and Morten Levin
    2000   Reconstructing the Relationships Between Universities and Soci-
            ety Through Action Research. In *Handbook of Qualitative Re-
            search.* 2d ed. Norman K. Denzin and Yvonna S. Lincoln, eds.
            Pp. 85–106. Thousand Oaks, Calif.: Sage.
Gupta, Akhil, and James Ferguson, eds.
    1997   *Anthropological Locations: Boundaries and Grounds of a Field
            Science.* Berkeley: University of California Press.
Guyer, Jane I.
    1988   The Multiplication of Labor: Historical Methods in the Study of
            Gender and Agricultural Change in Modern Africa. *Current An-
            thropology* 29(2): 247–72.
Habermas, Jürgen
    1983   Ernst Bloch: A Marxist Schelling. In *Philosophical-Political Pro-
            files.* Frederick G. Lawrence, trans. Pp. 61–77. Cambridge,
            Mass.: MIT Press.

Hage, Ghassan
   2003   *Against Paranoid Nationalism: Searching for Hope in a Shrinking Society.* Annandale, NSW, Australia: Pluto Press Australia.
Hanks, William F.
   1996a   Exorcism and the Description of Participant Roles. In *Natural Histories of Discourse.* Michael Silverstein and Greg Urban, eds. Pp. 160–200. Chicago: University of Chicago Press.
   1996b   *Language and Communicative Practices.* Boulder, Colo.: Westview Press.
   2000   *Intertexts: Writings on Language, Utterance, and Context.* Lanham, Md.: Rowman & Littlefield.
Harding, Susan Friend
   1987   Convicted by the Holy Spirit: The Rhetoric of Fundamental Baptist Conversion. *American Ethnologist* 14(1): 167–81.
   2000   *The Book of Jerry Falwell: Fundamentalist Language and Politics.* Princeton, N.J.: Princeton University Press.
Hare, Eric B.
   1985 [1969]   *Fulton's Footprints in Fiji.* Boise, Idaho: Pacific Press Publishing Association.
Harootunian, Harry
   2000   *Overcome by Modernity: History, Culture, and Community in Interwar Japan.* Princeton, N.J.: Princeton University Press.
Harvey, David
   2000   *Spaces of Hope.* Berkeley: University of California Press.
Herzfeld, Michael
   1990   Pride and Perjury: Time and the Oath in the Mountain Villages of Crete. *Man,* n.s., 25(2): 305–22.
   1997   *Cultural Intimacy: Social Poetics in the Nation-State.* New York: Routledge.
Hickson, Letitia
   1979   Hierarchy, Conflict, and Apology in Fiji. In *Access to Justice.* Volume 4. *The Anthropological Perspective. Patterns of Conflict Management: Essay in the Ethnography of Law.* Klaus-Friedrich Koch, ed. Pp. 17–39. Milan: Giuffrè.
Hobsbawm, Eric
   1973   The Principle of Hope. In *Revolutionaries: Contemporary Essays.* Pp. 136–41. New York: New American Library.
Hocart, A. M.
   1914   Mana. *Man* 14: 97–101.
   1915   Chieftainship and the Sister's Son in the Pacific. *American Anthropologist* 17(4): 631–46.
   1929   *Lau Islands, Fiji.* Bernice P. Bishop Museum Bulletin 62. Honolulu: Bernice P. Bishop Museum.

1952   *The Northern States of Fiji.* Royal Anthropological Institute Occasional Publication No. 11. London: Royal Anthropological Institute of Great Britain and Ireland.

1970 [1936]   *Kings and Councillors: An Essay in the Comparative Anatomy of Human Society.* Rodney Needham, ed. Chicago: University of Chicago Press.

N.d. a   Fijian Fieldnotes. Microfilm, Division of Pacific & Asian History, Research School of Pacific & Asian Studies, Australian National University (original at the Turnbull Library, Wellington).

N.d. b   The Heart of Fiji. Microfilm, Division of Pacific & Asian History, Research School of Pacific & Asian Studies, Australian National University (original at the Turnbull Library, Wellington).

Hollander, John
1959   Versions, Interpretations, and Performances. In *On Translation.* Reuben A. Brower, ed. Pp. 205–31. Cambridge, Mass: Harvard University Press.

Holmberg, David, and Kathryn March
1999   Local Production/Local Knowledge: Forced Labour from Below. *Studies in Nepali History and Society* 4(1): 5–64.

Holmes, Douglas R., and George E. Marcus
In press   Cultures of Expertise and the Management of Globalization: Toward the Re-Functioning of Ethnography. In *Global Assemblages: Technology, Politics, and Ethics as Anthropological Problems.* Aihwa Ong and Stephen J. Collier, eds. Oxford: Blackwell.

Hooper, Steven
1982   A Study of Valuables in the Chiefdom of Lau, Fiji. Ph.D. diss., University of Cambridge.

Hudson, Wayne
1982   *The Marxist Philosophy of Ernst Bloch.* New York: St. Martin's Press.

Husserl, Edmund
1964 [1887]   *The Phenomenology of Internal Time-Consciousness.* James S. Churchill, trans. Bloomington: Indiana University Press.

Irvine, Judith
1979   Formality and Informality in Communicative Events. *American Anthropologist* 81(4): 773–90.

Jaggar, Thomas J.
1988   *Unto the Perfect Day: The Journal of Thomas James Jaggar Feejee, 1838–1845.* Esther Keesing-Styles and William Keesing-Styles, eds. Auckland: Solent Publishing.

James, William.
    1981 [1890]   *The Principles of Psychology*. Cambridge, Mass.: Harvard University Press.
Jameson, Fredric
    1971   Ernst Bloch and the Future. In *Marxism and Form: Twentieth-Century Dialectical Theories of Literature*. Pp. 116–59. Princeton, N.J.: Princeton University Press.
    1991   *Postmodernism, or, The Cultural Logic of Late Capitalism*. Durham, N.C.: Duke University Press.
Jay, Martin
    1984   *Marxism and Totality: The Adventures of a Concept from Lukács to Habermas*. Berkeley: University of California Press.
Jean-Klein, Iris
    In press.   Palestinian Martyrdom Revisited: Critical Reflections on Topical Cultures of Explanation. In *Innovations around Property-Thinking: Dialogues Between Law, Policy and Ethnography*. Tony Crook, Andy Holding and Melissa Damien, eds. Oxford: Berghahn.
Jolly, Margaret
    1992   Custom and the Way of the Land: Past and Present in Vanuatu and Fiji. In *The Politics of Tradition in the Pacific*. Margaret Jolly and Nicholas Thomas, eds. *Oceania* 62, special issue (4): 330–54.
    1996   Devils, Holy Spirits and the Swollen God: Translation, Conversion and Colonial Power in the Marist Mission, Vanuatu, 1887–1934. In *Conversion to Modernities: The Globalization of Christianity*. Peter van der Veer, ed. Pp. 231–62. New York: Routledge.
Jolly, Margaret, and Nicholas Thomas, eds.
    1992   *The Politics of Tradition in the Pacific*. *Oceania* 62, special issue (4): 241–354.
Jones, John Miller
    1995   *Assembling (Post)modernism: The Utopian Philosophy of Ernst Bloch*. New York: Peter Lang.
Kahn, Miriam
    1990   Stone-Faced Ancestors: The Spatial Anchoring of Myth in Wamira, Papua New Guinea. *Ethnology* 29(1): 51–66.
Kant, Immanuel
    1929 [1781]   *Critique of Pure Reason*. Norman Kemp Smith, trans. London: Macmillan.
    1998   *Religion Within the Boundaries of Mere Reason and Other Writings*. Allen Wood and George di Giovanni, trans. and eds. Cambridge: Cambridge University Press.

Kaplan, Martha
  1988 The Coups in Fiji: Colonial Contradictions and the Post-Colonial Crisis. *Critique of Anthropology* 8(3): 93–116.
  1990a Christianity, People of the Land, and Chiefs in Fiji. In *Christianity in Oceania: Ethnographic Perspectives*. John Barker, ed. Pp. 127–47. Lanham, Md.: University Press of America.
  1990b Meaning, Agency and Colonial History: Navosavakadua and the "Tuka" Movement in Fiji. *American Ethnologist* 17(1): 3–22.
  1995 *Neither Cargo nor Cult: Ritual Politics and the Colonial Imagination in Fiji*. Durham, N.C.: Duke University Press.
  2004 Promised Lands: From Colonial Lawgiving to Postcolonial Takeovers in Fiji. In *Law and Empire in the Pacific: Fiji and Hawai'i*. Sally Engle Merry and Donald Brenneis, eds. Pp. 153–86. Santa Fe, N.M.: School of American Research Press.
Kaplan, Sam
  2002 Documenting History, Historicizing Documentation: French Military Officials' Ethnological Reports on Cilicia. *Comparative Studies in Society and History* 44(2): 344–69.
Kasuga, Naoki
  1994 Christ, the Devil, and Money: Witchcraft in Fijian History. *Man and Culture in Oceania* 10: 39–57.
  1999 Tochi wa naze shuchaku wo umuka? Fiji no rekishi to genzai wo tsujite kangaeru [Why does land engender persistent attachment? From the viewpoint of Fiji's past and present]. In *Tochi shoyu no seiji-shi: jinruigaku-teki shiten* [The political history of land ownership: anthropological perspectives]. Takashi Sugishima, ed. Pp. 371–89. Tokyo: Fukyo-sha.
  2001 *Taiheiyo no Rasupuchin: Vichi Kanbani undo no rekishi jinruigaku* [Rasputin of the Pacific: Historical anthropology of Viti Kabani]. Tokyo: Sekaishisho-sha.
Kaufmann, David
  1997 Thanks for the Memory: Bloch, Benjamin, and the Philosophy of History. In *Not Yet: Reconsidering Ernst Bloch*. Jamie Owen Daniel and Tom Moylan, eds. Pp. 33–52. London: Verso.
Keane, Webb
  1994 The Value of Words and the Meaning of Things in Eastern Indonesian Exchange. *Man*, n.s., 29(3): 605–29.
  1997a From Fetishism to Sincerity: On Agency, the Speaking Subject and Their Historicity in the Context of Religious Conversion. *Comparative Studies in Society and History* 39(4): 674–93.
  1997b Religious Language. *Annual Review of Anthropology* 26: 47–71.
  1997c *Signs of Recognition: Powers and Hazards of Representation in an Indonesian Society*. Berkeley: University of California Press.

Keenan, Elinor Ochs, Bambi B. Schieffelin, and Martha Platt
    1978   Questions of Immediate Concern. In *Questions and Politeness:
            Strategies in Social Interaction.* Esther Goody, ed. Pp. 44–55.
            Cambridge: Cambridge University Press.
Keesing, Roger, and Robert Tonkinson, eds.
    1982   *Reinventing Traditional Culture: The Politics of Kastom in Is-
            land Melanesia. Mankind* 13, special issue (4): 297–399.
Keesing, Roger
    1982   Kastom in Melanesia: An Overview. In *Reinventing Traditional
            Culture: The Politics of Kastom in Island Melanesia. Mankind*
            13, special issue (4): 297–301.
Kelly, John D., and Martha Kaplan
    2001   *Represented Communities: Fiji and World Decolonization.* Chi-
            cago: University of Chicago Press.
Kermode, Frank
    2000   *The Sense of an Ending: Studies in the Theory of Fiction.* Ox-
            ford: Oxford University Press.
Krause, Ernest G.
    1986   The Great Awakening in Fiji During World War I. In *Adventist
            History in the South Pacific, 1885–1918.* Arthur J. Ferch, ed.
            Pp. 174–88. Wahroonga, NSW, Australia: South Pacific Divi-
            sion of Seventh-Day Adventists.
Lal, Brij V.
    1988   *Power and Prejudice: The Making of the Fiji Crisis.* Wellington:
            New Zealand Institute of International Affairs.
Lal, Brij V., ed.
    1990   *As the Dust Settles: Impact and Implications of the Fiji Coups.
            Contemporary Pacific* 2, special issue (1): 1–146.
Lasch, Christopher
    1991   *The True and Only Heaven: Progress and Its Critics.* New York:
            Norton.
Lazarus, Richard S.
    1999   Hope: An Emotion and a Vital Coping Resource Against De-
            spair. *Social Research* 66(2): 653–78.
Lederman, Rena
    1986   Changing Times in Mendi: Notes Towards Writing Highland
            New Guinea History. *Ethnohistory* 33(1): 1–30.
Lee, Benjamin
    1997   *Talking Heads: Language, Metalanguage, and the Semiotics of
            Subjectivity.* Durham, N.C.: Duke University Press.
Levinas, Emmanuel
    1998   *Of God Who Comes to Mind.* Bettina Bergo, trans. Stanford:
            Stanford University Press.

Lévi-Strauss, Claude
  1962   *La Pensée sauvage*. Paris: Plon.
Lindstrom, Lamont
  1993   *Cargo Cult: Strange Stories of Desire from Melanesia and Be-
          yond*. Honolulu: University of Hawaii Press.
Lloyd, D. T.
  1982   *Land Policy in Fiji*. Occasional Paper No. 14. Cambridge: De-
          partment of Land Economy, University of Cambridge.
Lynch, Michael
  1993   *Scientific Practice and Ordinary Action: Ethnomethodology and
          Social Studies of Science*. Cambridge: Cambridge University
          Press.
Lynch, William F.
  1965   *Images of Hope: Imagination as Healer of the Hopeless*. Balti-
          more: Helicon.
Macnaught, Timothy
  1979   Apolosi R. Nawai: The Man from Ra. In *More Pacific Islands
          Portraits*. Deryck Scarr, ed. Pp. 173–92. Canberra: Australian
          National University Press.
  1982   *The Fijian Colonial Experience: A Study of the Neotraditional
          Order Under British Colonial Rule Prior to World War II*. Pa-
          cific Research Monograph No. 7. Canberra: Australian Na-
          tional University.
Malinowski, Bronislaw
  1922   *Argonauts of the Western Pacific: An Account of Native Enter-
          prise and Adventure in the Archipelagoes of Melanesian New
          Guinea*. London: Routledge.
Malkki, Liisa
  2001   Figures of the Future: Dystopia and Subjectivity in the Social
          Imagination of the Future. In *History in Person: Enduring
          Struggles, Contentious Practice, Intimate Identities*. Dorothy
          Holland and Jean Lave, eds. Pp. 325–48. Santa Fe: School of
          American Research Press.
Marcel, Gabriel
  1962   *Homo Viator: Introduction to a Metaphysic of Hope*. Emma
          Craufurd, trans. New York: Harper.
Marcus, George E.
  1988   Parody and the Parodic in Polynesian Cultural History. *Cultural
          Anthropology* 3(1): 68–76.
  1998   *Ethnography Through Thick and Thin*. Princeton, N.J.: Prince-
          ton University Press.
  1999   Critical Anthropology Now: An Introduction. In *Critical An-
          thropology Now: Unexpected Contexts, Shifting Constituencies*,

Changing Agendas. George E. Marcus, ed. Pp. 3–28. Santa Fe,
      N.M.: School of American Research Press.
Marcus, George E., and Michael M. J. Fischer
  1986   *Anthropology as Cultural Critique: An Experimental Moment
          in the Human Sciences*. Chicago: University of Chicago Press.
Maurer, Bill
  2002   Anthropological and Accounting Knowledge in Islamic Banking
          and Finance: Rethinking Critical Accounts. *Journal of the Royal
          Anthropological Institute*, n.s., 8(4): 645–67.
  2003   Please Destabilize Ethnography Now: Against Anthropological
          Showbiz-as-Usual. *Reviews in Anthropology* 32: 159–69.
Mauss, Marcel
  1966 [1925]   *The Gift: Forms and Functions of Exchange in Archaic
          Societies*. Ian Cunnison, trans. London: Cohen & West.
McDowell, Nancy
  1985   Past and Future: The Nature of Episodic Time in Bun. In *His-
          tory and Ethnohistory in Papua New Guinea*. Deborah Gewertz
          and Edward Schieffelin, eds. Pp. 26–39. Oceania Monograph
          No. 28. Sydney: University of Sydney.
Mead, George Herbert
  1959   *The Philosophy of the Present*. Arthur E. Murphy, ed. La Salle,
          Ill.: Open Court.
Merry, Sally Engle
  2000   *Colonizing Hawaii: The Cultural Power of Law*. Princeton,
          N.J.: Princeton University Press.
Mertz, Elizabeth
  1996   Recontextualization as Socialization: Text and Pragmatics in the
          Law School Classroom. In *Natural Histories of Discourse*.
          Michael Silverstein and Greg Urban, eds. Pp. 229–49. Chicago:
          University of Chicago Press.
Messick, Brinkley
  1993   *The Calligraphic State: Textual Domination and History in a
          Muslim Society*. Berkeley: University of California Press.
Methodist Church in Fiji
  1988 [1938]   *Ai vola ni sere ni Lotu Wesele e Viti* [Hymnbook of the
          Weseleyan Church in Fiji]. Suva, Fiji: Methodist Church in Fiji.
Metz, Johannes Baptist
  1969   *Theology of the World*. William Glen-Doepel, trans. New York:
          Herder & Herder.
Miyazaki, Hirokazu
  2000a   Faith and Its Fulfillment: Agency, Exchange and the Fijian Aes-
          thetics of Completion. *American Ethnologist* 27(1): 31–51.

2000b The Limits of Politics. *People and Culture in Oceania* 16: 109–22.
2003 The Temporalities of the Market. *American Anthropologist* 105(2): 255–65.
N.d. Documenting the Present. In *Documents: Artifacts of Modern Knowledge*. Annelise Riles, ed.
Miyazaki, Hirokazu, and Annelise Riles
In press Failure as an Endpoint. In *Global Assemblages: Technology, Politics, and Ethics as Anthropological Problems*. Aihwa Ong and Stephen J. Collier, eds. Oxford: Blackwell.
Moltmann, Jürgen
1993a [1967] *Theology of Hope: On the Ground and the Implications of a Christian Eschatology*. J. W. Leitch trans. Minneapolis: Fortress Press.
1993b [1974] *The Crucified God: The Cross of Christ as the Foundation and Criticism of Christian Theology*. R. A. Wilson and John Bowden, trans. Minneapolis: Fortress Press.
Munasinghe, Viranjini
2001 *Callaloo or Tossed Salad? East Indians and the Cultural Politics of Identity in Trinidad*. Ithaca, N.Y.: Cornell University Press.
Munn, Nancy
1990 Constructing Regional Worlds in Experience: Kula Exchange, Witchcraft and Gawan Local Events. *Man*, n.s., 25(1): 1–17.
1992 The Cultural Anthropology of Time: A Critical Essay. *Annual Review of Anthropology* 21: 93–123.
Muyskens, James L.
1979 *The Sufficiency of Hope: The Conceptual Foundations of Religion*. Philadelphia: Temple University Press.
Myers, Fred R.
1995 Representing Culture: The Production of Discourse(s) for Aboriginal Acrylic Paintings. In *The Traffic in Culture: Refiguring Art and Anthropology*. George E. Marcus and Fred R. Myers, eds. Pp. 55–95. Berkeley: University of California Press.
Myers, Fred R., and Donald L. Brenneis
1984 Introduction: Language and Politics in the Pacific. In *Dangerous Words: Language and Politics in the Pacific*. Donald L. Brenneis and Fred R. Myers, eds. Pp. 1–29. New York: New York University Press.
Nader, Laura
1990 *Harmony Ideology: Justice and Control in a Zapotec Mountain Village*. Stanford: Stanford University Press.

Nayacakalou, Rusiate R.
   1965   The Bifurcation and Amalgamation of Fijian Lineages over a Pe-
          riod of Fifty Years. *Transactions and Proceedings of the Fiji So-
          ciety* 8: 122–33. Suva, Fiji: Fiji Society.
   1971   Fiji: Manipulating the System. In *Land Tenure in the Pacific.*
          Ronald Crocombe, ed. Pp. 206–26. Melbourne: Oxford Univer-
          sity Press.
Nichol, Francis D., ed.
   1978 [1953]   *The Seventh-Day Adventist Bible Commentary: The Holy
          Bible with Exegetical and Expository Comment.* Volume 1.
          Washington, D.C.: Review and Herald Publishing Association.
Norton, Robert
   1990   *Race and Politics in Fiji.* 2d ed. St. Lucia, Queensland, Aus-
          tralia: University of Queensland Press.
Obeyesekere, Gananath
   1992   *The Apotheosis of Captain Cook: European Mythmaking in the
          Pacific.* Princeton, N.J.: Princeton University Press.
   1997   Afterword: On De-Sahlinization. In *The Apotheosis of Captain
          Cook: European Mythmaking in the Pacific.* Pp. 193–250.
          Princeton, N.J.: Princeton University Press.
Ong, Aihwa, and Steven J. Collier (eds.)
   In press   *Global Assemblages: Technology, Politics, and Ethics as An-
          thropological Problems.* Oxford: Blackwell.
Ortner, Sherry B.
   1984   Theory in Anthropology Since the Sixties. *Comparative Studies
          in Society and History* 26(1): 126–66.
Otto, Randall E.
   1991   *The God of Hope: The Trinitarian Vision of Jürgen Moltmann.*
          Lanham, Md.: University Press of America.
Otto, Ton, and Nicholas Thomas, eds.
   1997   *Narratives of Nation in the South Pacific.* Amsterdam: Har-
          wood Academic Publishers.
Parmentier, Richard J.
   1987   *The Sacred Remains: Myth, History, and Polity in Belau.*
          Chicago: University of Chicago Press.
Peirce, Charles Sanders
   1960   *Collected Papers.* Vols. 5 and 6. Cambridge, Mass.: Belknap
          Press of Harvard University Press.
Peters, Curtis H.
   1993   *Kant's Philosophy of Hope.* New York: Peter Lang.
Pickering, Andrew
   1995   *The Mangle of Practice: Time, Agency, and Science.* Chicago:
          University of Chicago Press.

1997   Concepts and the Mangle of Practice: Constructing Quater-
        nions. In *Mathematics, Science, and Postclassical Theory*. Bar-
        bara Herrnstein Smith and Arkady Plotnitsky, eds. Pp. 40–82.
        Durham, N.C.: Duke University Press.

Povinelli, Elizabeth
1993   "Might Be Something": The Language of Indeterminacy in Aus-
        tralian Aboriginal Land Use. *Man*, n.s., 28(4): 679–704.

Rabinow, Paul
1996   *Making PCR: A Story of Biotechnology*. Chicago: University of
        Chicago Press.
1999   *French DNA: Trouble in Purgatory*. Chicago: University of
        Chicago Press.

Rappaport, Joanne
1994   *Cumbe Reborn: An Andean Ethnography of History*. Chicago:
        University of Chicago Press.

Rapport, Nigel
2003   *I Am Dynamite: An Alternative Anthropology of Power*. Lon-
        don: Routledge.

Ravuvu, Asesela D.
1987   *The Fijian Ethos*. Suva, Fiji: Institute of Pacific Studies, Univer-
        sity of the South Pacific.

Reed, Adam
2003   *Papua New Guinea's Last Place: Experiences of Constraint in a
        Postcolonial Prison*. New York: Berghahn.

Ricoeur, Paul
1986   Foreword by Paul Ricoeur. In Bernard P. Dauenhauer, *The Poli-
        tics of Hope*. Pp. ix–xvi. New York: Routledge & Kegan Paul.
1995   Philosophy and Religious Language. In *Figuring the Sacred: Re-
        ligion, Narrative and Imagination*. M. I. Wallace, ed. Pp. 35–47.
        Minneapolis: Fortress Press.

Riles, Annelise
2000   *The Network Inside Out*. Ann Arbor: University of Michigan
        Press.
N.d. a Introduction. In *Documents: Artifacts of Modern Knowledge*.
        Annelise Riles, ed.
N.d. b Making White Things White: An Ethnography of Legal Knowl-
        edge.

Robbins, Joel
2001   Secrecy and the Sense of an Ending: Narrative, Time, and Every-
        day Millenarianism in Papua New Guinea and in Christian Fun-
        damentalism. *Comparative Studies in Society and History* 43(1):
        525–51.

Roberts, Richard H.

1990   *Hope and Its Hieroglyph: A Critical Decipherment of Ernst Bloch's Principle of Hope.* American Academy of Religion, Studies in Religion No. 57. Atlanta: Scholars Press.

Rorty, Richard

1998   *Achieving Our Country: Leftist Thought in Twentieth-Century America.* Cambridge, Mass: Harvard University Press.

1999   *Philosophy and Social Hope.* New York: Penguin Books.

Rutz, Henry

1978   Fijian Land-Tenure and Agricultural Growth. *Oceania* 49(1): 20–34.

1987   Capitalizing on Culture: Moral Ironies in Urban Fiji. *Comparative Studies in Society and History* 29(3): 533–57.

1995   Occupying the Headwaters of Tradition: Rhetorical Strategies of Nation Making in Fiji. In *Nation Making: Emergent Identities in Postcolonial Melanesia.* Robert J. Foster, ed. Pp. 71–93. Ann Arbor: University of Michigan Press.

Sahlins, Marshall

1972   *Stone Age Economics.* New York: Aldine.

1981   *Historical Metaphors and Mythical Realities: Structure in the Early History of the Sandwich Islands Kingdom.* Association for Social Anthropology in Oceania Special Publications No. 1. Ann Arbor: University of Michigan Press.

1985   *Islands of History.* Chicago: University of Chicago Press.

1991   The Return of the Event, Again; with Reflections on the Beginnings of the Great Fijian War of 1843 to 1855 Between the Kingdoms of Bau and Revu. In *Clio in Oceania: Toward a Historical Anthropology.* Aletta Biersack, ed. Pp. 37–99. Washington, D.C.: Smithsonian Institution Press.

1993   Goodbye to *Tristes Tropes*: Ethnography in the Context of Modern World-History. *Journal of Modern History* 65(1): 1–25.

1995   *How "Natives" Think: About Captain Cook, for Example.* Chicago: University of Chicago Press.

Said, Edward

1978   *Orientalism.* New York: Pantheon Books.

Sangren, P. Steven

2000   *Chinese Sociologics: An Anthropological Account of the Role of Alienation in Social Reproduction.* London: Athlone Press.

Sartre, Jean-Paul

1956   *Being and Nothingness: An Essay on Phenomenological Ontology.* Hazel E. Barnes, trans. New York: Philosophical Library.

Sayes, Shelley A.
  1982   Cakaudrove: Ideology and Reality in a Fijian Confederation.
         Ph.D. diss., Australian National University.
  1984   Changing Paths of the Land: Early Political Hierarchies in Ca-
         kaudrove, Fiji. *Journal of Pacific History* 19(1): 3–20.
Scarr, Deryck
  1980   *Ratu Sukuna: Soldier, Statesman, Man of Two Worlds.* London:
         Macmillan Education.
  1984   *Fiji: A Short History.* Laie, Hawaii: Institute for Polynesian
         Studies, Brigham Young University, Hawaii Campus.
Schutz, Alfred
  1970   *On Phenomenology and Social Relations: Selected Writings.*
         Helmut R. Wagner, ed. Chicago: University of Chicago Press.
SDA General Conference
  1988   *Seventh-Day Adventists Believe . . . : A Biblical Exposition of
         Twenty-seven Fundamental Doctrines.* Washington, D.C.: Minis-
         terial Association, General Conference of Seventh-Day Adventists.
Shapin, Steven
  1994   *A Social History of Truth: Civility and Science in Seventeenth-
         Century England.* Chicago: University of Chicago Press.
Shapin, Steven, and Simon Schaffer
  1985   *Leviathan and the Air-Pump: Hobbes, Boyle, and the Experi-
         mental Life.* Princeton, N.J.: Princeton University Press.
Shore, Bradd
  1982   *Sala'ilua: A Samoan Mystery.* New York: Columbia University
         Press.
Shryock, Andrew
  1997   *Nationalism and the Genealogical Imagination: Oral History
         and Textual Authority in Tribal Jordan.* Berkeley: University of
         California Press.
Siegel, James T.
  1997   *Fetish, Recognition, Revolution.* Princeton, N.J.: Princeton Uni-
         versity Press.
Silverstein, Michael
  1996   The Secret Life of Texts. In *Natural Histories of Discourse.*
         Michael Silverstein and Greg Urban, eds. Pp. 81–105. Chicago:
         University of Chicago Press.
Smith, Barbara Herrnstein, and Arkady Plotnitsky
  1997   Introduction. In *Mathematics, Science, and Postclassical Theory.*
         Barbara Herrnstein Smith and Arkady Plotnitsky, eds. Pp. 1–16.
         Durham, N.C.: Duke University Press.
Spencer, Dorothy
  1941   *Disease, Religion and Society in the Fiji Islands.* Monographs of

the American Ethnological Society 2. Seattle: University of Washington Press.

Steedman, Carolyn

1998   The Space of Memory: In an Archive. *History of the Human Sciences* 11(4): 65–83.

Steiner, George

1967   *Language and Silence: Essays on Language, Literature, and the Inhuman.* New Haven, Conn.: Yale University Press.

Steley, Dennis

1986   Advances and Reversals in Polynesia: 1890–1918. In *Symposium on Adventist History in the South Pacific: 1885–1918.* Arthur J. Ferch, ed. Pp. 164–73. Wahroonga, NSW, Australia: South Pacific Division of Seventh-Day Adventists.

1990   Unfinished: The Seventh-Day Adventist Mission in the South Pacific, Excluding Papua New Guinea, 1886–1986. Ph.D. diss., University of Auckland. Ann Arbor: University Microfilm International.

Stoler, Ann Laura

2002a   Colonial Archives and the Arts of Governance: On the Content in the Form. In *Refiguring the Archive.* Carolyn Hamilton, Verne Harris, Jane Taylor, Michele Pickover, Graeme Reid, and Razia Saleh, eds. Pp. 83–100. Dordrecht, Netherlands: Kluwer Academic Publishers.

2002b   Developing Historical Negatives: Race and the (Modernist) Visions of a Colonial State. In *From the Margins: Historical Anthropology and Its Futures.* Brian Keith Axel, ed. Pp. 156–85. Durham, N.C.: Duke University Press.

Strathern, Marilyn

1981   Culture in a Netbag: The Manufacture of a Subdiscipline in Anthropology. *Man*, n.s., 16(4): 665–88.

1987   Introduction. In *Dealing with Inequality: Analysing Gender Relations in Melanesia and Beyond.* Marilyn Strathern, ed. Pp. 1–32. Cambridge: Cambridge University Press.

1988   *The Gender of the Gift: Problems with Women and Problems with Society in Melanesia.* Berkeley: University of California Press.

1990   Artefacts of History: Events and the Interpretation of Images. In *Culture and History in the Pacific.* Jukka Siikala, ed. Pp. 25–44. Helsinki: Finnish Anthropological Society.

1991a   One Man and Many Men. In *Big Men and Great Men: Personifications of Power in Melanesia.* Maurice Godelier and Marilyn Strathern, eds. Pp. 197–214. Cambridge: Cambridge University Press.

1991b *Partial Connections.* ASAO Special Publications No. 3. Savage, Md.: Rowman & Littlefield.

1992 *Reproducing the Future: Essays on Anthropology, Kinship and the New Reproductive Technologies.* New York: Routledge.

1997 Gender: Division or Comparison? In *Ideas of Difference: Social Spaces and the Labour of Division.* Kevin Hetherington and Rolland Munro, eds. Pp. 42–63. Oxford: Blackwell.

Strathern, Marilyn, ed.

2000 *Audit Cultures: Anthropological Studies in Accountability, Ethics, and the Academy.* London: Routledge.

Szondi, Peter

1986 Hope in the Past: On Walter Benjamin. In *On Textual Understanding, and Other Essays.* Harvey Mendelsohn, trans. Pp. 145–59. Minneapolis: University of Minnesota Press.

Thomas, Nicholas

1986 *Planets Around the Sun: Dynamics and Contradictions of the Fijian Matanitu.* Oceania Monograph No. 31. Sydney: University of Sydney.

1989 *Out of Time: History and Evolution in Anthropological Discourse.* Cambridge: Cambridge University Press.

1991 *Entangled Objects: Exchange, Material Culture and Colonialism in the Pacific.* Cambridge, Mass.: Harvard University Press.

1992 The Inversion of Tradition. *American Ethnologist* 19(2): 213–32.

1997 *In Oceania: Visions, Artifacts, Histories.* Durham, N.C.: Duke University Press.

Thornley, Andrew, and Tauga Vulaono, eds.

1996 *Mai Kea ki Vei? Stories of Methodism in Fiji and Rotuma, 1835–1995.* Suva, Fiji: Methodist Church in Fiji and Rotuma.

Tomlinson, Matt

2002a Religious Discourse as Metaculture. *European Journal of Cultural Studies* 5(1): 25–47.

2002b Sacred Soil in Kadavu, Fiji. *Oceania* 72(4): 237–57.

2004 Ritual, Risk and Danger: Chain Prayers in Fiji. *American Anthropologist* 106(1): 6–16.

Toren, Christina

1988 Making the Present, Revealing the Past: The Mutability and Continuity of Tradition as Process. *Man,* n.s., 23(4): 696–717.

1990 *Making Sense of Hierarchy: Cognition as Social Process in Fiji.* London: Athlone Press.

1994 All Things Go in Pairs, or the Sharks Will Bite: The Antithetical Nature of Fijian Chiefship. *Oceania* 64(3): 197–216.

1995 Seeing the Ancestral Sites: Transformations in Fijian Notions of the Land. In *The Anthropology of Landscape: Perspectives on Place and Space*. Eric Hirsch and Michael O'Hanlon, eds. Pp. 163–83. Oxford: Clarendon Press.

1998   Cannibalism and Compassion: Transformations in Fijian Concepts of the Person. In *Common Worlds and Single Lives: Constituting Knowledge in Pacific Societies*. Verena Keck, ed. Pp. 95–115. London: Berg.

1999   *Mind, Materiality and History: Explorations in Fijian Ethnography*. London: Routledge.

2003   Becoming a Christian in Fiji: An Ethnographic Study of Ontogeny. *Journal of the Royal Anthropological Institute*, n.s., 9(4): 709–27.

Trompf, Garry W.

1990   *Melanesian Religion*. Cambridge: Cambridge University Press.

Turner, Terence

1988   History, Myth, and Social Consciousness Among the Kayapó of Central Brazil. In *Rethinking History and Myth: Indigenous South American Perspectives on the Past*. Jonathan D. Hill, ed. Pp. 195–213. Urbana: University of Illinois Press.

United States

N.d.   [U.S. Government memorial in support of] Fiji Land Claims of George Rodney Burt, Benson Robert Henry, John B. Williams [and] Isaac M. Brower. National Archives of Fiji, Suva, Fiji.

Valeri, Valerio

1985   The Conqueror Becomes King: A Political Analysis of the Hawaiian Legend of 'Umi. In *Transformations of Polynesian Culture*. Antony Hooper and Judith Huntsman, eds. Pp. 79–103. Auckland: Polynesian Society.

Vance, Laura L.

1999   *Seventh-Day Adventism in Crisis: Gender and Sectarian Change in an Emerging Religion*. Urbana: University of Illinois Press.

Verdery, Katherine

1995   Faith, Hope, and *Caritas* in the Land of the Pyramids: Romania, 1990 to 1994. *Comparative Studies in Society and History* 37(4): 625–69.

1999   *The Political Lives of Dead Bodies: Reburial and Postsocialist Change*. New York: Columbia University Press.

Verran, Helen

2001   *Science and an African Logic*. Chicago: University of Chicago Press.

Wagner, Roy

1981 [1975]   *The Invention of Culture*. Rev. ed. Chicago: University of Chicago Press.

Wall, Colman
  1920   Sketches in Fijian History. In *Transactions of the Fijian Society for the Year 1919*. Suva, Fiji: Fijian Society.
Ward, R. Gerard
  1969   Land Use and Land Alienation in Fiji to 1885. *Journal of Pacific History* 4: 3–25.
  1995   Land, Law and Custom: Diverging Realities in Fiji. In *Land, Custom and Practice in the South Pacific*. R. Gerald Ward and Elizabeth Kingdom, eds. Pp. 198–249. Cambridge: Cambridge University Press.
Weber, Elizabeth
  2001   Elijah's Futures. In *Futures: Of Jacques Derrida*. Richard Rand, ed. Pp. 201–18. Stanford: Stanford University Press.
Weiner, Annette
  1992   *Inalienable Possessions: The Paradox of Keeping-While-Giving*. Berkeley: University of California Press.
Weiner, James F.
  1992   Anthropology Contra Heiddeger. Part I: Anthropology's Nihilism. *Critique of Anthropology* 12(1): 75–90.
  1993   Anthropology Contra Heiddeger. Part II: The Limit of Relationship. *Critique of Anthropology* 13(3): 285–301.
  2001   *Tree Leaf Talk: A Heideggerian Anthropology*. Oxford: Berg.
West, Cornel
  1989   *The American Evasion of Philosophy: A Genealogy of Pragmatism*. Madison: University of Wisconsin Press.
West, Thomas H.
  1991   *Ultimate Hope Without God: The Atheistic Eschatology of Ernst Bloch*. New York: Peter Lang.
White, Geoffrey M.
  1991   *Identity Through History: Living Stories in a Solomon Islands Society*. Cambridge: Cambridge University Press.
Whitelaw, James Sutherland
  1966   People, Land and Government in Suva, Fiji. Ph.D. diss., Australian National University.
Williams, Raymond
  1979   *Politics and Letters: Interviews with New Left Review*. London: NLB.
  1989   *Resources of Hope: Culture, Democracy, Socialism*. Robin Gable, ed. London: Verso.
Williksen Bakker, Solrun
  1986   Ceremony and Complication in an Urban Setting. In *Fijians in Town*. Chris Griffin and Mike Monsell-Davis, eds. Pp. 196–

208. Suva, Fiji: Institute of Pacific Studies, University of the South Pacific.

Wittgenstein, Ludwig
 1953   *Philosophical Investigations*. G. E. M. Anscombe, trans. Oxford: Basil Blackwell.

Yankah, Kwesi
 1995   *Speaking for the Chief: Okyeame and the Politics of Akan Royal Oratory*. Bloomington: Indiana University Press.

Zipes, Jack
 1988   Introduction: Toward a Realization of Anticipatory Illumination. In Ernst Bloch, *The Utopian Function of Art and Literature: Selected Essays*. Jack Zipes and Frank Mecklenburg, trans. Pp. xi–xliii. Cambridge, Mass.: MIT Press.

Zournazi, Mary
 2002   *Hope: New Philosophies for Change*. New York: Routledge.

Index

In this index an "f" after a number indicates a separate reference on the next page, and an "ff" indicates separate references on the next two pages. A continuous discussion over two or more pages is indicated by a span of page numbers, e.g., "57–59." *Passim* is used for a cluster of references in close but not consecutive sequence.

Adams, Robert, 13
Adorno, Theodor, 10, 143n5, 144n6, 144n12
Aesthetics, 5, 56, 63, 71, 89, 99, 154n2, 157n31; and Christian rituals, 96f; of emergence 137–40. *See also* Analytical aesthetics
Agency, 7f, 16–18, 27f, 86, 92, 112, 124f, 138; of God, 2, 16, 98, 105, 116–20 *passim*, 143n1, 146n15; in abeyance, 97, 99, 105–8 *passim*; of humans, 105f, 112, 125
Alexander, Gilchrist, 40
Allardyce, William L., 36f, 77
Analytical aesthetics, 5f, 52, 137
Analytical distance, 18f, 132
Anamnesis, 15
Anare Matahau and Associates, *see* Matahau, Anare
Annuity, 40f, 51f, 59–65 *passim*, 149n30, 150n31, 155–56n13
Anthropology, 3–8 *passim*, 25, 29f, 52, 130–40 *passim*; of expert knowledge, 3, 132; and hope, 5, 129–40 *passim*; and philosophy, 24–25, 133–35; temporal strategies of, 29f, 146n16; as secular knowledge, 86; critique of, 135; of Fiji, 163n1. *See also* Historical anthropology
Anticipation, 14, 26f, 50, 70ff, 82, 110, 136–40 *passim*
Anti-essentialism, 17
Apology, 162n9, 165n25; Rabuka's, 29, 110–11, 120–28, 165n21

Apolosi Nawai, 153n43
Appadurai, Arjun, 157n31
Archival research, 3ff, 12, 24, 45–47, 49, 75–76, 153n43, 153n50, 160n5
Arno, Andrew, 88f, 100
Assemblage, 137
Atheism, *see under* Bloch, Ernst
Attendance, 85, 95, 98, 104, 106, 162n10. *See also* Response; Veiqaravi
Australian Aborigines, 42
Avorosa, Ratu, *see* Tuivuya, Ratu Avorosa

Bakhtin, Mikhail, 137
Battaglia, Debbora, 105
Bau, 31f, 63, 76, 78, 101, 113, 147n3, 147n6, 148–49n15, 157n22
Bauman, Richard, 161n1
Bau-Rewa War, 63, 78, 113
Belatedness, 29, 136, 139–40
Benjamin, Andrew, 144n11
Benjamin, Walter, 143n5, 144n12; and Ernst Bloch, 4f, 10, 12, 20–23, 139; and messianic historian, 21, 110; and critique of history, 22; and spark of hope, 24, 140
Bete, 74, 81
Bible, 13, 88–95 *passim*, 103–11 *passim*, 118, 120, 161n3; and parables, 95f. *See also* Psalms 127:1
Bible study, 90–93 *passim*, 103, 106, 161n3
Bloch, Ernst, 3ff, 11–16, 25–28, 128ff,

155n6, 162nn9, 13. *See also*
Attendance; Gift-giving
Viti Kabani, *see* Apolosi Nawai

Wall, Colman, 113
West, Cornel, 15
Whale's teeth. 7, 60, 72, 101f, 126
Wilkinson, David, 75f, 78,160n8
Winter, Sir Francis, 40, 149n31

Wittgenstein, Ludwig, 70, 133

Yaqona, 47, 87, 126, 164n7
Yavusa 51–67 *passim*, 74–83 *passim*,
156n15, 158n32, 159n33
Yavutu, *see* Origin place

Zipes, Jack, 144n6
Zournazi, Mary, 1–2